# LOOK ME IN THE EYE

*Caryl's Story*

About Overcoming Childhood Abuse,
Abandonment Issues, Love Addiction,
Spouses with Narcissistic Personality
Disorder (NPD) and Domestic Violence

# Caryl Wyatt
## with Anita le Roux

CCB Publishing
British Columbia, Canada

Look Me in the Eye:
Caryl's Story About Overcoming Childhood Abuse,
Abandonment Issues, Love Addiction, Spouses with
Narcissistic Personality Disorder (NPD) and Domestic Violence

Copyright ©2007, 2013 by Caryl Wyatt
ISBN-13  978-1-77143-098-2
Second Edition

Library and Archives Canada Cataloguing in Publication
Wyatt, Caryl, 1950-, author
Look me in the eye : Caryl's story about overcoming childhood abuse, abandonment
issues, love addiction, spouses with narcissistic personality disorder (NPD) and
domestic violence / by Caryl Wyatt; with Anita le Roux. -- Second edition.
Issued in print and electronic formats.
ISBN 978-1-77143-098-2 (pbk.).--ISBN 978-1-77143-099-9 (pdf)
Additional cataloguing data available from Library and Archives Canada

Cover artwork and design by Caryl Wyatt: http://www.abuseisnoexcuse.co.za/

Previously published in print by 30° South Publishers (Pty) Ltd.

Publisher:    CCB Publishing
              British Columbia, Canada
              www.ccbpublishing.com

# Dedication

This book is dedicated to my mother
who I learned to love and understand
through this painful journey.

ॐ

To my three beautiful daughters and my granddaughter,
stay as sweet as you are—who have my utmost respect
and I hope one day to regain theirs.

ॐ

To the men who are important in my life:
My father, brother, son-in-law, nephews and grandsons,
none of whom resemble the characters in this book.

"I am so proud of you and hope that in time I will be
forgiven for many of the wrong choices I have made."

# Contents

# Acknowledgements

Anita—I spent a week in Durban with you sharing my story. You laughed and cried with me, but *you* made the decision that my story was worth sharing. You understood my fear, my pain and persevered when I wanted to give up completely. I could never have done this with out you. Thank you.

Alison—for your courage and willingness to share your story. It gave me hope that anything is possible.

Dr. Tessa van Wyk—for telling me the truth and being willing to go the distance, supporting me throughout my divorce and taking my calls day and night. You are remarkable and I will always be thankful—you were my last hope.

Dr. Annemare Norvello, Trauma Specialist—who walked with me through the valley of death and helped me to heal from CPTS.

Kerrin and Chris Cocks—thank you for being so supportive and putting the first edition of this book together so well.

Dr. Sam Vaknin—for your dedication to helping people understand NPD, and for doing the review for this book. You made me realize the only person I can change is *me*.

# Foreword

I met Caryl several years ago at a conference in Zambia. I was a speaker at the conference and had a chance to mingle with the delegates afterwards. Caryl introduced herself to me and asked if she could meet me later as she had something to 'offer' me. This is when she offered to do a graphology analysis of my handwriting. What a special gift! I found her analysis incredibly insightful, sensitive and enlightening.

I was blown away when she later admitted to me that she—this confident, beautiful, warm, generous woman—was in a violently abusive marriage. She was not what I thought an abused woman would *look* like. Surely someone in an abusive relationship is broken and feeble? I have valued reading Caryl's story for many reasons. One of these has been discovering why many of us have this preconceived idea of what an abuse victim should *look* like. It is a direct result of the importance placed on keeping the abuse hidden—by both the abuser and the victim. In addition, society is very willing to turn a blind eye unless it is faced with abuse head-on, and so the cycle of secrecy continues.

I believe that one of the reasons that abuse has so much power is because we don't understand it. Those of us who are directly affected by it and those of us that are not—either way, none of us really understands the nature of abuse. We don't *understand* its power and that is why it continues to have so much.

I am the first to admit that I do not understand abuse. I have no understanding in my soul of people who would choose to abuse others. In fact, one of the stumbling blocks in my own healing after my rape and attack was my insistence on wanting to understand the two men who had so violated and abused me.

When I came to a stage of realizing that in order to understand them I would have had to also 'accept' them—I chose to turn away from the yearning to understand and to accept that I would rather not.

I have also never understood why someone would 'choose' to stay in an ongoing abusive relationship. However, in reading Caryl's story, she has enabled me to put myself in her place and I have to wonder if I would have been able to do it any differently given her history and her reality. And this is the gift that Caryl brings us with her story and the honest way in which it is told—she makes it possible for us to move outside of ourselves and our own realities, judgments and prejudices so that we are easily able to walk the journey of another. This is a rare opportunity for us to truly *live* the life of a victim of abuse and to understand—from a safe vantage point—the powerlessness, hopelessness and desperation.

What a powerful blessing this book is to us all. I am confident that it will benefit those people who still feel trapped by the incapacitating cycle of abuse and that it will give some understanding and hope where there is none. Caryl's acceptance of her own shortcomings and determined soul-searching are nothing short of inspirational. Following in the footsteps of another can make a frightening journey more achievable.

I also believe that Caryl's story is a rare gift to our society. It is an insight into an epidemic that brews behind closed doors in more homes than we would care to know. If the statistics are accurate (and the general understanding is that the prevalence of abuse is much higher because domestic violence is notoriously under-reported), then a quarter of the female population in South Africa suffers abuse at home every week. In fact, 80% of violence that women suffer is at the hands of the men who supposedly love them. This is already affecting our community on a daily basis and society as a whole needs to take up Caryl's mantra of 'Abuse is No Excuse' if we care at all for our humanity.

I, personally, want to thank you, Caryl, for what your story has meant to me. I am inspired and humbled by your willingness to share your difficult story. I had no idea how deeply moved I would be by your honesty and your gentle humanness. This is a story that I will never forget.

Alison
Author of *I Have Life*
Rape and attack survivor
Inspirational Speaker

# Introduction

Victimhood is an objective state of being—but it is undoubtedly, also a subjective state of mind. The author's tumultuous and tortured life led her to this epiphany, which allowed her to embark on a process of self-empowerment and healing.

The book is not for the faint-hearted or the politically correct. It mercilessly explores in excruciating detail the fraught relationships between men and women, co-dependents and narcissists, society and victims and therapists and 'clients'.

The author holds nothing back: date rapes, addictions, and domestic violence, incapacitating fears, warts and all. It is this candour that endears her to the reader. Early on in the book, we come to empathize with her and we become eager to join her in her voyage of self-discovery.

Rare in such confessionals, the author has never shut herself off from the big wide world out there. Her narrative is deliciously embedded in the story of her country, South Africa, its race relations, and the ancient wisdom possessed by its inhabitants.

The book opens with a thinly veiled metaphor: news about the tsunami in Thailand reverberates in the author's own quaking self and (third) marriage. Throughout this harrowing time the world and its representatives intrude, at times helpful, mostly obstructive and mean.

Having defied incredible odds, the author emerges, in front of the readers' astonished gaze, as a beautiful, self-confident, mature, and self-aware woman. She shares the wealth of her experience by simply telling a story that is bound to captivate, infuriate and educate.

One of the best personal odyssey books I have ever read.

Dr. Sam Vaknin
Author of *Malignant Self Love: Narcissism Revisited*

# The Tsunami in My Heart

We are never ready for disaster. No matter how painstakingly life prepares us for a crisis, we are simply never quite ready for the blow when it strikes.

On the 26th December 2004, when the loud roar of water from the tsunami came crashing down in Thailand, I was having a shower in a luxury hotel suite in Cape Town. My husband had never been one to penny-pinch on holidays. We had just been to South America and this was the last leg of our holiday before returning to our home in Johannesburg.

It hadn't all been fine and dandy, though. I didn't want to go with him on this holiday because, with a very emotional year behind, I had wanted to spend some time by myself.

I had suggested that he go on a 'bonding trip' with his teenage son from his first marriage, and initially he seemed quite pleased with this idea. I had also said that I wanted to move my art materials to another one of our properties because I thought it was an ideal setting to start a business, and at the last minute, as if he had reason to worry that I might 'clean him out' while he was on holiday, he begged me to join him. He even sweetened the deal by extending an invitation to my teenage daughter and so off we went on a two-week trip to Argentina and Uruguay.

The truth is he needn't have pleaded with me at all. I had never been able to refuse him any request. I would even pre-empt his wishes and spontaneously fulfil his unexpressed desires. In return, he fulfilled my material needs and abated my fear of abandonment.

This tacit exchange was often thwarted, though. On one occasion he refused to lend me R200 000 to start my own business and yet, somewhere on our glamorous holiday, he mentioned to me that we had already blown R350 000. I was very aware that the issue was never about the amount—it was about the control. This amount of money was petty cash in his pocket, but it was under *his* control all the same.

On the way back from South America, as we waited for our flight to Cape Town in Buenos Aires airport, he got a bit drunk (which was nothing out of the ordinary for him). This time I decided to tease him a little. I pretended to film his bad behaviour on my video camera. This infuriated him. I felt a bit guilty and wanted to pacify him, so I asked him one of my regular mollifying questions when I wanted to know what he was thinking.

"Babe, where are you?"

This would usually calm him a bit, but instead, he pinned me with his piercing blue eyes and said without much deliberation, "I'd like to rip your heart out." For a moment, I believed him.

On the flight home he insisted my daughter and I sit together while he sat with his son in the seats behind us.

As always, we managed to sweep that unpleasant little tête-à-tête under the carpet and arrived in Cape Town for the Christmas and New Year celebrations, the faultless picture of a happy family. My husband arranged for us to have a family dinner at an expensive restaurant in Camps Bay on Christmas Eve. When my stepdaughter asked if her mother could join us I didn't object, but I didn't expect their whole family to join us. I got on well with them but thought it inappropriate that my husband would entertain both his ex-wife's family and our family on Christmas Eve. We had never done it before, so why now?

While in the shower on Boxing Day, I contemplated what had happened when suddenly I heard my husband shouting from the lounge, "Shit! There's been an earthquake in Thailand!"

I rushed through to the lounge to see the news for myself. While I stood there staring at the devastating scene of people screaming and crying, trying to run away from death, my first thought was, *Thank God my newly wedded daughter and her husband's honeymoon arrangements had not worked out as planned, otherwise they would still be in Thailand!*

As I watched more of the horrific drama unfold on the television screen, I could almost taste the people's fear and I couldn't help wondering: *Is this an act of God—the same God that has been so merciful to me?* Then, quite involuntarily, another thought started to tug at me like a deeply buried truth trying to surface. *I know Thailand well. I even recognize some of the hotels and other settings where the tragedy is taking place. Why do my private memories of those idyllic places match the horror of the tsunami, rather than contradict them?*

I managed to distract my mind from that line of thinking and instantly returned my focus to the news. A short while later, my husband decided to go to Clifton beach for the day and half-heartedly asked if I was going to join him. In the thirteen years we had been together, his ability to switch off never ceased to amaze me. Even when we had had the most horrendous fight late in the evening, he could get into bed and (without making peace) fall asleep within a heartbeat and sleep like a baby. I must admit I resented this a little—lying awake next to him after a quarrel, wondering if he was faking sleep. Sometimes I wondered if he would put a pillow over my head and suffocate me after I'd fallen asleep!

I also resented the fact that he refused to comfort me. I was clearly deeply distressed about the tsunami and he simply ignored this fact. The beach he was on his way to, hosted a myriad of young topless girls with perfect bodies. I knew he would be eyeing them shamelessly, even if I accompanied him, and worse—they'd be eyeing him too! My husband has never been short of female admirers.

I had also married a man who didn't share my values. Unlike him, I am capable of expressing myself without the need to curse, and his habitual swearing was something I absolutely refused to get used to. Although I eventually learnt to swear like a trooper myself, my constant retort throughout the thirteen years we were together was, "Stop swearing!"

"Why can't you accept me for who I am?" he automatically replied.

In fact, we were well known for our constant quarrelling about his use of bad language. Once we were on a family holiday in Spain with his darling, old father and his cousins. One evening, after a whole day of drinking, we went to Barcelona Village for yet another round of drinks. My husband's incessant swearing was beginning to gall me more than usual because of his father's presence. I loved and respected the old man and I knew he felt the same way about me too. Eventually I sprouted forth my, now infamous, mantra: "*Please* stop swearing so much!" For some inexplicable reason I said, "If my brother was with me now...."

Like a pack of wolves, he and his cousins went for me. "Who the fuck do you think you are?

"What makes you think that you and your family are so special?"

I fled the scene, sobbing as I made my way back to the apartment. I had been fighting a losing battle all along. In his defence, I must say that he did warn me when we first met: "If you knew what a bastard I am you would leave me." At the time, I was so deluded I believed that if I loved him enough he would change.

My husband's lack of morals and my misguided belief in the power of love were at the back of my mind that day in Cape Town. I declined his invitation to go to the beach and stayed glued to the television screen as I watched the news about the tsunami. As soon as he walked out the door, I started to sob for those who had lost their loved ones.

৪৩

Once before, I had been as profoundly affected by an international tragedy. It was in 1997 when Princess Diana died. I remember sitting in my gown and slippers for days on end watching the latest news and the many flashbacks and references to her failed marriage. I completely identified with her pain of not being able to 'make' her Prince Charming love her. More than that, just like her, it was my deepest desire to have a loving family of my own. She clung to the dream of a functional family until her death.

Although my husband and I both genuinely loved children, the children and I seemed to be no more than by-products of his public image and esteem. My similarity to Princess Di was painfully clear to me.

৪৩

However, sitting in that hotel suite in Cape Town all by myself, day after day watching the news from Thailand, I couldn't fathom why I was so consumed with the tragedy. I had the instinctive knowledge that the event signalled a major change in my life, one way or the other.

New Year's Eve came and my mind was still on the people in Thailand. I felt dazed from staring at the television screen for days, trying to make sense of it all. I made a real effort to dress up for the New Year's Eve party and I especially wore the Dolce & Gabbana top with vibrant colours that I had asked my husband to buy for me in Argentina. By the time we entered the restaurant, he still had not commented on the way I looked and I began to feel insecure.

We were waiting for my newly wedded daughter and her

husband to join us for dinner. From where we were sitting, I could see two men at a table watching us and talking between themselves. I was convinced that they were commenting on the icy distance between my husband and me.

After a while they came up to the bar where we were sitting. My husband wished them well for the New Year and continued to converse with them in the usual jovial manner that made him such a successful salesman. During the ensuing chitchat, one of the men leaned over to me and said that earlier that evening they had been admiring me in my beautiful outfit. I was delighted that somebody had noticed, but simultaneously deeply hurt and disappointed that the way I looked went unnoticed by the man I loved.

The theme for the evening was Latin America and the restaurant had a wonderful atmosphere. The tables were beautifully decorated.

The evening consisted of soft candlelight, music, professional dancers and excellent food. But the atmosphere at our table was thick with tension. No one knew exactly what the problem was, but we could all feel that things were not the way they should be on a New Year's Eve. I was filled with fear and felt as if I wanted to cry. Something was wrong—horribly wrong!

The band played my favourite Gypsy Kings music. I had danced with my husband to their familiar tunes many times before. At that stage of our lives we were in love and so in tune with each other that people used to say it looked as if we made love on the dance floor.

The male lead of the cabaret was a brilliant dancer. Once the show was over, I went to the table where he was sitting. "I thought your show was excellent, thank you," I said. Then I added half-jokingly, "You danced like my husband and I used to, but I think I could teach you a few new steps!" He laughed and pulled me onto the dance floor.

There was no one else on the floor as we started to dance. He led so expertly that I felt like a professional, even though I didn't know the moves at all. I hoped I looked as regal and sensual as I felt and that (perhaps this time) my husband would notice me. When the dance was over, I went back to our table a bit flushed. I expected my husband to take me onto the dance floor and dance with me the way we used to, but he remained seated with a snide grin on his face. Embarrassing a narcissist is a dangerous game.

Suddenly he stood up and walked across the room to where the professional female dancers sat. I saw him lean over and say something that inspired two of the dancers to get up and take to the floor with him!

I felt the walls crushing in on me. I went outside the restaurant onto the patio for some fresh air, to compose myself. When my daughter joined me, I expected her to ask me what was wrong. Instead she asked, "Mom, how long are you going to take this?" Apparently everyone else in the restaurant, on that inimitable New Year's Eve, understood the message he had sent me loud and clear.

A couple of days later I was sitting on the patio of our hotel suite in Cape Town writing in my journal while my husband took a shower. It had been on my mind to phone my brother to wish him well for his birthday, when my husband's phone signalled that he had a text message. Without thinking, I picked up his phone and looked at the message. As my eyes traced the words of the message, I felt the earth shake beneath me.

The tsunami survivors say that when the first wave hit, it sounded like an express train bearing down on them. It was no different to the tsunami that was happening in my heart. I felt like screaming, crying and running away, but I was hypnotized by the message on the phone's screen. My husband came out of the shower with a towel wrapped round his waist, looking at me wide-eyed.

"What are you doing?"

"You have a message," I replied flatly.

He grabbed the phone from me and read the message. "Why are you reading my messages?" He was angry with me, as if I was the guilty party. He put the phone down and went back into the bathroom. As if programmed, I quickly went back to the message. There it was, large as life, staring back at me. "No, I'm not horny, but when are you due home?"

My mind started to race out of control as I quickly wrote the number down. I thought of the incessant phone calls he had made and received over the past few weeks, with the excuse that he had advertised one of his properties in order to rent it out. Then I thought of our family, which consisted of his two teenagers and my three daughters. Our children had bonded closer than blood brothers and sisters.

I thought about the rumours I'd heard about his infidelities. My mind moved to the beautiful house with a marble staircase we'd just bought and our wonderful dogs that would wag their tails on our return home. I was feeling pretty shaken when my husband finally approached me again. "What are *you* going to do now?"

I'm not sure where I found the strength to respond so calmly. Perhaps I was numb from the shock, rather than composed.

"What *am I* going to do?" I asked him with a hint of sarcasm, "You've already decided that for me. This was your choice, not mine."

"Does this mean you want to go back to Johannesburg?"

It was the day before we were due to return from our vacation.

"If you want to go back now, it's up to you. I am going to leave tomorrow as planned." With this he briefly left the hotel suite.

When he eventually returned, he had a brand-new suitcase.

He made two phone calls, packed and left. I was in a trance, I couldn't cry. I immediately went into denial and doubted that I had read the message correctly. But when I phoned the number I knew I was right. I knew the person. More shocking to me was that she was a doctor client of his and she was married. She denied sending the message and blamed her daughter.

I sat for several hours in the hotel room alone and in shock. I kept telling myself that this couldn't be happening. Every fibre of my being wanted to rewind the clock and deny the truth. I berated myself: *I have never read his messages before, what made me do it this time? I didn't even want to come on this holiday; I should have stuck to my guns and stayed at home!*

The pain was so intense that I thought I would die with each new breath. I sat on the patio and started to piece parts of the puzzle together. I thought of my daughter's wedding the previous month when my husband made a tearful speech, apparently from the depth of his heart. He was confessing his love and pride for the bride and groom and everyone reached for the tissues!

One guest was overheard to say, "It costs the movie industry millions to get Mel Gibson in *Brave Heart* to bring a movie theatre to tears. All it takes is for this guy to make a speech at a wedding!"

"I haven't seen this many people cry at a *funeral*!" remarked another.

Throughout his speech he didn't once mention me, the mother of the bride. The bride was, after all, his stepdaughter and she did not even live with us! Later that evening, he danced with me once and then proceeded for the rest of the evening to ignore me, occupying himself by dancing with all the other women for the rest of the evening.

I thought of his frequent golf trips and his in-your-face motto: "What goes on tour stays on tour." Next, I remembered his 'boys' nights out', drinking and partying, staying out until late. Once I asked him where he had been. He replied facetiously, "Out fucking. Why, do you have a problem with that?"

Finally, I remembered something that nearly broke my heart. At the beginning of our relationship he told me that even if I caught him red-handed (lying naked on top of another woman) he would deny his infidelity in order to preserve our marriage. Now that it had practically happened, he was not denying anything!

I couldn't bear the pain of my own thoughts anymore. I phoned my Forever-Friend who had been my confidante over the past twenty-two years. Thankfully, she lived in Cape Town and came over to the hotel. When I told her about the latest event, I thought she was going to weep. We had been through so much together, but this time she couldn't find the right words to comfort me. I was yearning to hear the words, "Don't worry Caryl, he'll make amends and it will all turn out okay", but they didn't come. All she could offer was: "You don't deserve this Caryl."

When she had left and I was on my own again, I started to sob. The sense of loss was unbearable. I instinctively knew that the thick wall of denial was finally tumbling and threatening to crush me in the process. For thirteen years I had managed to keep it in place, restoring the cracks as they'd occurred.

Then suddenly, without warning, there was complete chaos in my psyche. It felt as if I had been dumped in a sea of emotion and desperately had to tread water. As I tried to take my next breath I felt as though I was choking. Although I was breathing, it felt as if I was drowning. I was certain that I was going to die. My whole life started to flash before me in a kind of slow-motion slide show. The second wave had hit.

Finally, I caught my breath, calmed down a bit and started to weep again. I'm not sure how long I lay there, completely exhausted with tears streaming down my face, but it was as if the tears had melted the ice and a memory that I had kept frozen for so many years projected itself onto the screen of my mind.

ॐ

It was early December 1995 and we were in Thailand. My husband and I were getting married for the second time and we were on honeymoon, sitting at a sidewalk café. We had already drunk quite a lot that day when a stunning-looking young prostitute walked past and pulled her slinky black dress over her head, revealing her beautiful bare body. My husband suggested that we follow her to see what she was advertising. After a short walk, we ended at a strip club.

Once inside the club, I went to the ladies' room. When I returned to our table, I found three naked girls entertaining my husband. One of them was sitting on his lap. He appeared to be dumbstruck and said to me, "We'd better go before I get into trouble." I was instantly enraged and hooked into his game.

I baited him, "If you want her, you can have her." Of course I wanted him to reject the idea and to prove to me that he wasn't interested. It was after all our honeymoon.

"Are you sure?" he asked with much anticipation.

That moment I made a choice between the unknown and the known. If I showed my hurt and disgust, we would certainly have a fight that could end in yet another separation. I had been locked out of my home, and all my belongings put in storages—many times, so that was not an option for me.

I chose the unknown, and said with feigned indifference, "Sure!"

Without much hesitation, he led the lap-dancing prostitute out of the club, hired a scooter and drove off with her to our hotel room. I followed, crying as I walked the streets of Phuket to our hotel—the very hotel room in which I had seen the news of the many lives that had been destroyed by the tsunami.

When I arrived, they were in the throes of intercourse. I was drunk and recklessly distressed and I lay on the bed next to him while he finished what he had started. When the prostitute left, my husband looked at me and said, "We are going to live to regret this."

"No 'we' are not. We are never going to mention this to each other or to anybody else, ever again!" I replied plainly.

ೞ

Until that moment I had buried that memory so deep in my subconscious that I thought I was safe from the damage it had done in my life and in my marriage. How dreadfully misguided I was! Since childhood, *the truth* has been my greatest value. By allowing this incident to happen, I proved that I would go to any lengths to please and to keep this man. I had sold my integrity for material security, regardless of the spiritual cost— just like the prostitute.

In my hotel suite in Cape Town I was filled with unspeakable remorse for what had happened that day in Thailand. In the forefront of my mind was the verse from Scripture, "Do not cause your brother to stumble". That is exactly what I was guilty of on that fateful afternoon. I was the more mature Christian of the two of us and should have prevented the whole scenario. Instead, I was also party to the abuse of another woman.

It became perfectly clear to me that I had given myself over so completely to my charming husband that I had lost myself in the process. It was this knowledge that caused me an overwhelming sense of loss, more so than the thought of losing him. It felt as if I had compromised my spirit, sold my talents and dreams and it felt as though there was almost nothing left of the original me. I wanted so badly to be real with others, but I didn't know what real was anymore. This realization was devastating.

I suppose when a person's sense of security is challenged, it is a natural tendency to hold onto whatever one can. I could feel myself slipping back into denial. I wanted my husband to look me in the eye and tell me he was sorry; that it was all a terrible mistake and that he loved me so much he couldn't live without me (exactly like he did the day he asked me to go with him and his son to Argentina).

"No amount of money in the world could replace you. I really do not want to go without you. I would give up everything I have for you," he said.

Yes, I was willing to turn a blind eye to absolutely *all* our problems, not just the 'No-I'm-not-horny' situation in Cape Town. With the wisdom of hindsight, I can say that *fortunately* this is not what happened.

As soon as we arrived back in Johannesburg, it was clear that I was no longer welcome in the house. I had never really felt that our home was a safe haven for me, but suddenly I got the sense that my teenage daughter and I were actually in substantial danger of his wrath. I immediately contacted an attorney to set up an appointment.

Before my attorney had time to act, I was served a summons for divorce! My husband was divorcing me on grounds of incompatibility; was stating that we had different values and that we did not share the same friends. Irreconcilable differences maybe, but incompatibility was a joke. If I'd had any emotional energy left, I would probably have laughed out loud. His cousin was acting as his lawyer and the irony of the situation was that this very cousin and his wife were the 'friends' I had objected to entertaining at our home and for good reason. I wondered if they'd had a giggle between themselves when conjuring up legitimate grounds for *him* to sue *me* for a divorce. It was not the first time that the two of them had made a mockery of the legal system.

Anger was starting to mount in me. He had always been very public about our compatibility in bed. He openly bragged about how good we were together, which both embarrassed and annoyed me. We had been hailed as 'soul mates' by our friends and regarded as such by ourselves. I had bent over backwards to accommodate his so-called shortcomings.

This man had physically abused me many times. Over the past thirteen years with him, I had suffered broken bones, received black eyes, experienced split lips and grazed flesh. I had also made many trips to the hospital, to the lawyers and to the police station. I had felt isolated and was treated for depression—still I would forgive him!

The two of us had been caught up in the most macabre dance since the day we'd met. I'd accepted his neglect and abuse; I'd tried to control him; I'd tried to rescue him; I'd enabled him and I'd compromised my integrity and honesty. In fact I'd done absolutely everything in my power to 'take care of' him. I had done this in the hope that he would not leave me, or that someday he would reciprocate and treat me with kindness.

Unfortunately he was as dependent on this dysfunctional, unholy alliance as I was. He had been draining power from me as if his survival depended on it. He had been as powerless as I to put an end to our relationship. In sheer desperation he declared one night, "I will do whatever it takes to get you out of my system, including fucking someone right here [gesturing towards our bed] if I have to!"

Surely, we were in this mess together? *Both of us* allowed this addictive pattern to have authority in our marriage. He had the nerve to call us incompatible! Facing the prospect of being homeless and penniless again was a big wake-up call for me. I'd been there so many times before. The events of my life revealed a pattern that I could no longer ignore: I had always surrendered my life to someone else, because I never really believed that I could look after myself, or that I had enough talent or value to offer the world. Moreover, I constantly placed the power to provide a roof over my head and a safe home for my children and me, in someone else's hands.

I moved into my teenage daughter's room the moment we arrived back from Cape Town. Many nights I held her close to me and we cried together. She had nightmares most nights and I would reach out and stroke her to console her. He stayed out late; he came home drunk and tried to provoke us. We could feel the tension mounting, but tried to control the panic and uncertainty of the future.

I was stuck between a rock and a hard place. I knew he was going to stoop very low to get me out of the house, but I had nowhere else to go. I felt as though I was in solitary confinement and tried my best to avoid any arguments. I stayed out of his way as much as practically possible. In contrast, he continued to go to work, to play golf and to party all night.

One would think that these circumstances would make me hate him, but my sense of security was so deeply challenged that I decided to bargain with him instead. I genuinely thought we could reach a compromise for the time being, so I requested that we take turns to have friends over to the house. I was reaching breaking point and thought it would be a good idea to invite my two older daughters around (on occasion) for moral support.

He jumped at the gap I gave him and sent me a phone message, "Good idea, starting this weekend I want you out of the house. I am going to have a party ..." He added that he would be inviting my 'arch enemies', his Lawyer-Cousin and his wife, to this party.

I am not sure what happened in my husband's childhood to make him such a callous man. I am loathe to believe that it was only his mother's doing. It truly grieves me when I think what women do to other women, and then we wonder why we are so disempowered. We sleep with each other's husbands; we gossip and humiliate each other and, worst of all, we treat our sons less than lovingly, so that they grow up to hate women. It turned out that there was, indeed, another woman at the core of my husband's obsession to get me so swiftly out of the house. To my surprise, it wasn't the 'No-I'm-not-horny' woman, but a psychologist, mind you, whom his Lawyer-Cousin had introduced him to, a sex therapist, to be exact. Apparently, at the suggestion from his Lawyer-Cousin that they would make a perfect pair, my husband set up a fake appointment with her and then proceeded to charm the pants off her. Their affair was well underway by the time he planned this party.

On the Friday morning of the party weekend, I left the house to see my attorneys. When I arrived back, there was a huge marquee in the garden, chairs and tables were being delivered, and our home was inundated with deliveries. My blood was beginning to boil. My husband was simply doing what he had always done—whatever he damned well liked!

To add insult to injury, it turned out to be a party to celebrate his daughter's eighteenth birthday. I had met this man when his daughter was five years old and I love her like my own. Just a few months prior to this event, she was a bridesmaid at my daughter's wedding, alongside my other two daughters, and Star would be a bridesmaid in just a few years, at her wedding—but neither my daughters nor I were invited to her party! Another woman had already taken my place and a new 'family unit' had already been formed under our noses. For what it's worth, I don't believe that the "No-I'm-not-horny" woman and the sex therapist were aware of each other.

The night before the party, I was sitting on the patio attempting to calm down, so I wrote in my journal. Our teenage daughters were out for the evening, and so was he. The journal writing didn't really help. As each hour passed I became more and more stressed and angry about my situation.

At about eight o'clock I heard his car. By then the house was dark and empty and I could actually hear my heart pounding. Although he would have seen my car parked in the garage, I sat quietly, without drawing any attention to my whereabouts. The patio light was off, and I was writing by the light of the kitchen.

The next minute I heard his voice and realized that he was not alone. He and one of his friends, a stocky and cocky little man whom I knew well, walked through the kitchen towards the drinks cabinet. They were chuckling like two little schoolboys, clearly highly intoxicated. My heart sank as I realized they were going to pour themselves yet another drink. From where I sat I could see that the cocky, little man was nervously looking around the house.

"Where is she ... is she here?"

"Fuck her, we're getting divorced. I don't give a shit!" My husband said, full of false bravado, as he downed another drink.

I was terrified, but sat there watching them. Then they headed towards the patio where I was sitting and where the sound system was. I realized that they were planning on having a very late night. As they came onto the patio, I stood up and looked them squarely in the eyes.

"Please, if you're going to have another party go and party somewhere else. This is also my home!"

The Cocky Man was quite unnerved, but my husband took it in his stride. "Bloody good idea! Come on bud, let's go party somewhere else." His suggestive tone wasn't lost on me, but they left and I sighed with relief. For the moment I had managed to avoid unnecessary conflict.

In the early hours of the morning I was woken by loud music. The two of them were back in full force. I decided to sit outside on the bedroom balcony, out of hearing distance from the lounge. But they moved their raucous party to the study, which was right below the balcony where I was sitting. They

17

were talking about women and having affairs. Overhearing my husband talking about his infidelities with such conceit, felt like acid being poured into my soul.

I couldn't contain my anger anymore. I marched downstairs and confronted them. With as much self-control as I could muster, I made an appeal to the Cocky Man.

"Please understand, we are going through a very stressful time at the moment, as I'm sure you can imagine. It's three o'clock in the morning and I am trying to sleep. *Please* will you go home?"

He became very defensive and said, "My bud has asked me to be here!"

I couldn't understand why. *Was it so that he could witness my husband humiliating and provoking me?*

"Fuck her! You're my mate and I say you stay!" my drunken husband barked.

Then he pointedly removed the photograph of his father and me from the frame on his desk and tore it up. This mortified me. It was the only picture of the two of us and his father had passed away the previous year.

"How can you do that?" I pleaded.

"Oh, I'm sure he'll understand under the circumstances," he replied.

"In that case, you wouldn't mind if I do this," I retaliated by tearing up a little album that I had made for him which consisted of photos of the highlights of his life. It was something that I knew he cherished.

Suddenly I was beginning to see his ploy. My husband was trying to provoke me, hoping that I would lose the plot and then he could have me removed—either to a clinic or locked up in a holding cell at the local police station. I'd been down that road with this man before and I was quite determined not to rise to the occasion again, so I retreated and they continued their loud conversation.

I was still wide awake due to the noise they were making when I heard my husband say, "Come on bud, let's go to bed." I listened as they stumbled up the marble staircase, and to my utter shock, they made their way towards the master bedroom! I became absolutely enraged. *Here I am sharing a bed with my daughter, and my husband invites his drunken friend to sleep in my bed!*

Finally, I lost the plot. I got into my car and drove to the police station. When I explained to them what was going on in my home, and the abuse I had been subjected to over the years, they agreed to come back with me and ask the Cocky Man to leave.

I arrived back at home, armed with four police officers by my side. Without any further ado, I marched them up to the master bedroom and flung the door open. Those few seconds of seeing the two men jump out of bed and the Cocky Man trying to get his pants back on in a hurry was almost worth the grief and discomfort that followed!

Absolute pandemonium broke loose. My husband started cursing at me, saying I was demon possessed and insane. He called me a variety of unmentionable names. The police did nothing, except prevent him, a couple of times, from beating me up.

The timing couldn't have been worse, though. The fight progressed to the driveway, just as our two teenage daughters arrived home from their night out. Suddenly, from being friends and partying together all night, they turned on each other. Of course, my daughter immediately jumped to my defence.

"Why are you doing this to us? My mom has done nothing to you! Why are you hurting her like this?"

"How can you shout at your father like that?" the Cocky Man screamed at her. My daughter was becoming almost hysterical.

"He's not my father! And look how he's shouting at my

mom!"

My husband turned his wrath on her and screamed, "Why don't you fuck off and mind your own business!"

Tears flowed down her cheeks as she faintly replied, "I'm a child of God. How can you speak to me like this?"

This comment seemed to provoke my husband into a near frenzy. He literally started to froth at the mouth like a crazed demon and screamed, "You are the daughter of Lucifer!"

At this point I went into the garden to get a cell-phone signal to call my newly wedded daughter and to ask her to come and rescue us. The situation was out of control and the police did nothing to help. Several times my husband lunged at me or at my daughter while threatening, "I'll fucking kill you!" I kept anticipating that the police would take control and order him to calm down, or at least warn him that they would take him into custody, but that only happens in the movies. That night, my daughter and I had to fend for ourselves.

When my daughter and her husband arrived to fetch Star and me, my husband became so enraged that the veins in his neck bulged.

"Why the fuck are you here? What's this got to do with you?"

"This is my mother and my sister," my daughter said, as dignified as ever and then she pointed at the Cocky Man, "Tell me, what has this got to do with *him*?"

This seemed to shut my husband up for a while and I ran into the house to get an overnight bag.

"I hope you get what you deserve! You provoke my father and then you blame him when he beats you!" his teenage daughter shouted after me.

I was stunned. She and her brother had experienced her father's wrath. What was more, she knew he had abused her own mother. Did everyone who provoked him deserve to be beaten up? There seemed no point in asking the question.

As I climbed into the car, I noticed someone throwing my cell phone into the fishpond. I asked one of the policemen to get my phone. In front of the policeman, the Cocky Man leaned into the pond, picked up my phone and then proceeded to smash it a couple of times against the wall. As he handed it over he said sarcastically, "Oh, so sorry, it broke while I was shaking the water out."

I have no idea what the police must have thought of us, but as we all departed, my intoxicated husband and the Cocky Man sang the national anthem as loudly as they could, just in case the police thought they gave a damn.

This was not the first time I'd left home with my teenage daughter after a quarrel with my husband but, as it turned out, it was the last. The next day he had all the locks and the security codes of the remote controls changed. All our belongings were boxed and sent off to storage. My teenage daughter and I had an overnight bag and nothing else—no money, no phone and no car. We slept on the lounge floor in my newly wedded daughter's home, powerless and exhausted.

Over the next couple of weeks it felt as if I was on a roller-coaster ride—I went from depression, to bargaining, to anger and back again. Acceptance was a long way off for me. I was too sore to even contemplate accepting the realities of my life.

If there was a barometer to measure emotions, I'm sure the desperate pain I felt that night would have blown the instrument to pieces. In fact, all the emotions I'd experienced over the thirteen years I'd been married to my third husband would have been able to explode any feeling-barometer: pain, pleasure, joy, despair, loneliness, euphoria, love, hate—there was just never a middle ground with him.

As I lay in my daughter's lounge, I contemplated my future. I knew I had to gather my strength and courage for a merciless divorce battle. I realized that the only advantage I had over my husband was that I was smarter than he thought I was.

It was then that I made the decision to not *be a victim* for another second. Not for him—or anyone else for that matter. It was clear to me that something would have to change drastically if I was to avoid engaging in these dreadfully abusive relationships. And that 'something', I realized, would have to be me.

In the Bible it states that: "There is a time for everything, and a season for every activity under heaven." Clearly, time had come for me to examine how I could be so untrue to myself that I could let myself get involved with a man who seemed determined to brutalize my very soul? And more to the point— how had it happened that I could love such a man so deeply?

# I Met My Soul Mate

To make mistakes is part of the game of life. I believe that it is through making mistake upon mistake that we finally *learn* our own personal truth. After all, everything and everyone around you teach you something.

Way back, when I was happy and free, a colleague of mine arrived at work one morning very excited. With great animation she told me that she wanted to introduce me to a man whom she had met on a blind date the previous evening. She explained that they hadn't 'connected'; but that he had made such a favourable impression on her that she wanted to be the matchmaker—as if she couldn't let such a glorious 'find' go to waste!

I was quite surprised by this show of friendship towards me because we hardly knew each other and I certainly had never expressed the need to be paired up with a potential lover. I laughed it off, saying that I wasn't interested.

This was in fact the absolute truth. I was forty-one years old and had been divorced twice already. I had three gorgeous-looking girls whom I have given the pet names of my Sun, Moon and Star. They were my universe and for the first time ever, I truly didn't feel lonely, nor did I have that nagging feeling of wanting a man by my side. When anyone asked me if I would ever consider marriage again, my response was: "If it happens, it happens, but I am not looking." I was perfectly at peace, and felt on top of the world.

I wasn't exactly wealthy at the time. I owned a few outfits that I apparently filled out well—and one coat in particular, that when I wore it, turned heads. It was a designer item in spectacular peacock colours; it reminded me of the Biblical figure of Joseph and his multicoloured coat that he received from his father to mark him as the favourite child. I used to wear it with a cheeky little upright Zulu-style hat when I went to church and the whole ensemble certainly did make me feel very 'chosen' and special.

I had been a re-born Christian for nearly ten years by then and in spite of the pinch I felt towards the end of every month, my heart was filled with the spirit of generosity that was grounded in my faith. I had often noticed one of the congregants in particular, staring at me when I swept into church with my coat on. I would catch her eye every so often during the service as she sneaked a peek in my direction.

One Sunday morning after the service I decided to ask her why she kept looking at me.

"I just love your coat. It is stunning," was the reply, and without any ceremony, I took the coat off and handed it to her.

"It's yours." She tried to protest of course, but I simply gave her a warm smile and walked away, feeling that inexplicable comforting feeling of Agape.

My faith was gloriously unshakable. Often, when I was running out of money to feed my own children, I would make egg sandwiches, fill all the bottles I could find with tea, pack the kids in the car and drive off to Hillbrow, the so-called Sodom and Gomorrah of Johannesburg, and hand out the food and tea to those who were more needy than we were. The spiritual law of sowing and reaping worked for us every single time. We never went hungry. I firmly believe in the principle of giving what you need to receive.

It was in the light of all this that my colleague, on that fateful day in 1991, tried to sell me the idea of going on a blind date. She was one of the best sales representatives in the company we worked for, and I was starting to succumb to her tactics. It had been eighteen months since my second divorce, and although I had been very attracted to a 'certain someone' for a long time, there was no chance of a romantic relationship with him. He belonged to the same church as I did and had recently ended a relationship with a woman, like myself, who was quite a few years older than he was.

In fact, the esteemed members of our church advised him not "to go down that road again". Obedience to our faith was paramount to both of us and I sadly accepted that nothing was going to come of our mutual attraction.

My colleague, on the other hand, was relentless. "He's absolutely gorgeous! I just know you will like him ..." And she wasn't wrong. I have often wondered over the thirteen years, how such an apparently insignificant person, in terms of the grand scheme of my life, had such a major role to play in it.

Anyway, the 'absolutely gorgeous' man invited me for drinks to a venue, which left a lot to be desired. It was a pub that was reputed to be one of Johannesburg's favourite pick-up joints. And to crown it all, I was not even in the habit at the time of drinking alcohol! So, I wasn't trying to be witty when I told him that it wasn't my "cup of tea".

I am perfectly convinced that not even the heavens above knew how I managed to miss this first and momentous red flag. Clearly we were poles apart. My guardian angel must have been exasperated when I impulsively agreed to meet him at his office for a cup of coffee, instead of going for cocktails to the infamous pick-up joint.

Be that as it may, during this negotiation over the phone, he casually mentioned that he wanted me to meet a colleague of his when I got to his offices. "She has a business opportunity that may be of interest to you," he said.

I arrived at his office wearing an electric-blue jacket with a short black skirt, black stockings and high heels. My hair was cut into a Cleopatra-style, shiny black bob. I felt unusually confident that decisive morning. His colleague with the business opportunity, an attractive blonde, seemed to be caught off guard by the sight of me. She nervously introduced herself and led me into a boardroom where she attempted to sell me a motivational program that cost nearly double my salary! I was a little annoyed and somewhat suspicious about all the unnecessary 'foreplay', but by then my curiosity was aroused.

The minute I laid eyes on him, the super-confidence with which I entered his office vanished and this absolutely gorgeous apparition of a man instantly intimidated me. They say beauty is in the eye of the beholder, and in all my life no one has had that impact on me. He was definitely well over six feet tall with a bush of slightly wavy, dark-blond hair. A charming, almost shy little smile lit up his whole face and he practically hypnotized me with his piercing blue eyes. Even writing this I feel anxious.

I wanted to run away and now I wish I had, but instead I exploded into one of the worst episodes of verbal diarrhea I have ever had. He casually handled the situation like a professional casting director. He offered me a cup of coffee and sat there listening to my babble, while smiling ever so faintly at me. Very soon I ran out of things to say and I fled. I thought I had made a bad first impression, but less than a kilometre away from his office he called me on my car phone and asked me out to dinner. I was hooked.

There's a saying: "Don't underestimate love at first sight— many of us will not pass a second inspection!" This certainly applied to our first meeting. He admitted some time later, when we were already in a committed relationship, that he had not at first found me attractive. I was apparently not his type, but there was something he found irresistible about me. And I, on the other hand, instinctively knew that he spelled Trouble.

However, neither of us took time to undertake a second inspection of our thoughts and feelings—we just charged headfirst into a romantic relationship. How I wish now, nearly fifteen years later, that we had each stuck to our initial gut feelings.

At dinner that evening, his beautiful blue eyes didn't leave my face for a minute. He listened intently to every single word I spoke. I had craved this kind of attention my whole life and it felt as though I had finally found my promised Knight in Shining Armour. I was smitten. We shared a bottle of red wine over dinner. I was too embarrassed to admit that I did not drink, and of course, I got tipsy and lost my inhibitions.

On the way home I did not resist his suggestive advances. For the first time in my life, I encountered the femme fatale part of me that had not come to light with any other man before. At first I felt guilty for letting my guard down on our first date, but then again, I had fallen hopelessly in love with this man and I was willing to go to any lengths to keep him.

Our sexual encounters in the car became a pattern because I didn't want my daughters to witness my affections towards this new man in my life. An incident occurred on one such occasion on our way home from a party.

Immediately after we'd made love, he promptly zipped up his pants, put the car in gear and drove off. He was heading towards a nearby garage to put petrol in the car. My blouse was still half undone when we pulled into the garage!

The whole scenario made me feel like a typical rape victim—powerless and humiliated. I reacted by becoming sulky and tearful. The second he stopped the car, I got out very pointedly and, without saying a word, headed for the ladies' room at the side of the building. My show of disapproval annoyed him immensely. He followed behind me and screamed at the top of his voice, "What the fuck is your problem now?"

I wasn't going to let him off the hook that easily and persisted with my martyred attitude. "Just leave me alone, will you?"

"For fuck's sake, get in the car!" He was running up behind me and before I reached the ladies' room, he grabbed me by my blouse and pushed me up against the wire fence. He was very rough and squashed the one side of my face against the fence so forcefully that it left an imprint.

"Just get back into the fucking car!" With this he gave me an extra-hard shove against the wire fence and I lost my footing and fell to the ground. "Now!" he added, and started to walk back towards the car.

I followed him like a lamb to the slaughter. I knew as sure as the nose on my face that this was the first sign of the physical violence in store for me if I were unwise enough to continue down this slippery path. At the same time, I also knew I was already too addicted to this man to walk away from what was going to prove to be a roller-coaster ride.

The only defence mechanism I had was to rationalize. I convinced myself that I was entirely to blame for his reaction and that I should be more considerate of his feelings in future. I was guilty of crossing my boundaries and having sex with him in his car. This occurred only a couple of months into the relationship and I was beginning to negotiate myself away for the 'love' of this man.

On the one hand he treated me so well. He bought me flowers—two hundred roses at a time to be precise—he took me to the finest restaurants and gave me his undivided attention. He often took me shopping and bought me anything that lit up my eyes. "Do you want this watch, Babe? Come on; let me buy it for you." The next thing I knew, I would be the proud owner of an exquisite diamond-faced wristwatch!

Yet, on the other hand, I began to discover that he could be desperately mean to me. I had never been one to use pet or nick names for the men in my life, however, with this one, there were two such distinct personalities that I started to call the one 'Hitler' and the other 'Babe'.

Whenever I spotted that cold look in his eyes, I would say, "Hello Hitler, where's my Babe?" This usually circumvented the emotional abuse that was forthcoming, albeit only for a short while.

In his Hitler-mode one day, he told me with glee in his voice, that his blonde colleague, who had the business opportunity for me, was actually his girlfriend at the time I had met her in his office. Then he added that I was "geographically unsuitable"—meaning she lived closer to him and he didn't want to date me anymore!

I wish I could say that this was the end of him. But he didn't leave me alone. He would call me at work and send messages on my pager. At first I was hurt and angry when he asked how I was. I resentfully thought, *What does it matter to you?* However, I soon started to convince myself that he was legitimately confused about what he actually wanted, and I became more and more willing to pardon his callous treatment of me.

Eventually, his obsession with me became contagious—I started to crave his calls. I kept everyone else on a string, making no commitments on the off chance that he might call and ask me out.

The invitation finally came. He called to invite me to a fortieth birthday party not far from where I lived. (I suppose I was 'geographically suitable' that night.) He also asked me if I would invite one of my girlfriends along to accompany his ex-brother-in-law. I was aware of the dubious bond he maintained with his former brother-in-law. The two of them had been on a holiday together in the Comores not long before I'd met him, and as far as I could gather, they'd had a pretty raunchy time with a couple of married women.

Nevertheless, I obliged him and invited an attractive young friend of mine along. The four of us had a wonderful evening. We sat around a huge bonfire in the garden until late into the night. It felt so natural to be with him again that I thought we would spontaneously resume our relationship. However, he simply didn't contact me after that evening.

A couple of weeks later, I bumped into my young girlfriend

and told her that I had not seen him since that night. She replied facetiously, "No, because he's been taking me out!" Needless to say, that was the end of the friendship and of him, as far as I was concerned.

His obsession with me surfaced again after a couple of weeks, and the pager messages started.

"Would be nice to hear from you again."

"Call me, I miss you, we need to talk."

"Please stop playing hard to get."

When he came back into my life, he did so in a grand style. He invited me to lunch at an upmarket shopping centre. Next to the restaurant was a travel agency advertising a week's trip at a very special price to Mauritius.

"Can you take leave from work for a week?" He was eager and very convincing. "Come on, let's go!"

I told him that I was booked to go into hospital for a hysterectomy and he said, "That's fine, we can go when you get out of hospital." Then after a brief pause, he added nonchalantly, "If you could change anything about yourself, what would it be?"

Without a moment's hesitation, I replied, "My boobs!" Since I was thirteen years old I'd desired larger breasts. I'd even scraped the money together and sent away for creams advertised in magazines promising to produce breasts the size of Pamela Anderson's. Needless to say, the creams didn't work, and although my flat chest stood me in good stead during my modelling career, I'd been hankering after full breasts for many years. The long and the short of the story is that I received a pair of beautiful breasts paid for by him!

Two weeks after my release from hospital, we went on our promised holiday to the glorious topless beaches of Mauritius. It turned out to be one of the most enjoyable and romantic holidays the two of us ever went on. At the airport, before we departed, he bought me a bottle of Coco Chanel perfume. It is still my favourite to this day and it always conjures memories of a very idyllic time in my life.

We began to get into the holiday spirit after quite a few drinks in the departure lounge. He started to tease me about joining the 'mile-high club'. I teased back, flirting and getting him to anticipate the idea. We giggled and laughed like two teenagers. Once we were on the plane, he ordered more wine and we started to continuously joke and laugh. He kept asking, "Are you still keen to join the mile-high club?"

I kept teasing him by asking, "How's that possible?" He came up with several imaginative schemes and the more we talked about it, the more aroused he became and the more I giggled. By the time we arrived in Mauritius we were both quite pickled and feeling very amorous.

It was dark by the time we boarded the bus for the short journey to the hotel. There were only three other couples on board and the two of us were sitting right at the back of the bus, kissing and laughing. Apparently the men were straining to have a peek and cracked a joke or two about us. I was so enamoured that I was totally oblivious of this voyeurism. He told me later that it spurred him on! He knew that I was an intensely private person or "toffee-nosed" as he called me, and if I'd been aware I was providing a sideshow I would have stopped dead in my tracks. This he couldn't let happen and at some point he asked me, "Seeing as though we didn't join the mile high club, can we join the back-of-the-bus club?" We both laughed uncontrollably at our silly private joke.

At the hotel a large group of tourists was checking into the hotel and while we waited, one of the couples from the bus asked if we would mind exchanging rooms with them. It turned out that their party of three couples had been spilt and we were booked into a room that would unite them. We told them that we would inspect the rooms first before we agreed to the exchange.

When we arrived at our room and saw the beautiful view from the patio, we decided to stay. Without wasting any more time, he grabbed me. We fell onto the bed and made passionate love. In the excitement, I forgot to lock the patio door, and while we were in a very compromising position, the patio door opened and the man, who had asked us to exchange rooms, walked in unexpectedly. When our eyes locked, he cursed loudly in Afrikaans and then fled! This left me feeling degraded and trashy. Babe, of course, felt as proud as punch that another man had been witness to his sexual prowess.

The rest of our holiday was extremely romantic. We were good together and our chemistry was strong. We did on one occasion, however, have a disagreement, and he spitefully hired a scooter and disappeared for the whole day, leaving me at the hotel alone and without money! We made up quickly though, and that evening at dinner he spoke about getting married, which I thought was premature but I was flattered.

Before we left the island, he wrote me a letter on the hotel stationery, telling me how much he loved me. He committed to writing that I was the most amazing woman he had ever met. I was certainly the happiest woman in the world that day.

When we arrived home in Johannesburg I made tea and while he was relaxing on the sofa, I massaged his feet. It was the end of the most wonderful week of my life. I was deeply in love. Absolutely nothing prepared me for his comment as he stood up to go home.

"I think you are amazing. I think you are the most awesome woman I have ever met. You seem too good to be true, but I can't do this. I don't want to see you again." With that, he left me at my front door reeling from shock. I wrestled with what had happened and re-lived our relationship over and over. Even though I was hurt and confused I decided to let it be and move on.

A couple of weeks later the pager messages started again.

"I can't stop thinking about you."

"What are you up to?"

"Can I see you?"

I'm not sure where or when I crossed that so-called invisible line of no return. By then it was no longer a question of pride—I needed him. I began to understand that the two of us were trapped in a deadly unison, and that neither of us knew how to disengage. It was terrifying. The roller-coaster relationship that had started moving down the slope over the previous six months had not only picked up momentum, but was now entering the sharp turns, flipping me upside down, inside out, and any which way—except the way I expected.

We resumed dating, and the prospect of marriage came up again. He persuaded me to give up my job and join him in business. I was reluctant at first, but eventually gave in to him. We found a house to move in to together and the future was beginning to look a bit brighter after our rocky start.

On the day of the move, he took a load of household items to the new house while I finished the last-minute packing. He took an awfully long time to return for the second load. Dinnertime was approaching and my five-year-old daughter was tired, but I reasoned that he had no help on the other side and exercised some patience. When he finally came back, I immediately noticed that familiar icy look in his eyes. "I can't do this, Caryl," he said coldly.

At first I thought he meant that he couldn't do another load that evening because he was too tired. I suggested that we drag out some linen to make a bed and finish the move the following day.

"No, you don't understand, I don't want to do *this*," he gestured to the two of us.

I looked around the empty house and when I found my voice, I asked him how he could do that to me.

"Just wait a minute," he mumbled and went outside to the

car. I looked out of the window and through my tear-filled eyes I saw that he had the trailer with all my belongings hooked to the car (just the way it had been when he'd driven off earlier that afternoon). Only this time there was also someone else with him.

When he came back into the house, none other than the attractive blonde colleague, who had tried to sell me the motivational programme the day I first met him, accompanied him. This time she did the talking.

"I am sorry Caryl, I know this must be hard for you, but we've been seeing each other all this time. He's been very confused about whom he wants, but now he's decided—and it's not you."

I had little to say to that except, "Please, I want you both to leave." They unhooked the trailer and left.

I made a bed for my daughter and once she was asleep, I sat on the kitchen floor with the packed boxes all around me and sobbed. The curtains were packed and the house was dark and cold. I had no home, no job, no phone, very little money and no car. He was completely aware of my situation and the fact that I had returned my company car after I resigned to go and work with him. I was crushed.

All through the stormy time with this man, I had fortunately not neglected my commitment to the church. I was part of the healing ministry and at the same time publicly shared my personal experiences with bulimia. I was also one of the trusted hostesses of the church and had 'meet and greet' duties at the Sunday services.

I had stepped down from this commitment some time before, due to the emotional mess I was in. When I explained my predicament to the decision-makers at the church, they agreed to help me with groceries for a week. Of course, they also prayed for me.

I contacted the owner of the house to see if I could stay on, but they had already committed to other tenants. I had one week's grace, but then I had to vacate. Within that week of living off charity and on borrowed time, he came back to me! He called and asked me to meet him for lunch at the same shopping centre where we had seen the advertisement for the Mauritius holiday a few weeks earlier. I accepted like an obedient little lap dog whose loyalty has literally been beaten into it.

He appeared sad and sorry for the mess he'd put me in. He said he couldn't live without me and if I could forgive him, he really wanted to try and make it work. He said he'd been very confused. His first marriage had been to a woman who was older than him and she also had a small child, just like mine. He was afraid of repeating the same pattern. I was ten years his senior and I knew that the blonde was younger than him and had never been married. I thought that he was deciding whether to make a practical or an emotional decision. I understood that.

With hindsight, and in my defence, I'm pretty sure that had I not been in such dire straits, I would have ended the unhealthy entanglement at that stage. My allegiance with the church was strengthened by the previous episode, and with their support, I could easily have gathered the courage to rise above my obsession with the relationship. I also knew that the more you become persuaded by forces outside yourself, the more you are at their mercy and eventually you become completely *dominated* by them.

Anyway, when we walked into the shopping centre, we passed a jewellery store. We stopped to look in the window and he asked me which ring I liked. I pointed to a reasonably modest one. He in turn, pointed out another rather flashy ring and asked if I liked it. I had never been in a position to consider such extravagance before and I said gaspingly, "Of course I do, it's beautiful!"

With that he ushered me into the shop and asked the

assistant to bring the ring to us. He slipped it onto my ring finger and asked me again if I really liked it.

"Of course I do!" I gushed. I was both thrilled and shocked; I realized that he was actually proposing! He promptly bought the ring and instructed the jeweller to size it while we were having lunch.

During the meal I questioned him about his blonde colleague, and he replied that he was totally in love with me and couldn't get me out of his system. He had made up his mind; he wanted to be with me.

A couple of weeks later, we attended his office Christmas party, and to my dismay the blonde was among the party crowd. I was shocked to see her there, but he wasn't fazed at all. In fact, while we were mingling with a group of people, he announced in a loud voice, "Do you know that Caryl and I are engaged?" From where I was standing, I saw two people trying to console the completely devastated young blonde. The roles were reversed and all I could do was ignore her, though I did feel her pain. After all, I had been in the same situation just weeks before.

Shortly after that incident, I was told that she had suffered an emotional breakdown and went to stay with her family in Swaziland. In retrospect, she was the lucky one.

The chemistry between him and me grew progressively stronger. We moved into a townhouse, and things seemed to be going a lot better. We both made compromises—I relaxed a little on my puritanical approach and started having a drink or two with him on a regular basis. He joined the church I was attending and even signed up for Bible School. He told me that he had a desire to improve his relationship with God. This news pleased me tremendously, until he arrived home late one night from Bible School and said that he had to take a fellow student home after class—a female. This made me feel very uneasy and the familiar haunting pain started to surface again. In no time, the downward spiral had begun.

I'd become so entangled in my relationship with this man, that I was incapable of making rational decisions when it came to my children. I acted like a complete zombie most of the time. My eldest daughter, Sunshine, was at boarding school, and my middle daughter, Moonie, asked if she could go to boarding school as well, rather than change to a school in our area.

Truth be told, she wanted to get away from the constant tension in our lives because of this man. Even though there was relative peace at the time, or rather a kind of truce in the home, we were forever walking on eggshells around him. One minute he would be charming and the next, he would be rude. (I later discovered that she used to communicate with him without my knowledge and she had expressed her concern to him about our relationship.) This yo-yo effect threw me completely off balance all the time and my mental health began to deteriorate.

One Sunday afternoon, while we were driving Moonie back to her boarding school after a weekend visit, I leaned over towards the back seat to talk to her. I specifically wanted to give her my undivided attention before she went back to school. He didn't like this at all, and after a while he barked at me, "Why are you talking to her? She's not the only person in the car, you know!" With this relatively innocuous statement, he finally produced the straw that broke the camel's back.

I started to scream at him, "What is your fucking problem? All I'm doing is talking to my daughter before she goes back to school!"

My outburst was so forceful that he pulled the car over to calm me down, but instead, I jumped out and headed for the bushes. All the while, I was sobbing like a hysterical lunatic. All I wanted was to be close to her before she went back to school. Together, they managed to get me back into the car, but I was crying uncontrollably. We dropped Moonie off at her school and still, all the way home, I sobbed hysterically.

He had the good sense to take me to the clinical psychologist he was in therapy with at the time. She recommended that I immediately be admitted into hospital.

I had finally suffered a complete mental and emotional breakdown and I was placed under psychiatric care for two weeks. I had officially become a bona fide victim of an abusive relationship (which continued until the night in my daughter's lounge when I decided that I would no longer be his victim). I was subjected to his customary expression: "Stop playing the victim!" If only he knew how ludicrous such an injunction was. How could I stop playing the victim while he continued to be the perpetrator? The one requires the other in order to exist—surely?

The day I was due to be discharged from hospital, he collected me and seemed sorry for the distress he had put me through. I didn't dare ask him why he had only visited me once, just in case I annoyed him.

I managed quite well, until one evening when he came home late from Bible School. I sensed something wasn't quite right, and when I asked him why he was late, he became angry and defensive. Then he promptly started to change his clothes, explaining that he had to meet a client at a hotel. This was not a good sign in my book—my first husband did the same thing (a change of clothes before he would go out to have an affair).

When I made my disapproval clear, he offered the client's name as a sign of innocence. Eve Fisher was the name. On hearing the name, my stomach turned and I instantly flew into a rage.

"If you get into that car, don't expect to find me here when you get home!"

He didn't go, and I knew my suspicions were correct—he would never leave a client hanging or jeopardize a sale because of my petty jealousies. The tension mounted over the next few days. Things appeared to go on as usual while he attended Bible

School regularly—or did he?

One evening, he returned home very late again from Bible School. A huge fight ensued. The following day I called my friend, Crystal, to 'rescue' me. We managed to pack up my belongings in less than an hour. I was in rather high spirits at the prospect of getting away from him, and the two of us were so impressed with our efficiency that we jokingly thought of starting a removal business called Girls-On-The-Move.

I stayed with my friend, Crystal, for a couple of days until the predictable pager messages started. I allowed him to see me, and he begged me to come home. Of course he said he loved me and swore that I was the only person that mattered to him. And so, I returned.

Around this time, my mother became seriously ill and he drove me all the way to Zululand to see her. When we got to her bedside, he slipped into the same kindly role as he played when he'd offered to pay for my breast enlargement during our courtship.

"If you could wish for anything, absolutely anything, what would it be?" he asked my ailing mother. She couldn't think of anything other than pears and ice cream, and sure enough, she got it! Where exactly he found it in the backwaters of Eshowe, I wouldn't know, but he delivered her wish all the same.

"He's a good man, Caryl," she whispered as I leaned over to kiss her goodbye.

When we arrived back in Johannesburg, he told his ex-parents-in-law to move out of the apartment that they rented from him. I was shocked and felt sorry for them because they were pensioners and were kind, good people. I knew their financial resources were limited. He had told me how fond he was of his father-in-law and I just couldn't understand this callousness towards them. At the same time he had bought a cluster home off-plan in a very exclusive area. This was the first of many more property investments he would make and the beginning of his rise to remarkable wealth.

I helped choose the tiles and landscaped the garden for our new home, but we weren't happy. Warning bells shook my core. In spite of our public and legal commitment to each other in the light of our official engagement, I did not feel secure at all.

One day my brother phoned to say that our mother had deteriorated suddenly. I immediately decided to go see her. She had always been so scared that she would die alone and that her life would not have meant anything to anybody.

On the way to Eshowe, I was inconsolable and couldn't stop crying. I thought of how fragile my relationship with my mother had been and that she had never really been available to either my brother or me, or even to her beautiful and talented grandchildren. While we were driving through the misty mountain range, my five-year-old daughter, Star exclaimed, "Look mom, I can see Nana dancing with Jesus in the clouds!"

When I arrived at my mother's bedside, she had already slipped into a coma. There was a lady from her church sitting beside her and I wanted her to leave, but I didn't want to be rude, so I sat down beside my mother and said a prayer. I gently stroked her arm and whispered, "Mum, I'm here, you're not alone …" A tear rolled down the side of her nose and onto the crispy white sheet. Then she was gone. All I wanted was to be alone with my mum, but the friend from the church was not about to leave.

My fiancé phoned me at the very minute that my mother died. It was typical of the bond we had that he could sense the moment of my intense grief. Yet, for some inexplicable reason, I could not bear to be with him during the period immediately after my mother's death. Instead, I went to stay with the family of an old boyfriend with whom I had maintained a close friendship. His mother knew how to comfort me as I was so distraught about my mother's pitiful life.

After her death, I began the habit of tearing up photographs of myself where I was not smiling, as I do not possess a single photo of my mother where she looks even the least bit happy.

During the time of my mother's illness and death, my eldest daughter, Sunshine who was in her final year at school, fell pregnant. I was devastated by the news, but would not consider abortion as an option.

I barely had time to digest these shocks, when the kind Babe disappeared and Hitler made his untimely appearance again. He told me, with his familiar cruelty, that he no longer wanted to be with me—and then he added that he had invited someone over for lunch the following Sunday, and would prefer it if I was not there. Apart from the fact that I had nowhere to go, I didn't believe he could actually be that callous. Sadly, I was wrong.

That Sunday, Star and I were sitting in the television room when I heard a woman's voice, followed by children's chatter. I peered into the kitchen and saw a blonde woman with her two young sons perched on our kitchen stools, while *my fiancé* chopped salad and salted the meat! They looked very comfortable around each other. After a while I gathered the courage, took my daughter by the hand and walked up to them. He casually introduced her to me as if it were the most natural thing in the world, "Oh, this is Eve Fisher."

On hearing the name, I was outraged and said, "How you can do this to Star and me is one thing, but how you can do this to *her* too, is beyond me!" and I stormed out of the house. This was of course a Freudian slip. I meant to say it the other way round, because I really could not fathom how he could find it in his heart to treat my innocent five-year-old child and me so atrociously. When I got outside the house, I saw her white Mercedes Benz parked next to his burgundy one. I was completely numb with pain, humiliation, stress and fear.

So this was 'the client' he was preparing to see that night when I stopped him from going. *At what stage did she become his new love interest?* I wondered.

I had nowhere to go with my daughter. I did not even possess a car, so we walked around the neighbourhood, while I tried to distract her by pointing out the birds, the doggies and the kitties, and tried to prevent myself from bursting into tears. I felt so completely alone. I had no idea how I was going to get myself out of the situation, and even less of an idea how I had managed to get myself in so deep in the first place. I hated myself for being so weak. It felt as if I had slipped too far into the abyss to be saved. Sunshine was having a baby, and I was not even able to provide a stable home for Star and me. My whole world was collapsing—again.

Horrible situations seem to stretch our coping abilities beyond their limits. We become bigger than ourselves. I had one of two choices, as I saw it: either have a breakdown or use the anger that was mounting in me to have a breakthrough. I chose to pursue a breakthrough. I went back to the house and for once stood my ground. I told him that I would not leave until I had transport, cash and a place to stay. In the meanwhile, I would move into the spare bedroom with my daughter.

In the middle of all this chaos and turmoil, I was blessed with one of the most awesome experiences life has to offer. Even though my five-year-old and I had to share a bed, my pregnant daughter wanted to be near me and moved in with us. She was due to give birth. In this small room, with the three of us sharing a bed, her water broke. My first grandchild was born after an eleven-hour labour, and a perfect baby boy was aptly christened, Sky. It took an event of this magnitude to take my mind off my dysfunctional relationship with my fiancé Hitler-Babe, albeit for only a couple of hours.

My daughter Sunshine and my beautiful grandson moved in with a relative after they left the hospital, and I shared a room with my five-year-old. I would get up early every morning and get dressed as if I had a job to go to. I would put on stockings, a suit or whatever made me appear as if I was on my way to work. I would walk to a nearby supermarket and browse through the job section of the newspaper. There weren't many jobs to choose from.

One morning I spotted an ad for a job with a security company. It was a far cry from the more glamorous jobs I had had in the past, but I was desperate.

The following day, I dressed immaculately and went to a building site neighbouring our complex to ask them if I could use their phone. Hitler was making it as difficult for me as possible. I did not even have the money to pay for the call, but there I was balancing in my high heals on a wooden plank, clutching the clippings of the job ad and encouraging myself with affirmations: *I already have the job; I am working in a nice place; I am earning a good salary ...*

A hard-hat engineering type approached me. He was a real gentle old man. He asked if I was okay and seemed genuinely concerned about me. It had been quite a while since someone had cared to ask about my well-being, and before I knew it, I told him my whole pitiful story. He came to the rescue immediately. He let me use the phone and his driver gave me a lift to the interview in a dirty old van strewn with building plans and rubble. By the end of that day, I was gratefully employed and had negotiated an advance on my salary, as well as a car, which was not part of the original offer.

I had taken my power back. I had authority over my own life again. My eldest daughter and grandchild were safe for the time being I thought and Moonie was still at boarding school. I moved well out of harm's way of Hitler's house and into a place of my own with Star.

I sincerely intended for it to be the end of my obsessive relationship with this man. It had already stolen eighteen months of my life. However, after having been away from him for a while, I realized that it wasn't going to be that easy to get him out of my system. I still longed for him. It occurred to me that I might be able to sever the bond if I made myself 'geographically unavailable'. I had lived in Cape Town before and always wanted to go back, so I didn't even unpack my boxes in my new place.

As I was planning how I would manage to get to Cape Town, the infamous pager messages came again.

"I hope you are okay…."

"Thinking of you!"

"Can I see you?"

I was instantly hooked. There was a public phone in the complex where I stayed and he got wise to this. He would page me to go to the phone box, sometimes as late as eleven o'clock at night and I'd rush off to get his call, desperate to hear his voice.

Soon we started seeing each other again. Then he suggested that we move to Cape Town together and "start from scratch". I was keen. Whether we both genuinely thought that a change of location would change our relationship, I'm not sure. As far as I was concerned, he was offering me a way to get to Cape Town and I was going to take advantage of the opportunity. I reckoned that I would eventually figure out a way to get my other two daughters to join me there. So I resigned from my job.

We moved to Cape Town over the festive season and I spent the holiday looking after the children—his two and Star. The minute his children went back to their mother in Johannesburg, my au pair services were apparently no longer required, he asked, "So when are you going to get a fucking job?"

"By the end of this week I will be working," I said rising to the challenge.

Again I proved my ingenuity—I started a nail salon in a prestigious hairdressing establishment on the Waterfront. I focused my attention on my new business and started to enjoy the interaction with all the clients—many of whom had celebrity status. More importantly, my clients liked me, and I became closely acquainted with members of high society in Cape Town. I was invited to their homes for lunch and I was happy. My growing confidence and the development of a circle of new friends sparked his jealousy, and our relationship became strained again.

On the night we had a Christmas party for the salon staff, he asked me to wear a sexy little red dress that we had bought together. It was a mini dress with three-quarter sleeves, made of a stretch fabric that clung to my body and left little to the imagination. I was somewhat alarmed at this request because I carried a lot of emotional baggage regarding jealousy. My first husband had been insanely jealous. He didn't like me being sexy in any way at all and, for fear of his wrath, I used to cut my hair short and dress modestly.

However, the salon crowd was mainly gay and I was eager to please my man, as always. So, I wore the little red dress to the party and caused quite a stir during the course of the evening. My landlord's hairdresser lover remarked quite candidly, "If any woman could make me go straight, it would be Caryl!"

When I walked back to the table from having been to the ladies' room, the gay men at the table whistled and shouted, "Wow sexy, show us some leg!" Having had a few glasses of wine by then, I stood behind a pillar in the middle of the room and lifted my leg in a can-can pose. We all found it quite hilarious—except my jealous fiancé.

We didn't stay long after that and when we got to the car his false smile slipped from his face. Hitler appeared and growled at me, "Do you fancy the guy? Would you like to screw him?" We argued for a while and I said that he was being pathetic. As an old victim of the green monster, I kept quiet the rest of the way home.

When we arrived at our apartment he went straight to bed. I poured myself another glass of red wine, fetched a pair of scissors and sat drenched on the floor in the shower and cut my red dress into tiny little pieces while I sobbed! This overreaction to the situation had some reasoning behind it. I thought: *Here I go again, another jealous relationship with a man who, incapable of faithfulness himself, fears that I won't be faithful. Wearing that red dress again wouldn't be worth the trouble and heartache it would bring.*

The following day I found the whole incident quite funny. Hitler didn't. He interpreted it as an attack, a crafty manoeuvre to punish him so he threatened to cut up a negligée he had bought me. It did indeed take some very crafty manoeuvring to calm him down, explaining with all my convincing powers that it was such a cheap dress, it had only cost a few rand and I didn't want the same reaction every time I wore it. He calmed down.

Soon after this incident, he decided to return to Johannesburg without me, and I was glad to see him go. I just wanted to get my own life back. Of course, once he was away from me, his obsession surfaced again and he started to make compulsive contact with me. I absolutely refused to go back to Johannesburg and continue the same co-dependant game.

He drove to Cape Town several times to persuade me to go back, but I was adamant: "Not unless we get married." I stupidly thought at the time that a marital commitment would change the playing field. In the months that followed, he made lots of promises, but the actual proposal was not forthcoming.

In the meanwhile, I had made contact again with a man I'd met many years before, a really charming and sensitive man with a special love for pianos. He would courteously stay away while I was trying to make the arduous relationship with Hitler-Babe work. In those earlier years I used to be a fairly regular customer in his music shop to buy guitar strings and plectrums. In my first few years as a re-born Christian, I learnt to play a few gospel songs and to this day, those are the only songs I can play on the guitar.

On one occasion I went into his shop with one of my teenage daughters. The young shop assistant who usually attended to me asked who she was. I told him she was my daughter and then added, "Isn't she gorgeous?"

Before he could answer, a voice from the office said, "Yes, but not half as gorgeous as the mother!" As I turned round, I saw a man with a very long dark ponytail. Gosh, he was cute! The artist in me always liked a man with long hair.

Over the next couple of months we became friends and I was flattered that this good-looking younger man found me so interesting.

We flirted a lot with each other but the relationship was to go nowhere. The piano-man sadly did not have the stomach for a divorcee mother of three.

Now that my ex-fiancé was making a comeback in my life I was beginning to get quite frustrated with my situation—I had two men hanging on, but neither of them wanted to make a commitment, and yet, neither of them wanted to let me go!

On one occasion Hitler-Babe came to Cape Town to convince me to return to Johannesburg with him. He walked into my nail salon while Piano-Man was visiting me. Courteous as ever, Piano-Man excused himself and the minute he disappeared, my ex-fiancé proposed! We got married in court within a couple of days. A drunk, old coloured man was delighted to be our witness and we went to the beach for the rest of the day.

My newly wedded husband returned to Johannesburg and I followed soon after. The letter he wrote before he left was something out of a Hollywood love story. He apologized for all the pain he had put me through over the years and confessed his undying love. He said that he didn't want me to work and that he just wanted me to be with him. "I can't be without you. I can't concentrate on my work. I can't think of anything except being with you." We were in love all over again, and this time, I thought, we would be just fine.

&#8478;

We had been married for less than three months when the physical violence started. We were staying with my husband's parents, because he was suddenly short of cash. He had fallen victim to a scam and had subsequently been declared insolvent. Together we were going to "start from scratch". But for the time being, we were so poor that we ate egg sandwiches for Christmas lunch that year!

The situation was not ideal, to say the least. From the very first visit to his family, in the beginning of our courtship, I felt uncomfortable around them. When I was growing up in Rhodesia (now Zimbabwe), my mother and I used to go camping in our caravan at a dam on the outskirts of the city of Salisbury most weekends. The young boys belonging to the Sea Scouts would come to the dam and learn skills such as tying knots and sailing. There was one boy I really took a fancy to and I looked forward to seeing him every weekend. We used to kiss and cuddle on the weekends, but didn't see each other in town during the week.

One day, I asked him where he lived and only then did I realize that he came from the poor area where the railway workers lived. I dumped him immediately because even though he was good looking and an absolute gentleman, we were not from the same class—it could never work out between us in the long run.

This was the way I felt about my husband's family. However, I had matured somewhat since my camping holidays, and more importantly, I had become a Christian. I felt that it was imprudent to judge him or his family. I thought that, as a Christian, I was 'bigger' than our differences in background but

I was beginning to seriously doubt it. Apart from the strain of staying with his family, the lack of money was a constant source of tension between us.

One day, out of the blue, he asked me to make him the beneficiary of my life insurance policy. I was quite taken aback and said, "Absolutely no way! If anything happens to me, I want the father of my five-year-old to have some money to look after her." I added that I would at least know that, in the event of my death, she'd be taken care of. His history had shown me that as her stepfather, he was certainly not going to do that!

Of course it developed into a hefty argument. Eventually I rose to leave the room. With this, he slapped me so hard that I fell. I stumbled to my feet and I ran into his father's room. He caught up with me, tackled me, then climbed on top of me and beat me repeatedly over the head. At first I screamed at him to let me go, and then I begged him not to beat me like that in front of Star. Mercifully, he lost interest and said, "Why don't you fuck off back to Cape Town?"

Escape had always been my first option in a conflict situation. I packed my personal belongings into the car, even though I didn't know where I was going. As I was about to leave, he stood in the driveway, holding my car radio and said facetiously, "You forgot something!"

In that moment I recalled a memory from my childhood, which stabbed my heart like a dagger.

*I was thirteen years old, sad, lonely and hurting because of my mother's total disinterest in me. I decided to run away from home in the hope that she would recognize the pain she was causing me. As I headed off, my mother called after me with much sarcasm, "You should take a jersey, it's getting cold!"*

*To this my elder brother added, "I would have something to eat if I were you, you might get hungry!" They were in cahoots with each other and ridiculing me.*

Now, my husband was doing the same. I grabbed the car

radio from him and threw it back at him in a rage, leapt into the car and reversed out of the driveway. In my blind fury, I smashed into a car parked behind me. Without stopping to assess the damage, I drove off to the nearby garage. When I got there, I noticed that my husband had followed me. There is nothing to say when rage becomes so intense. I collapsed, and suffered a complete mental and emotional breakdown. I was put in hospital yet again.

When I came out of hospital we moved into a place of our own but I soon realized that Eve Fischer was back on the scene. My husband said he was doing business with her—what kind I wondered? This circuitous journey was torturing me. Round and round we'd go with no ending and no new beginning.

In a desperate ploy for transformation of *any* sort, I exposed his infidelity at a dinner party. His pride was so utterly wounded that he immediately started divorce proceedings. Moreover, to show his condescension, he was going to perform a 'do-it-yourself-divorce'—wasting no time and money on lawyers—he gave me R50 and left a note saying "Have a nice life!"

# No Happily-Ever-Afters

When I was a teenager, the craze was a film called *Love Story*, and in this film the famous phrase, "Love means never having to say you're sorry" was coined. At the time, we were all hypnotized by this story of perfect love in spite of the painful reality most of us were facing in our homes. My own mother's anguish over the men in her life after she divorced my father was not enough to open my eyes to the Hollywood lie.

Nearly thirty years later, attending my third divorce case, I was still trying to untangle myself from the web of denial I had woven around romance.

As I sat in the gallery in court (with a friend for moral support) he stood in the witness box, filled with self-righteous arrogance, as he attempted to obtain a 'do-it-yourself-style' divorce from me. The judge fumbled through the paperwork presented to him and with some irritation pointed out that the most important piece of paper was missing—the Return of Service, giving my consent for the divorce proceeding to go ahead!

"Does your wife even know you're here?" he was drilling my suddenly flustered husband, "Where is she?"

I put my hand in the air like a dutiful schoolgirl, "I'm here Your Honour."

"Do you want to get divorced?" He was giving me a chance to air my views—which was more than my own husband ever did—and I wasn't going to let this chance go by.

"No, I don't your honour!"

The judge clicked his tongue and without any further ado, threw the case out of court. He told us to see a counsellor to try and resolve our differences. "Failing which, I will see you back here in two weeks time," he said.

My friend and I skidded out of there as fast as we could. As we turned the corner of the long hallway, we heard my exasperated husband shouting after us, "Caryl! Caryl …" Before his stint in court, he and I had lived in a fully furnished home that belonged to a friend of mine. It was a beautiful 'girlie' townhouse filled with crystal glasses, ornaments and roses in crystal vases. In fact, if ever I ran out of ideas of what presents to give her, I'd buy her something crystal, knowing that she would always find a place for it in her ultra-feminine home.

So, when my husband decided to divorce me, I thought it was right that he would be the one to move out and that I'd be safe from him while I stayed there. It was after all, my friend's home.

It should come as no surprise to learn that I was wrong— again. Apparently he thought that as he had paid the rent for the month, it still gave him the right to simply come and go as he pleased. On one such occasion he walked into the house and spitefully threatened me with eviction. Naturally we got into an argument. He picked up my car keys and I tried to grab them away from him. We got into a struggle and eventually, with sheer brute force, he managed to get my keys away from me, hurting my hand in the process before storming off.

A while later I walked to the shops. As I turned the corner of the townhouse complex, I saw one of the wheels of my car had been removed. I had bought my car with the money I'd earned from my nail salon business in Cape Town.

Adding insult to injury, over the next few days the pain in my hand became unbearable and when I had it X-rayed I realised that a bone in my wrist was broken and a plaster cast was needed. I had reached a point where I took all these things in my stride. Fixing my broken bones would become the norm.

Within the two-week period ordered by the court, he called to say that he was sorry. I took for granted that he wanted us to be reconciled and to cancel the divorce—I was thrilled by this thought!

Yes, it is true that the relationship with this man had caused me tremendous pain and humiliation. Yet, absolutely nothing compares to the pain of rejection and intense emotional turmoil that comes from feeling abandoned. It was this that I couldn't bear to go through. The power that these so-called co-dependent and abusive relationships have over one's psyche is staggering.

There is no doubt in my mind that it is the power struggle within such relationships that makes it so highly addictive. The negative energy from one partner to the other boomerangs and it is almost impossible to stop playing the game once you've started—especially while you are in denial about your part in the game. When your partner suddenly stops playing, the sense of rejection and loss is enormous.

One evening during my time of separation from my husband, my friend, Crystal, invited me to join a group of women for dinner. We were all in the throes of divorce or break-up of some sort, and in no time the majority of us were commiserating with one another about the inequity of it all.

One of the women present told us the story of how she was the one who had had an affair and was caught by her husband. As it happened the husband phoned Crystal just after his life-drama had been related to us. It became clear that he was in a highly emotional state and needed much consoling. In the end, Crystal convinced him to come to where we were rather than aimlessly drive around Johannesburg. The soon-to-be ex-wife didn't seem to mind and said that she was about to leave the party anyway.

When he arrived, all the women consoled him and spoke with him until we established that he was alright. I, in particular, came to the rescue. I gave him my number and said that I had become single quite recently and would be available for him anytime he might need someone to talk to.

One day, soon after this encounter, he called. I was about to meet my husband for lunch and asked him to call me later in the day. Of course, in my benevolence, I'd forgotten to mention that the offer was not open if Hitler-Babe should snap his fingers.

At lunch my husband declared his undying love for me. I believed him as I had done so many times in the past. After lunch he drove me to a secluded off-road spot and he made love to me, passionately, in the car. While I was still fixing my hair and make-up, he presented a document and asked me to "Just sign here, babe". I thought I was signing the cancellation of the divorce, or something to that effect.

However, it turned out that I had signed the much-revered Return of Service, and we were divorced, against my wishes, within a few days. With all this drama—the comedy and tragedy of it all—I completely forgot about the desperate man to whom I promised a shoulder to cry on. Or shall I say I forgot about him until Crystal called to say that he had shot and killed himself. Playing the co-dependant relationship game can be deadly.

Since that incident, I became very conscious of the way in which we tend to deal with another person's grief. When someone loses a loved one, we generally seem to be so respectful of their pain: we give them space, empathy and support. But when someone grieves over the loss of a loved one through divorce, there is hardly any compassion at all. Our lack of empathy gives the message: "You made your own bed; you lie in it—on your own". It is this aloneness that the person fears more than death itself.

My husband managed to convince the court of the urgency of our divorce by stating that I was planning to get married in Mauritius the following week! I call that perjury. He also succeeded in cancelling my gym membership by convincing them that he was marrying another woman.

In spite of his antics and the official divorce, I was not free from the emotional attachment to this man. I still wanted to rescue him, to love him and to make all the trouble between us go away. What's more, I realized with horror that I did not know how to survive outside this love-hate relationship. Although I used to complain bitterly about the emotional turmoil in my marriage, I was blindly addicted to the drama! Life with him was hell, but life without him was just as bad.

When we first got married, I had a peculiar dream about the two of us. *We were driving on a farm road in Zimbabwe. My husband was speeding and I was trying to convince him to slow down, pointing out that the farm workers' children often jump into the road out of nowhere.*

*He wouldn't listen to me as he drove along in his new, executive car. I could smell the genuine leather seats. Eventually he pushed a button and a soundproof glass divide came up between us—all the while driving faster and faster.*

*Suddenly in my head I heard God say, get out of the car. I was afraid because we were going very fast but I obeyed. I jumped out the car and rolled down a steep slope.*

*When I dusted myself off and worked my way back to the top of the hill, I witnessed his car driving into a tobacco barn, setting the car alight. I watched as people threw sand on him to try and save him. And then I saw he was still alive.*

"But he's still alive, Lord," I declared in surprise.

"By my grace," came the answer. As I recalled the details of this dream, a rebellious feeling came over me. I simply could not accept that this was the end of the road for us—not yet. Over the years, I had been praying daily for guidance with my struggles in the relationship, sometimes on an hourly basis! But at the same time it was a case of saying to God, "Please give me guidance, but don't give me the bad news," I couldn't bear the thought of being wrong about us. We were soul mates—everybody could see that!

§

After the divorce, my life was in a shambles and I couldn't see any way of getting it back on track. My eldest daughter, Sunshine, was struggling. She was trying the best she could with her baby and I was painfully aware of her situation, but at the same time I was completely powerless to help her. It was as though I was drowning and could hardly rescue myself.

Adding to my despair was the guilt that I carried about her situation. During the early stages of her pregnancy, I promised her that I would go all out to sell my paintings in order to help her financially and that I would stand by her and help her cope with the baby. Now the time had come to put my money where my mouth was and it felt as though I was abandoning her.

Her father couldn't be counted on either, and I watched helplessly as my beloved daughter started to descend into an ever-deepening spiral of despair.

Moonie, my second eldest decided to go overseas with a group of friends. I was heartbroken because I knew that this was not just a youthful whim to travel the world—she wanted to get away from the stress of our lives.

I couldn't blame her, but I felt rejected all the same. I remember saying to her, "I won't let you go, and I will have you arrested at the airport for being under age!" I felt that she was far too young to face the real world—I couldn't cope, how could she?

I forgot, of course, that my dysfunctional relationships and broken marriages had empowered and matured her way beyond her years. In fact, she had been the adult in our relationship all along. Needless to say, she left and I went to the airport to say goodbye.

I was simply too depressed to go out to work. I survived by falling back on a business idea that worked for me many years before, just after I got divorced from my first husband—making little gift frogs. When I initially came up with the idea, I was living in Natal and the local newspaper had this to say about my endeavour: "If you want to light up someone's life, give him or her a matchbox, but make sure there's a frog in it. An inventive Durban girl has thought up a new way of sending messages that can't easily be spoken person to person. The gift consists of a matchbox painted with flowers and inside she places a frog made out of a homemade clay mixture and a note of good wishes."

Thirteen years later, I again made ends meet with these little gifts and was slowly getting on my feet emotionally and financially. After a couple of months I eventually transcended the 'froggie stage' and found myself a well-paid job. I was making a huge effort to get my life back on track. I even made a new friend at work and Christmas was beginning to look less lonely. But sometimes it's not goodbye, it is until we meet again.

The day before Christmas I received an unexpected phone call. It was Hitler, disguised as Babe. He said that he wanted to see me so that he could wish me a Merry Christmas. He seemed to be genuine, and promised to "put the past behind us and be friends". I was dreading the idea of seeing him, but it was Christmas after all, and he had apparently bought me a gift.

The minute I walked into his flat, I cringed. I didn't know why I kept doing it, but when he spoke—I obeyed. I fell into hypnotic mode and couldn't stop myself. The first thing I noticed as I entered his home was my coffee table and some kitchen utensils from my first marriage, which had somehow ended up with him! It made my gut wrench.

The next thing I noticed was the snack platter that he had obviously specially prepared for us. As I stood there, not really knowing what to make of it all, he promptly started to pour Champagne. We sat down on the sofa and began to chat about mundane things. Suddenly the conversation turned. He told me how much he loved me, but added that we were simply "not good together". I fell hook line and sinker for this story and became tearful. He comforted me and tried to kiss me. I put up a very weak resistance and in no time we were making love. After a shower I expected him to tell me that he wanted me back. Instead, he gave me my present and kissed me goodbye.

As I was leaving, he mentioned casually that he was going to Thailand the next day. He was fully aware of the fact that Thailand had been my dream destination for a holiday since childhood. On my way home, I cried and cursed his malicious game. When I got home I opened the present. I was hoping for something special, but instead I got a cheap, childish, blue plastic radio that he had bought from a vendor at a traffic light!

The girl I befriended at work had been through much the same with her boyfriend. We spent Christmas together and empathized with each other. Fortunately my children were with their respective fathers. I did not want them to see my unhappiness – I could barely breathe, let alone put on a fake Christmas-smile.

I remember lying by the pool with my friend, drinking wine and crying. We tried to console each other. She kept repeating, "Just remember, your kids love and need you." Did she know what I was thinking?

We both went back to work between Christmas and New Year. I was feeling so raw that all I wanted to do was to stay in bed. However, it was my forty-fourth birthday on the twenty-eighth of December, and I needed to be around people.

On the day of my birthday, my friend came into my office and judging by the look on her face, I thought that someone had died. She looked scared.

"God, I don't know what to do!" She was close to tears and I asked her what was wrong. She replied, "I really don't know what to do. I'm tempted to tear up the fax—but perhaps you should read it." I took the fax from her.

*I am in Thailand and all I can do is think of you. There is nothing worse than being in such a beautiful place with someone who you are not in love with. I really wish that I could speak to you and hope that it's not too late. Please can I see you when I get back?*

When I saw him to collect my Christmas gift, he conveniently omitted to mention that he was taking someone with him to Thailand. At first I was upset, but almost instantly I was willing to forgive him—after all, he was thinking of *me* while he was away with his new lover!

My friend and I started to cry. She was much younger than I was, but she had enough life experience to understand why my relationship with him could flare up again. And, of course she felt guilty for giving me the fax. How I wish I could have ignored that fax.

He returned home, dropped his lover off and came to see me with all the gifts he had bought for me while he was in Thailand with her. I didn't care about her feelings. In fact, all I could think of was that at least someone else was hurting like I had so many times before. I was gearing up for my next 'joy ride'.

∞

A wise man once said, "Be careful what you wish for, you might just get it!" At the time, I was still learning this lesson—the hard way. We got married for the second time on a houseboat in the middle of a dam. My friend Crystal, who had helped me move out of home a couple of times during my first marriage to this man, was now helping me get dressed for the wedding. She bought me a wedding present of lingerie and earrings, stating rather sardonically, "He can't take this away from you!"

Crystal decided not to attend the wedding, but stayed with me until I was collected from the jetty. While we were standing there, she said with much trepidation, "Let's hope this time it'll work out."

I replied quite wistfully that it was a bit too late for hope, and then I added, "Unless we get in the car now and drive away." Just for an instant, I seriously contemplated doing exactly that. There was no getting away from the fact that I was entering into a marriage with Hitler-Babe for a second time with my eyes wide open, and I knew all too well—'first time victim, second time volunteer!'

At the wedding reception, my husband made a sentimental speech in which he confessed how much he had hurt me in the past and how dreadfully sorry he was for doing that. With tears rolling down his cheeks, he said, "I know that I've taken Caryl to hell and back, but this time round I'm going to clean up my act. I am going to do my best to make her happy." Absolutely everyone present was reduced to tears, including me.

It was after this charade that we went to Thailand on that regrettable honeymoon. There is something about the incident with the Thai prostitute, which I did not mention. When I arrived at the hotel to be part of the so-called 'three-some', I heard him ask the well-paid whore a question with apparent concern, "Did you come?"

For goodness sake! Surely such tenderness should have been reserved for me, his bride? The prostitute couldn't even speak English.

The following day he took a photograph of me sitting in a restaurant having breakfast. I clearly remember thinking, "You just don't understand me, do you?" And even to this day, when I look at that photograph I can barely look myself in the eye without feeling the pain of humiliation and the powerlessness of my anger on that deplorable morning.

Many years later I had some negatives developed thinking they were pictures of us on our honeymoon in Thailand, but instead they were of him and the girlfriend he had taken with him when I received that crucial fax. It happened exactly one year before we went there on our honeymoon.

In several of the photographs I noticed he had done exactly the same things with her that he had done with me, including wearing the same clothes and holding her hand across the table in the same way he held mine. In one of the photos he was wearing his favourite blue T-shirt, sitting at a sidewalk café, with one hand in his pocket and the other resting on the table, while smiling sincerely into camera. She was sitting next to him. It matched a photo taken of the two of us down to the T-shirt he was wearing! The photographs were probably even taken by the same waiter ...who knows? The similarity of the photographs, even down to her long dark hair, was painful.

Soon after our return home from honeymoon, we were woken in the early hours of the morning by the pungent smell of smoke. My husband went out onto the balcony of our apartment and saw that one of the neighbouring apartments was on fire. Several people were attempting to extinguish the fire with water, to no avail.

The following day we were told that the occupant, a young woman of about thirty-five years, had taken an overdose and fallen asleep with a cigarette in her hand.

She apparently had 'relationship problems'. I knew just how she felt. It was clear to me that life was no love story and the idyllic 'happily ever after' only happened in fairytales.

# All's Not Fair in Love and War

The Bible says, "Love keeps no record of wrongs." That's fair enough, but first we have to keep record of the wrong done to us in order to deal with the events, make sense of them, before we can eventually take responsibility for our part in them. Only *then* can we move on to forgiveness and learn to wipe the slate clean.

With my second marriage to Hitler-Babe, every aspect of our lives accelerated in a similar way to the dream I had. There was more money, more property investments, more overseas travel, more partying, more drinking and more violence.

There had never been any doubt in my mind that when I spoke out about the domestic violence, I would have to shoulder very uncomfortable comments and invite close scrutiny into my personal life. Most women, who have been in the same violently abusive situations as I have, usually choose to suffer in silence. People with little or no compassion for human frailty are quick to offer their harsh criticism and judgments. "Why the hell don't you get out of the situation?" "What's wrong with you that you tolerate this behaviour?" "Shit! I wouldn't put up with that crap!"

Let me assure you that comments like these do nothing more than make the victim of abuse feel even more useless and helpless. They erode your depleted self-esteem even further and confirm your worst suspicion—"I am not good enough". And it is this particular self-defeating lie that time and time again convinces you to go back into the arms of the perpetrator. "Nobody else would want a loser like me anyhow ..."

Be that as it may we are, after all, only human and I am sure that a lot of people have a curiosity born from a genuine need to try and understand. Questions like, "How many times did he beat you?" and "What caused the fights?" may well be a spontaneous response to my story. Or perhaps there are some who are still naïve enough to wonder, "Whose fault was it?" And, of course, the inevitable question from absolutely everyone, except, of course, from those who are caught up in, or who have experienced domestic violence: "Why didn't you leave?"

It is this thoughtless question—"Why don't you, or why didn't you leave?" These questions never cease to amaze me. Nobody would ask a cocaine addict or an alcoholic, "Why don't you stop?" There seems to be an intrinsic understanding that if the addict and alcoholic *could* stop ruining their lives, they would! So, my question to the world is: "Why do you think it would be any different for the victim of abuse?" Surely if it were as easy and effortless to walk away from the relationship as one thinks, more victims of abuse would!

Well, I have made the decision to tell my side of the story as honestly as my heart can bear. There are still some things that are merely too painful to face. And then there are other things that I cannot yet make sense of—and probably never will. So, forgive my human frailty, if you would.

ജ

I can't remember how many times I had been beaten up—too many to recall. How these violent eruptions happened, what or who caused them is a matter of perception. The truth is: "There are always three sides to a story—yours, mine and the truth." I happen to know from bittersweet experience that only the truth, without self-pity or blame, will set you free.

On one occasion, Hitler-Babe was working from home. Our security gate was broken and we had summoned a company to come and fix the problem. On completion, they obviously wanted payment, so I went to my husband's study and asked for a cheque.

He was instantly annoyed at the interruption and barked at me: "You sort it out!"

I didn't have signing power on any of his accounts and the monthly allowance he gave me was certainly not enough to cover the repair jobs required around the house. When I insisted that I wanted the money from him to pay the workers, he lost his temper.

"You fucking pay them!"

I didn't have the money and I knew the security company would not leave without it. The angrier he became the more anxious and desperate I became. Finally I lost my nerve and screamed at him, "For fuck's sake, it's your problem, not mine!" I will never know why I did what I did next, but I went to the lounge and fetched an ornamental little *knobkierrie* (miniature walking-stick) and stormed back into his office, holding it in my hand. I screamed, "Please just listen to me, they have to get paid. I don't have the money."

At the sight of me with this 'weapon' in my hand, he flew out of his chair, grabbed me around the throat and screamed while he shook me about. "Fuck off! Can't you see I'm busy?"

At this point, filled with adrenaline, we were getting out of control. He chased me down the passage and I ran into the kitchen. There was a set of kitchen knives in a wooden container standing on the counter. I grabbed one of the knives, turned around, and holding the knife threateningly out towards him I shouted, "What do you want me to do?"

This was the last straw. When I recognized that familiar angry look in his eyes, I ran back into the lounge in an attempt to reach the patio door. He overpowered me before I got out the door. Once I was on the floor, he sat on my chest and started to beat me. Hard, cold, painless punches started to rain down on my face—over and over again, until he had enough.

Usually at this stage of the game there are no more

histrionics. So, I simply went upstairs and cleaned up my bloodied face, and he paid the workers. There you have it. If provocation is any excuse for abuse, who was provoking who? You be the judge.

There is one thing left to mention—the *knobkierrie* was a gift I had received from my youngest daughter. She had bought it for me on a trip to Zimbabwe a couple of months earlier. When I asked her why I had got such an unlikely gift she said, "In case he ever beats you again!"

Arguing and quarrelling aside—there was always the hope that the violence would end, but at the same time, nobody truly believed that it ever would.

To answer the question, "Why didn't you leave him?" Well, I had laid charges of assault against my husband, and I had left the house with my daughter on several occasions and had moved in with one of my friends, Crystal. On this particular occasion, as with the many before, I knew I couldn't stay indefinitely. I felt like a burden to her, but I had nowhere else to go. I had no money to move into a rented place of any description and nor could I afford to feed us.

Always, after moving in with Crystal, I would feel guilty. I would begin to think that the whole scene was entirely my fault and that I should learn to deal with the stressful situations in our marriage differently. This occasion was no different. The feelings of guilt are the killer. If I could have found a way to stop the guilt, I might have had a chance to get away from my abusive situation. It is certainly the most destructive emotion of them all and leads straight to self-doubt and worthlessness. From here on the spiral downwards is lightning-fast.

I would start to castigate myself for the fact that I had been forewarned about my husband. The familiar cruel tape would start to run through my head …

A good friend of his explicitly told me that I was making a big mistake by getting involved with him. Another warned me,

"Caryl, he has issues. Do you know what you are letting yourself in for?" A person with whom he worked took the trouble to tell me that he was a "pathological narcissist". I had no idea what that meant at the time.

He had even warned me himself that he was a real bastard. "Treat them mean to keep them keen," was his official and shameless *modus operandi* with women.

Yet, I stubbornly rejected the advice and got myself immutably entangled with this man. Why, why, why? If only, at this point, there was someone, who could switch the tape off and get me out of my mental aberration. Perhaps if a kindly soul had asked me some empathetic and constructive questions it might have helped to clear away the fog that clouded my mind and trapped me in the perception of myself as a hopeless victim.

They could have asked: Are you ready to leave him? Is there anyone whom you trust that you can talk to? Do you have family who can help you? Do you have any money stashed away? How can I help—is there anything I can do?

Not even the hospital personnel during my countless breakdowns over the years had the good sense to engage me in a dialogue that would help me out of the situation I was in.

While all the self-blame was going on, my husband would call and say he was sorry for what he had done. Uncanny, but true; he never missed a beat. Not once. It was as if our minds were synchronized.

At this point, many thoughts go through one's mind, such as: *This time I will do things differently. I will never annoy him again.* But the decisive thought is the most infamous lie of them all—*I have no choice, I have nowhere else to go; I have to go back home.*

ॐ

Many times over the years I had fantasized about packing up

my things and simply disappearing from his life forever. Why didn't I? Would it be possible for you to understand the inexplicable spell he had over me? I know that to ask you to consider the possibility that I truly loved this man would be too preposterous.

Consider instead that invisible sticky bond and those silent hooks: the fear of the "unknown", and the most prevailing belief of them all, the lie that—I deserve this. All these trappings and beliefs overpowered the desire to be whole and free. It is the most desperate and powerless feeling.

It was clear to me even *then* that my husband and I were two immature adults who had never learnt to handle conflict—, which is a natural part of the human experience. We were both frightened by it, just as a child would be, scared that any conflict might lead to being thrown away, abandoned. I could see that we both used rage to mask our hurt and fear. I just couldn't figure out how to change this reaction.

On the one hand, I would use my rage in a passive manner. For instance, when we moved (yet again) into a new home, Max, our adorable white Labrador, decided to show my darling poodle, Sushi, exactly who was going to be boss in the new house. He started to mark his territory all over the house—including the Persian carpets I had just had cleaned at great expense.

The situation was so out of control that the whole family attended sessions with a dog psychologist in an attempt to deal with the behavioural problems we had with our pets. The sessions were quite fun, and we had lots of laughs with our friends about it, but the truth was—it took an animal-behaviour expert to tell us how to control our pets, and it worked! If only we had applied the same principles to our own lives.

In spite of our efforts, Max still acted out now and then. On one occasion he defecated on a rug in the living area and my husband called my daughter and told her to clean it up. This enraged me because Max was *his* dog and *his* two children were in the living area at the time—he could have asked them to do the dirty job.

My bitterness grew as I allowed myself to think of how badly he treated my daughter and me in general, which was *worse than the dog, and more like dog pooh!* I thought resentfully. But true to style—I zipped my lip and bottled up my anger, instead of dealing with the situation, as a 'normal adult would have done.

A few weeks later, my daughter went upstairs to her room and found a new deposit in the middle of her carpet. She stormed out of her room dramatically and complained loudly, as teenage girls normally do. In response to this little display, I overheard my husband say to her, "Stop making such a fuss. Just clean it up!" I blew a fuse! Without thinking twice I barged into her room.

"Oh no! You won't clean it up!" I said as I marched into her bathroom, pulled off yards of toilet paper, picked up the mess, went into the master bedroom and dropped it on the floor next to *his* side of the bed. Then I stormed past him on the way to my art studio and snapped, "Clean up after your own damn dog! Star is not doing it!"

This kind of conduct is apparently classic 'passive-aggressive behaviour'. Whatever the label is, I knew no other way of dealing with my anger. Since childhood, this was the only way I knew.

ॐ

When I turned six, there was to be a joint birthday party for my brother, one of my cousins, and me in order to cut down on the cost and effort. We had a big cake with three sections to it—one strawberry, one vanilla and one chocolate. Sometime before then, I had made friends with a girl who was quite a bit older than me. I was extremely proud of this friendship and desperately wanted to show her off at my birthday party. However, by the time the special birthday cake was about to be cut, she had still not arrived.

I remember experiencing an intense and very familiar, yet indescribable sensation in response to what I experienced as rejection. *How dare she not turn up?* I thought. I became sulky, and when no one took any notice of my mood, I promptly went into the kitchen, emptied the bottom cupboard, climbed into it and packed the pots and pans back into the cupboard from the inside. I stayed there, knowing that if nothing else, my absence from the cake cutting ceremony would at least be noticed.

This was the first time I can remember when I actually caused a scene to 'force' my mother to take notice of my hurt feelings. The only problem was—she didn't. She wasn't stirred at all, and the result was that my 'acting out' became more frequent and eventually it became a habitual response to pain and anger, and also a response to power issues with my mother.

One occasion I remember well was when I had to attend a wedding with her and I was just reaching the stage where I was eligible for pantyhose (with two little bee stings and about five pubic hairs I was *so* aware of myself). My mother refused the pantyhose and made me wear white socks with patent-leather shoes. I sulked, I 'stonewalled' her, I did the victim-martyr routine but nothing moved her.

So, when we arrived at the reception, I moved my chair out of the way so that I was obviously apart from the group of people at my table. I thought that nobody could ignore it. I was going to show my mother up, come what may. Everyone present that day, knew exactly just how unhappy and angry I was—I made sure of that.

The sad thing was that my mother never responded to this behaviour. If only she had realized that the core of the problem was that I didn't possess the emotional skills or tools to express my feelings. That was all. I wasn't 'naughty' or difficult, I was just a little messed-up emotionally and tongue-tied as a result.

℘

My father had abandoned me when I was only three years old. I wasn't even warned that he was going to leave and given the chance to express how I felt—which would have been to scream at the top of my little lungs: "Daddy, daddy don't leave me!" This didn't happen. One fine day he was simply gone. I had already bonded with him and loved him dearly. Until the day he left, I had trusted him with my whole heart and thought that he felt the same love towards me.

At that tender age, I took his leaving home *very* personally. I guess, ever since then, I have been saying: "Daddy, daddy please don't leave me" to all the men in my life in one way or another. just didn't know how to express it in an adult way.

When they wouldn't hear me, I would be hurt and angry and become passive-aggressive. I've always known that this kind of resistant behaviour made my partners extremely angry. In a sick sort of a way, noticing their anger towards me was better than experiencing no response at all. And I guess it's true to say that when you give me a black eye and a few broken bones, it is impossible for you *not* to see just how much you hurt me.

On the one hand I wished my mother knew how easily she could have prevented this pattern of behaviour in my life. All she needed to do when I became sullen was to talk to me about the situation that caused me such grief. Perhaps she could have hugged me and told me she loved me, but until the day she died she never did either.

On the other hand there was my husband who would use violence in reaction to any conflict. Where exactly he learned this response, I wouldn't know. But I'm sure that it stemmed from childhood wounds accompanied by inadequate parenting, just as my responses did.

I was not the only victim of his violent outbursts. On many occasions I protected his own children against his violent outbursts. He had often beaten up strangers for 'giving him lip'. Sometimes, but very seldom, someone would have the courage to stand up to him.

On one such rare occasion he was standing in a queue at an automatic teller machine and speaking loudly on his cell phone. His arrogance apparently irritated the man in front of him, who told him to "shut up". Without any hesitation, he punched this stranger in the face.

Now, usually, he would get charged with assault and then somehow his lawyer cousin would make the whole thing 'go away.' However, this time, my husband met his match. The stranger unceremoniously went to his car, fetched his gun and boldly held it against my husband's head in front of all the other people in the queue. It took the security guard with his automatic rifle pointed at this man much coaxing before he calmed down. When my husband arrived back home and told me the story, he was shaking like a leaf. The bully had been transformed into the coward!

On another occasion, he was taken to task by a nineteen-year old staff member for unfair dismissal and lost the case. She hurt him where he could least handle the pain—his pocket!

∞

For thirteen long, suffering years, I did not have the courage to stand up to my husband in an adult way. Or perhaps I could not remember where I had hidden my courage. More likely, I was simply not ready to awaken the giant within me and take up the challenge to be true to myself. Being true to myself would have been to pack up and leave voluntarily, like a lady. This was not to be—not then and not eventually, either. Courage only came to me later in my life.

The expensive make-up that I could easily afford would usually cover all the bruises. After a beating I would literally feel myself splitting into two distinctly separate people. It was the adult Caryl that took the abused and forsaken child by the hand and said: "Come now, let's fix you up and make you pretty so that you can face the world." I actually used to verbalize those words while I nursed myself and covered up the wounds! This manner of splitting into two separate personas was a method I had cultivated since childhood when I needed to console myself.

As always, I would wait for the arrest, hoping that someone would intervene and help me deal with 'the problem'. That of course never happened, either. I suspect that my husband's money in combination with Lawyer-Cousin's disdain for the law had everything to do with my case files disappearing. I, on the other hand, never followed up on the process. I waited and hoped, instead of doing the right thing.

&#8467;

Denial is a very curious creature. This was not my first violent marriage. When I turned twenty-one years old, I moved from Rhodesia to South Africa. A friend and I had plans to travel the world and I needed to make some money. In South Africa I was offered a well-paid job and a company car with one of the top cosmetic companies. I had been modelling since I was fourteen years old and this job suited me like a glove. I was promoted quickly from sales representative to Public Relations Officer.

It was 1972 and a British band, The Troggs, came to South Africa on tour. The company I was working for sponsored the band, and as their official PRO, I had to travel with them wherever they were performing.

On the night of their first performance, I met them at their hotel in a mining town called Welkom, for drinks. In the ladies' bar there was a one-man show. He was absolutely gorgeous. He looked just like Andy Gibb of Bee Gees' fame. After admiring him quietly for a while, I asked the waiter for a sheet of paper and cheekily wrote down a special request and sent it over to the Andy Gibb lookalike.

After he performed my request, he took a break and joined us for a drink. While we were chatting I brought up the subject of graphology. This had been my passion for a long time. Ever since I can remember, I had been fascinated by other people's handwriting. By that stage, I had taught myself all I could from the few books I could find on the topic. Andy wasted no time in asking me to analyze his handwriting. He gave me a sample with the words: "I am just a discontented citizen."

Sadly I wasn't very proficient in graphology, or else I would have noticed the warning signs. Instead, I was so taken by this man that I only noticed that the lower zones of his letters were over-exaggerated. This I thought reflected a good sexual appetite. And of course, I didn't hesitate to inform him of that.

I went back to Johannesburg the following day and Andy and I started corresponding in the old-fashioned way. We struck up a friendship and every time he came to Johannesburg we would go out together. We were physically attracted to each other, but I definitely didn't think it was going anywhere. In fact, we went out to a house party and Andy got so drunk that we had to stay over. I slept next to him in my gold, scratchy cocktail dress (which scratched both of us the whole night). He suggested I take it off promising not to do anything funny, but I refused.

I had only had one serious boyfriend by then and regarded myself as a decent young woman, rather than someone who was 'playing hard-to-get'. A couple of months after we met, he landed a gig in Cape Town. By then I was ready for some fun and when he asked me to join him, I instantly applied for a job transfer. The cosmetic company offered me the only position they had available in Cape Town. This didn't suit me, and I promptly resigned from a job that most girls could only dream of! Andy was perfectly happy with the decision because he earned a sufficient amount of money. He also worked all night and with me not working, we could both sleep late.

During the course of the following three months he showed his lesser attractive side, to say the least. It turned out that he had a drinking problem and a controlling, abusive personality to go with it. I broke up with him on many occasions. Each time he would beg me to come back, promising that the abuse and drinking would not recur. Of course it never stopped and when I discovered that I was pregnant, I ran away from him.

&#8734;

My mother was living in one of Rhodesia's finest tourist towns—Kariba, and I went straight to her. At that stage, she was married to her third husband and it probably comes as no surprise to learn that he was violent and abusive to her as well—like mother, like daughter. This third husband was an absolute creep. When I was introduced to him he undressed me with his eyes and then tried to give me a French kiss!

One evening they had a fight in the local pub and my mother and I went home, leaving him there to carry on drinking. She made me sleep on a stretcher next to her bed, which would force him to sleep in the lounge. The temperatures in Kariba reach into the forties and most people sleep without pyjamas on. When he came home in the early hours of the morning he crouched down next to me and tried to lift the bed sheet off me to peer at my scantily clad body. I pretended to sleep, but turned over to make him think I was waking. He did it again, and I stirred some more. Eventually he stood up, stared at my mother and me for a while and then mercifully left the room. I was absolutely terrified.

This was not the first time I was molested by my mother's husband. The previous creep had more success because I was only seven years old at the time.

One would think that my mother, under the circumstances of her own unfortunate choices, would have had some empathy for the circumstances I found myself in. However, when I told her that I was pregnant, she was furious.

"How could you do this to me? After all I have done for you!"

Even though we had a screaming row, I didn't challenge her on exactly what she had done for me. She wanted to know what I was going to do, and made it very clear that she was not going to be part of the problem. It was mine.

In a ploy to solicit assistance from her, I threatened to give the baby up for adoption. She went ballistic and screamed at me. "This baby is *my* grandchild!" That was it—no solution, only this inexplicable possessiveness over my unplanned child. Then she chased me out of her home.

Kariba is not safe at night. There had been a leopard in the area that had killed a few pets, but I walked down the road to the home of a friend of my mother's, not caring if I lived or died. I felt abandoned and lonely. And yet, this feeling strangely comforted me because of its familiarity. Neither my mother nor I knew at the time that this friend was having an affair with my stepfather, and that this affair would eventually be the cause of the break-up of my parent's relationship.

The next day I left to go and stay with my brother, who lived on a farm outside Salisbury (Harare). He was about to get married and agreed that I could stay on the farm with him until the wedding.

In the meanwhile, Andy drove from Johannesburg to Kariba in a battered hippy-style van, in order to find me. I will never know how he tracked down my mother, but she phoned to let me know that he was on his way to meet me at my brother's place. My mother had always been a sucker for a good-looking man—just like me.

I remember vividly how I watched through the kitchen window of my brother's home as the blue van came down the driveway. My heart missed several beats—not because I was thrilled to see him. Andy begged me to go back to South Africa with him. My mother had still not softened her heart to my predicament, and as I perceived my situation at the time—I didn't really have another choice.

I was going to be a bridesmaid at my brother's wedding and I didn't want Andy to be there. Once before, when he attended a family wedding with me, he was most unpleasant, accusing me of "dancing with all the men". Yes, it was true, but they were all family members, mainly my cousins with whom I had grown up. He was extremely jealous and was certain to spoil the occasion for me. So, I promised solemnly to return to South Africa after my brother's wedding. He accepted and left Rhodesia.

Before he left, I made sure that he understood that even though I would keep my word and return to South Africa to be with him, I was not prepared to marry him. At the time, he didn't object. Andy and two of his friends met me at the airport in Johannesburg. After collecting my luggage he suggested we go for a drink in the bar. The minute he ordered a whisky, I wanted to run through to the departure lounge and get straight onto the plane. When I objected, he gave me one look that said: "Don't you try to mess with me." I sat quietly while they got drunk.

On the way home he asked me with a sarcastic smile: "So, when are we getting married?" I made the fatal mistake of replying that we were not. He screeched the car to halt in the underground parking of the apartment block where he lived and told me to "get out of the fucking car". He frog-marched me all the way up to the flat. I was absolutely terrified. I knew that each step I took I was closer to the consequences of rejecting his proposal—although I did not know at the time exactly what that might entail.

Once we were inside the apartment, he went crazy. He called me a whore and said that if I was good enough to carry his child, I was good enough to marry him. "How dare you try and leave me with *my* child in your stomach?" he screamed.

I was flabbergasted. It sounded just like my mother in a man's body! If I thought that Andy would react to this narcissistic injury by chasing me away and giving me a cold shoulder as my mother had done, I was gravely mistaken. He proceeded to physically abuse me by grabbing me by the hair and throwing me across the room, kicking and hitting me repeatedly.

Eventually, I managed to escape into the bathroom and while I sat on the floor sobbing, he walked in and laughed loudly.

"Bravo ... bravo!" he taunted. "You should get an Oscar." Then he picked up a tin of baby powder and hit me several times on the head until the tin exploded. He simply went to bed and with a smirk on his face he said, "Clean it up."

I don't know how many people have tried to gather up talcum powder from a wooden floor. Believe me it's pretty damned difficult. The more I tried to scoop it up, the more it simply shifted elsewhere. As Andy turned over in the bed to make his drunken carcass more comfortable, he muttered, "This better be clean in the morning." Then he promptly fell into a deep, peaceful sleep. The message was clear—I was back in his prison. (For those who are interested—I added a little water to the powder and made porridge on the floor. Eventually the floor was spotless!)

ജ

Over the days that followed I gave a lot of thought to my dire situation and decided to go to a home for unmarried mothers. When I arrived the matron settled me in a room and I curled up into a ball, clutching my swollen belly and cried. I was inconsolable.

The following day the matron soberly explained that I would not be able to stay unless I was prepared to give the baby up for adoption. Alas, it was too late. I had fallen hopelessly in love with the little person inside me and couldn't let the baby go. I instinctively knew it was a baby girl and I wanted her—in fact I needed her. So, I picked up my bags and went back to my prison.

Nothing was said for a few days. Then one day Andy came home and announced we were getting married the following day. He presented me with a beautiful engagement ring. Surely, the size of the four diamonds clearly stated that he loved me and that he was obviously going to treat me better from there on.

I was six months pregnant on my wedding day and it was not a happy day for me. I had nothing nice to wear and not *one* of my family members was present—they didn't even know I was getting married. After the court proceedings we went to the nearest hotel. While Andy got drunk in the bar, I went to the ladies' room, sat on the toilet and sobbed.

I knew from that day on that I had officially relinquished my right to protest against the treatment that he was going to dish out on a regular basis. I had been silenced.

I couldn't fathom what had become of my life. My mother may have been the black sheep of the family and she certainly had her problems, but we were from good stock all the same. My biological father was a professional man and so was every member of his family. I was his beloved 'Popsie', his only daughter in whom he delighted. There was such promise for me with all my talents. I had always dreamed of the traditional white wedding and my father proudly walking me down the isle. What in God's name had happened?

My situation went from bad to worse. When I was in the final stages of my pregnancy, we left for Lesotho where Andy had a nine-month gig at the Holiday Inn in Maseru. I tried hard to change my attitude and fake happiness. I had faked enough orgasms so I was getting quite good at pretending! Of course, all the feigning in the world didn't make the abuse go away. He was insanely jealous and watched me like a hawk.

He played music in the hotel at night from about 7 p.m. until the early hours of the morning. I was tiring easily with my pregnancy and would remain in the little bungalows where all the staff from the casino stayed. The southern part of Africa didn't have television in those days, so I would listen to stories on the radio and knit booties for my baby. I had fallen in love with my little baby girl and she had become my only reason for living.

ಬ

One night while I was fast asleep, I woke up to the sound of the front door being kicked open. At first I thought it was a terrorist attack and lay paralyzed in the dark, expecting to hear gunshots any minute. Suddenly Andy walked into the lounge and started to laugh like a crazed maniac. He came into the bedroom, walking deliberately. I stupidly pretended to be sleeping—I mean *really*! The whole complex would have heard the commotion.

He walked up to me, grabbed a handful of my waist-length hair and in one yank ripped me off the bed and threw me across the room, straight into the cupboard door. He beat me and started to kick me all over while screaming, "You fucking bitch! Whore! I will fucking kill you!"

The more I asked him what I had done, the more his fists rained down on me. Due to my total lack of defence, he eventually got bored with me and went through to the lounge, picked a lounge chair up above his head and while screaming like a Viking, he crashed the chair down on the floor.

I hesitantly approached him and asked once more what I had done to cause him such uncontrollable rage. Without answering, he started to make a fire. Slowly but surely he pulled the chair to pieces and fed it piece by piece into the fireplace, all the while mumbling threats and accusations at me! I was dumbfounded and bewildered. Was I somehow to blame for his anger?

&#8523;

Nearly thirty years later, with my third husband, I was to experience a carbon copy of that baffling night in Maseru. It was as if my soul was asking me—*when are you finally going to get it?*

The occasion was when my husband and I were out to dinner with friends and I walked out on the three of them and went home after our conversation became argumentative. Because I anticipated a violent reaction, I purposely locked him out of the house. I thought that the locked-out-husband would sleep off his intoxication in the car. I was wrong. When Hitler-Babe came home and found the front door locked, he simply kicked it open.

I thought of escaping through the back door, but that meant I would have to pass him in the passage. So I decided to pretend that I was asleep. (Don't I ever learn?) This deliberate passive-aggressive behaviour never helps any situation. He walked into the bedroom, and just like Andy did all those years ago, grabbed me by the hair and in one movement ripped me out of the bed and threw me across the room, straight into the cupboard door, screaming, "You fucking bitch! How dare you lock me out?"

He swore abuse and threats. As with Andy, I tried to reason

with him, but with the amount of alcohol he had consumed, it was impossible. He kicked me and pushed me around the room and eventually threw me down on the floor and started to punch me in the face. I refused to fight back which at first seemed to annoy him even more. He punched me hard in the face and threatened to kill me, but eventually he got bored with me and stopped.

The whole drama felt surreal. I was so hazy from the adrenaline pumping through my veins that it was difficult to tell if it was a new experience or if I was having a nightmare recalling the previous time I was flung from my bed by my hair. I somehow ended up sitting on a chest of drawers, totally dumbfounded. He kept asking me the same question over and over: "Why did you lock me out? I am not going to leave you alone until you answer me." I refused to answer him, but in utter frustration I started banging my head on the overhanging beam. I just wanted him to go away.

Life was clearly trying to tell me something. I was the common denominator in both scenarios! I was either causing the abuse or allowing it to happen. But if I was the problem, why did these men move heaven and earth to make me stay? Perhaps I was missing the point all together.

∞

Sometime after this event and in an effort to make sense of it all, I confided in a female friend about the violence in my marriage. She was our interior decorator and had endeared herself to me by sharing her own marital problems, and the affair she was having with a married man. Not even my oldest friends knew the extent and the details of the trauma I was experiencing.

As far as most people were concerned, my life was to be envied—I was a talented artist; was able to buy anything my heart desired; I drove the latest German sports car; lived in a dream home with a landscaped garden in the best area money could buy; was married to a handsome, successful and jovial husband and I was always smiling. That's right—I would show a happy face to the world—not the long-suffering look of a martyr, or the pained expression of the victim.

I would use my clothes as mood-enhancers, always dressing up to help me achieve the 'happy-look'. If I were to commit suicide, (a thought that was never far out of my mind), my friends would have been surprised. "Sure she had difficulties in her marriage, but hell! Don't we all?"

I believed that I could trust this new friend, the interior decorator, and I shared my heart with her, telling her all about the latest fight with Hitler-Babe in detail. But to my dismay, when my husband and I were engaged in the divorce battle, she became so 'friendly' with him that she produced an affidavit in which she stated that I had confessed to her that I would habitually beat myself up and then lay charges of assault against my husband! How had she been promoted from our interior decorator to my husband's closest confidante? I couldn't help but wonder about their friendship.

The mind boggles. Did he seriously think that the judge would believe that I was in the habit of sporadically breaking my own arm and nose several times, giving myself black eyes and a couple of 'shiners' on the jaw, bruising my body, cracking my ribs and sternum and pulling clusters of hair out of my head, over a period of thirteen years? Interestingly enough, the cause of that particular fight on the night when I banged my head on the beam, was due to yet another woman's betrayal of my confidence.

ॐ

That same evening my husband and I were out to dinner with

another couple. The husband was a director of a prestigious institution and he was Hitler-Babe's golfing buddy. Several weeks prior to this dinner date, the wife had arrived at my house in an hysterical panic with her three teenagers in tow. They were literally fleeing from home because her husband 'was losing the plot'. He had apparently smashed up the furniture and was threatening them.

I soon gathered that this was not an unusual occurrence. In fact, she confessed that their marriage had been violently abusive for years and that he had once put her in hospital. Of course, she was too scared to leave him—he was a very powerful man but only in her eyes. At dinner, after several drinks, our two husbands with their typical misogynistic arrogance, started to make derogatory comments about women. Abusive remarks like "Oh that dumb blonde with the plastic tits…" were commonplace in the company of men like my husband and his friends.

Believing that I had an ally in this woman, I decided to challenge them. To my horror, instead of closing ranks with me, she started turning on me! I was deeply hurt. In fact, her betrayal enraged me. Men stick up for each other—why don't women? As always, I dealt with my anger in a passive manner, and it was at this point that I left the restaurant, went home and locked the front door so that my husband couldn't get into the house.

Whatever wisdoms life was attempting to communicate to me, one thing was for sure—my honing device was so faulty that I could not trust it any more. When I became a Christian all those years ago, my intuition was razor-sharp. I would never have made errors of judgment in character or trusted the wrong kind of people in the past. It occurred to me that constantly asking God for guidance and then ignoring it when it came had obliterated this gift of the Holy Spirit.

Another insight that became apparent, however dimly, was

the unwarranted power this woman and I had bestowed on our husbands. Sure, they were both successful men with contacts in high places, but that shouldn't have been a threat to us—it should have been a bonus! Instead we cowered at the Boys' Club and diminished our solidarity even further through acts of betrayal and jealousy of one another. How sad! It was completely unnecessary.

ॐ

I was about to turn fifty in December 2000 and my husband forty the following April. My birthday falls between Christmas and New Year and as a result my birthday often went ignored or even forgotten. In fact, since I've had a family of my own, we were usually travelling on my birthday going somewhere for New Year's celebrations. I used to joke about it, saying things like, "On which airport shall we spend my birthday this year? Or shall we just make a quick stop at a garage shop? Why don't we have it on the bridge between Pretoria and Johannesburg— that way friends from both cities will only have to drive halfway?"

Yes, I was quite bitter about the situation, but I genuinely believed that, for once in my life, an effort would be made for my fiftieth birthday. Someone, perhaps the man who was hailed as my soul mate, would congregate all the people I loved and give me a party that would make up for the countless ones I had not had. My birthday was approaching and there was no discussion as to what we would be doing. I became increasingly resentful that this was a big occasion and even so, no one seemed to care—least of all my husband.

At the same time, Hitler-Babe's involvement with Round Table added more tension to our strained marriage. He spent many nights attending their functions and came home very late, sometimes even in the early hours of the morning. I was fast becoming a real WART—that is, a Woman Against Round Table.

One afternoon, my husband went off to play cricket at a Round Table function. We had been bickering and arguing a lot at that time and I decided not to go and watch him play. Apart from the 'happy face' I would have to fake, I would be keeping company with all the other wives. They were all much younger than me and we had little in common. They had young children and bragged about 'little Johnny's' achievements in grade one, while my own were already experimenting with drugs and bunking high school!

Later that day, I received a phone call from one of the Round Tablers to say that my husband had been seriously injured and was on his way to an emergency clinic. He had broken his leg so badly that the doctors were concerned that an embolism would form and cause a heart attack. He was admitted into High Care.

I was amazed at how suddenly fearful I was that he would die. My heart spontaneously turned from acid anger to concern. Just a month before this accident, we had found and bought our dream home. Up until that point, we had already moved nine times in six years, so instead of feeling excited about moving into this exquisite home, I was filled with angst about his health.

At the same time, my beloved father-in-law was bravely being treated for cancer, but the writing was on the wall. I was spreading myself thin visiting his father in a hospital on the one side of the city; rushing to attend to my husband in a clinic on the other; attempting to prepare our new home and packing up for the move. I was completely overwhelmed with all the responsibility, and the anxiety about my husband's health was beginning to choke me.

For the first time in our relationship I wondered how I would feel if he died. I cried many nights while he was in hospital. I thought of the huge responsibilities I would have to face with his business, the properties, our children, his father and, most of all, my broken heart.

It may be confusing for some to consider the love I had for a man who habitually beat me up and caused me untold pain and humiliation. The frustrating truth is that this man had another side to him. When we were alone together we laughed a lot and he made me feel that I was the only person he truly cared about. Wherever we went, he would take my hand and hold it with such purpose that it gave me a sense of belonging that nothing else on God's earth could match. When we drove in the car he would put my hand on his leg. When we sat in the movies he would take my hand onto his lap and stroke or tickle my arm so tenderly that it was impossible to remember that he had broken bones in that very hand without any mercy on a previous occasion. He would often look at me and say, "You are so beautiful."

Apart from this, it had been my third attempt at a happy marriage. I was stubbornly insisting that we still had a chance to sort things out and live happily ever after. I was too proud to admit defeat at that stage. I absolutely *had* to be right about us. I simply could not believe that God would be so cruel as to have led me to this man, after five arduous years of celibacy, while I was practising my faith.

It was my deepest desire that the accident would provide my husband and me with an opportunity to heal the divide between us. I saw the accident as a chance to nurture him in a way that I had been yearning to do for many years. Truth be told, I wanted him to need me.

To my utter irritation, a friend of his completely thwarted my intentions for increased intimacy between us. I had long been ill at ease with this particular Aggressive Friend. They were golf buddies and the two of them repeatedly made homosexual innuendos like, "Your turn to bring the Vaseline to the golf course today!" My husband also used to buy him curiously personal little gifts, like a dressing gown with his initials embroidered on it, when we went on our overseas holidays. Now, every time I arrived at the hospital this golfing buddy would be sitting at his bedside like the proverbial consoling wife!

In the meanwhile, the doctor asked to see me privately. When I met with him, he asked if my husband was a 'drinker' because he was apparently not responding well to the treatment. They thought he might be going through withdrawal symptoms from alcohol abuse. They were quite correct of course, but when the doctor suggested that I bring his usual drink to the hospital so that he could get his 'fix', I was shocked. I had not realized that his drinking habit was already out of hand and with this, of course, came the knowledge that I would happily join in whenever I was with him.

I recalled the days long gone when I was a teetotaller, before I met him. There was no denying it—alcohol played a big part in our habitual violent fighting. As predicted, my husband started to hallucinate. He had dreams that he was in a fire and that someone in the hospital was trying to take his life. He contacted Lawyer-Cousin and insisted he be taken out of hospital "before they killed him".

When his cousin phoned to inform me that he was on his way to discharge my husband, I flew into a rage and forbade him to do that. I had had some nursing experience as a young woman and understood what my husband was going through. I was also piqued—it was not his cousin's right to release him from hospital—if anybody's, it was mine. In the end, I had to get the support from the medical staff to prevent my husband's untimely release!

ᛒ

At home once more, it became obvious that my husband and I had separate concerns—he was worried about how he was going to continue doing business and pay the bills and I was distressed about the neglected state of our marriage. I wanted everyone else out of the picture so that we could spend time together while he was convalescing at home.

However, he had created close bonds with his Round Table friends and other people, which totally excluded me. I was becoming acutely aware of the lack of status I occupied in his life as his wife.

One evening, while he was watching television, I decided to confront the situation. Of course I was taking advantage of the fact that he had a leg in plaster and thought that for once he would sit and listen to me. When he was dismissive of my appeal about paying attention to our marriage, I lost my temper and started to yell at him. I was standing right in front of him and without warning, he picked up a glass of water from the little side table and threw it in my face. Almost robotically, I slapped him across the face. All hell broke loose.

He jumped up on his broken leg and hit me so forcefully that I fell over onto the floor. My youngest daughter, Star, by now a teenager, came running downstairs to intervene. She had heard the screaming and shouting from her room upstairs.

As she tried to help me, he screamed at her to mind her own "fucking business". When she persisted in her attempt to save me, he slapped her and she fell backwards onto the couch. All the while he managed to keep kicking me in my ribs, as I lay flat on the floor. As soon as my daughter regained her stance she grabbed a hold of my arm and started to pull me along the floor to try and get me away from him. He simply continued kicking me while I was in this extremely vulnerable position. Naturally, he and I were both swearing and shouting at each other like two crazed lunatics.

How that particular evening actually ended is a complete

blank to me, but I do recall finding it absolutely amazing that he could even beat me up with a broken leg. I probably spent the rest of the night driving around in my car with my teenage daughter by my side.

His kids never interfered in our fights. They were terrified of him. My teenage daughter, on the other hand, regularly came to my rescue during a fight and always suffered abuse of some sort as a result. These days, it breaks my heart to think about this young and frail girl-child who would fearlessly face the big bully, just as David did with Goliath. Star was also the one who took the photographs of my wounds after a fight.

I admittedly never discussed the situation with her, or with my other two daughters for that matter. The reason for this was that I knew the minute I opened the proverbial can of worms for a discussion, I would inevitably have to take some corrective action. I simply was not ready for that. Believe me when I say that this self-centred, cowardly, behaviour on my part is as difficult to write about as it was to live with. I couldn't face myself, let alone my children.

℘

As a child I was also dragged into my mother's traumatic fighting with her husbands. I was also bundled into the car and driven off to 'God alone knows where'; I was also forever leaving home and finding refuge with friends; I also bore witness to my mother's irrational and desperate reactions to the chronic abuse she subjected herself to.

One evening she was so insane with desperation that she swam across a crocodile-infested river to 'escape' from her situation without giving my well-being a second thought.

I knew the damage this had done to me and that one day I will have to look my own daughters in the eye and say the very words my mother could never get past her lips—"I am sorry". I sadly also realize that when I finally do get round to that day of freedom from obsession with destructive relationships, "I am sorry" may very well be too late.

Yet, for the time being, I dared not challenge the fact that I had become a mother like the one I'd grown up with—the very person that I'd promised myself I would never become. Facing the emotional wounds that I was inflicting on my three beloved daughters in addition to the unremitting burden I had been carrying since childhood was too much to bear. Perhaps it is as a result of my past, but for as long as I can remember, I was certainly not my own best friend.

# What's in A Name?

When I was about thirteen years old and very unhappy in my own skin, I asked my mother why she gave me the name of Caryl, and specifically why she decided to spell it with a 'y'. She stopped what she was doing, tilted her head back and a wistful smile spread across her face. It looked as if my question had conjured up a fond memory for her, but then, quite matter-of-factly she told me.

"When I was pregnant with you, I was first going to call you Jill, after your father's sister. But then I read a story about a serial killer called Caryl, and I liked the spelling of the name."

At the time, I was living with my mother in Salisbury, the capital of Rhodesia. She was a working and a drinking mother. Be that as it may, after I received the unwelcome information regarding my name, I decided instantly that I wanted to have a new name. As a solution to my predicament I initiated a game in which my friends and I chose nicknames for each other. To my mind, nicknames symbolized perfect happiness. My popular elder brother had one—Fish, and all those who called him by that name would smile when they said it. He loved fishing as a teenager and as far as I could tell, his nickname was perfect—it described his greatest passion; it reminded his friends that they enjoyed fishing with him and it embodied the special bond he had with my mother—she shared his enthusiasm for fishing. I had no part in this twosome.

When the nickname game was on, one of my friends said that I reminded her of the character Pebbles from the popular animated TV series, entitled *The Flintstones*. A great source of humour is the way in which animals are used in the place of technology. For example a baby woolly mammoth is used as a vacuum cleaner. The animals, from time to time, will look straight at the audience, shrug and remark: "It's a living."

Although most of the episodes have stand-alone storylines, one of the most memorable stories is the episode surrounding the birth of the sweet child, Pebbles, to the lead characters, Fred and Wilma Flintstone. I welcomed the nickname 'Pebbles' with open arms. It felt great to be associated with something like *The Flintstones*, a show that spread such joy to all who came into contact with it.

My best friend was duly nicknamed Bamm-Bamm, after Fred and Wilma's abnormally strong adopted son! She didn't mind this at all, yet, out of our whole group who were christened that day, I was the only one who retained my nickname. I adopted the persona of Pebbles with my whole heart. I was no longer Caryl the serial killer, but Pebs the innocent child of Fred and Wilma Flintstone. She was cute, warm and friendly and I managed to completely convince myself that I was this new personality. I spontaneously started to feel happier and wittier. I simply loved my newfound freedom and to this day special friends still call me Pebs. When they do, it reminds me of those special times when I managed to trick myself into self-love and acceptance. "It's a living," I guess.

After that day, Caryl continued to have many traumatic experiences. Pebs, on the other hand, remained light-hearted and funny, perfectly untouched by any of it. She was without a care in the world—just like her two-dimensional fantasy counterpart on television. There was one particularly nasty ordeal, however, that was difficult to separate. It was one of those childhood experiences that leave an impression that is difficult to erase. We all have them. This one happened when I was nearly fourteen years old.

∞

My group of friends and I decided to bunk school and meet at a boy's house who was regarded as a classic high-school dropout. His house was a regular meeting place for school kids, especially the boys, to listen to music and to smoke.

On this particular day, we were about six boys and four girls. I somehow ended up in one of the bedrooms, talking to the dropout. In the meanwhile, my girlfriends left the house without telling me. They had apparently become aware that the boys had 'ulterior motives', but for some reason they omitted to inform me. At that stage of our lives, we were all still innocent and not ready to experiment with sex. I, in particular, was pretty naïve and determined to remain a virgin until my wedding night. There were quite a few 'scrubbers' in our grade, but no member of my group was one of them.

The next thing I knew, all the other boys came into the bedroom and strategically draped themselves around the dropout and me. Some sat down on the bed, while the others hung around the bedroom, or lowered themselves onto their haunches. I suddenly became afraid and decided to leave. When I tried to open the door, one of the guys beat me to it and locked it. They were laughing among themselves and I realized that something was seriously amiss.

Then the dropout, being the eldest, grabbed me and started to kiss me while he tried to unbutton my school uniform. I resisted and struggled to untangle myself from his grip. It became perfectly clear that they were planning to 'pull a train' – or in other words, to each have sex with me. At that stage of my youthful life I had never even heard of this sordid practice or encountered it in any way. However, I instinctively knew that something bad was going to happen, if I allowed it. When all my other brave defences failed, I started to sob loudly, and eventually the tears did the trick. They let me go, taunting me as I ran off.

"You're childish! Pathetic! Why don't you go home to your

mama?"

Even though they did not manage to rape me, they spread the rumour that I had participated in a 'gang bang'. I felt violated and so defenceless against their vicious lie, that I begged my mother to take me to a doctor to prove that I was still a virgin. I wanted a medical certificate to that effect.

My father had moved to Zambia with his new wife some time before then, and to my surprise, my mother decided to stand by me. At that stage she had already started the sinister and intimidating routine of calling me a "common hussy" whenever I put on my legendary pink lipstick, Mary Quant style, or attracted attention from the opposite sex with my mini skirts and baby-doll dresses that were flared into tent shapes with halter necks and cut-away arm holes. I feared that the situation I was in could give the appearance of fulfilling her prophecies.

Yet, she went to see the dropout's father in the hope that he would convince his son to tell the truth about what had happened on that particular day. The father unfortunately seemed to be a lot like his son and summarily dismissed the event, as well as my mother and me as "childish".

With this effortless sentence, my lot was sealed and my reputation was ruined. I became known as the "common hussy"—just as my own mother had already labelled me.

My mother's concerns about my respectability were decidedly unfounded, but not entirely out of place. The Rhodesia of the sixties was under sanctions from the rest of the world for intensely displeasing the Crown but that story belongs in another book. The fact was, we still had access to international television shows and the youth were exposed to the worldwide fashion revolution and faithfully followed the trend.

I am quite sure that my mother, having grown up during the Elvis Presley era, also shocked and displeased *her* mother with the way she dressed, but nothing could have prepared parents of teenagers in the sixties for Mary Quant and her mini skirts, 'hot' pants, the geometric hair cuts and almost theatrical make-up. And of course, the attitude to go with it was revealed in Mary Quant's cheeky statement, "Snobbery has gone out of fashion and in our shops you will find duchesses jostling with typists to buy the same dress."

The point I am making is that the change was radical. And what was more, Mary Quant's bold new 'mod' or 'Chelsea look' made London the centre of fashion, and as a British colony, or ex-colony (the teens didn't really care one way or the other) we were right there doing our thing with the rest and the best of them.

It breaks my heart to realize how out of touch my mother was with my tender and young soul at that exciting time of my life. It could have been so different for us, so beautiful. My brother had already left home by then. My mother was without a husband and the scene was set for the two of us to be each other's close confidantes and chums. I was no "common hussy", not by a long stretch of the imagination.

My friends and I were searching in encyclopedias to find some form of sex education. When we first saw drawings of the human anatomy we guiltily thought we were looking at porn. We had never seen genitals in all our lives—not each other's or our own for that matter!

We were vaguely aware about something called 'the curse', and that it came to all girls at the age of sixteen or once they developed breasts. So when I saw blood 'down there' at the age of fourteen, I became quite hysterical and phoned my mother at work.

"Mum … I think I'm dying! Come home quick!"

Without demanding an explanation, she simply replied, "Don't worry Caryl, you won't bleed to death. I'll deal with it when I come home tonight."

Those were the days of suspender belts and stockings. Due to the sanctions, Rhodesia had no access to the latest trend in tights. How we managed to wear our mini dresses with no protection from the elements and the occasional glimpses of unsightly stocking tops is beyond me, but we did.

When my mum came home, she gave me a little 'party pack'. A quick and clinical explanation of how to strap the 'nappy' to a thin belt and then to my body, and that was that. There was no invitation from her to discuss the matter any further. I took all my queries to my girlfriends at school. And they gave me the private and confidential details that my mother had omitted to part with.

"It's like you are on heat. Guys can tell by looking in your eyes and that is when you can fall pregnant."

Most of my sex education came from my husbands. I remember my first husband laughing until I thought he would pass out when I asked him what happened to the bone after his erection disappeared! I had no idea what an orgasm was until I finally experienced an orgasm at the age of forty-two. My third husband had the honours, and I'm not sure who was more surprised—him or me!

୫

It was many years after that awful experience in Salisbury with the aspiring 'gang bangers', after I had already moved to South Africa and was sharing a flat with a girlfriend in Hillbrow, that I heard the expression 'pulling a train' for the first time. One Sunday morning, several girls whom we had befriended were lounging around in our flat. Two really unsavoury men came to visit one of the girls. She was from 'the other side of the railway tracks', as it were, and I wasn't too sure how she had ended up in our group of friends to begin with.

After a while in the company of these men, I decided to go

and read my book in my bedroom. As I walked out, I heard one of the men say to the other, "So, who's going to pull the train?" As I closed the door behind me, I smugly thought to myself, "No wonder I don't like them … they work on the railways!" Only once the men were gone and I shared my snobbish opinion of them with my girlfriends, did they educate me to the squalid meaning of the expression. I shuddered when I realized that I had come close to the experience as an unsullied teenager without even knowing what the term meant.

All in all, that incident in Salisbury was the reason for the cultivation of a habit I continued from then on. I would keep a record of absolutely everything that I might need to prove a 'truth'—be that a letter, a note, print-outs of pager messages, cell-phone text messages, photos—whatever it took. If it looked like something, which could bear witness in an instance when my word could be doubted, I would preserve it.

The near 'gang bang' and my wrecked reputation was the final straw to convince me that Caryl was always going to have some kind of problem: I would get abused and be left helpless. I had become super-sensitive to rejection and other people's opinion of me, and that made me easy prey for the cruelty of the boys around town.

One day, a friend and I decided to dress up to go to the movies. We tried out new hairstyles and clothes, and felt very unsure of ourselves as we walked down the road with our mini skirts and (forbidden) pink lipstick. Adding to this ensemble, my long hair was neatly done up and sprayed as stiff as a board.

As we turned the corner, we heard someone whistle and shout "Hello dreamboat!" When we turned around to see who it was, we saw a bunch of guys standing together in a group. Once they got our attention, they shouted, "Not you bloody shipwrecks!" I took this typical teenage prank very personally and never risked going out on the town dressed like that again. Plain Jane was safer.

After that incident with the 'dropout', my mother came to the conclusion that we would be happier living in a smaller community where it was 'safer' for me. So, we moved to a small farming town called Marandellas. She had been divorced twice by then and little did she know that the biggest threat to my safety up to that point had come from within the confines of our household.

℘

When I was six years old my mother married for the first time after she and my father had got divorced. He was a smooth-talking pig who molested me on many occasions during their short marriage. One of his favourite tricks was to hold me on his lap while feeding me sweets, pushing his hard erection against me while at the same time casually talking to my mother. She knew nothing of what was going on and I was far too afraid to tell her.

My mother and her new husband would drink up a storm. I used to dread their drunken fights and would hear my name bandied about with much accusation and bitterness, particularly from him. He was violent and I was terrified of him.

One night during such a fight, my mother stormed into my room, locked the door and climbed into the bed with me. When she refused to unlock the door and let him into my room, he went outside and threw a beer bottle through the window, shattering glass all over the room and on my bed.

℘

Many years later this scene repeated itself—only this time I was storming into my six-year-old daughter's room. While I was lying in the bed next to her, my third husband, threw mud from the garden onto the bed. Like my own daughter, I had nightmares and I wet the bed for the entire time that my mother was married to her second husband. Fortunately theirs was a short-lived marriage. My mother left him after a year or two.

The thought of my stepfather and what he had done to me was all the more reason for me to reject Caryl. In fact, I had started to despise her. So when we moved to the clean-living and unchallenging community of Marandellas, Pebs left Caryl behind in Salisbury. Pebs was in control of her life and was full of fun—she was never angry. What was more, she had blossomed into a very attractive long-legged teenager with long jet-black hair, big dark eyes and an olive-toned skin. "Mysterious looking girl", some people called her, quite different to her mother with her auburn hair and freckles.

The most attractive quality about me, however, was that I had developed charisma, a certain charm that others found hard to resist, and in spite of my mum's assurance that I would "never grow up to be a lady" I started at the new school and felt ten feet tall. Until then I had received a lot of attention for my sporting achievements in athletics, netball and swimming. Suddenly, I had lost the desire for sport. I was getting enough attention for simply being me! And to top that, I was the new girl in town—everybody at school noticed me.

Soon after my arrival there, I was asked to be a model in the school's fashion show. Being a model was a secret dream of mine, and I decided to start paying more attention to my appearance—particularly to my weight. I had been quite chubby as a child and as a result, whenever I was chosen to appear in a school play or ballet concert, I always portrayed the sun, a tree or anything else as long as I didn't have to move around.

Now, with my dream to be a model becoming a reality for the first time, I went on my first diet. It mainly comprised of starving myself, and it worked! The more I lost weight, the more I started to eat like a bird. I would starve myself for days and then lie on the floor to see if my hipbones stuck out far enough for me to see down my pants. And if it was impossible to shave my armpits because they were too hollow, I considered this to be a good sign for my modelling aspirations.

This was also the time when I started my love affair with books. The first novel I read outside of children stories and setwork books was Wilbur Smith's novel *When the Lions Feed*. It is the story of South Africa at the burgeoning time of the gold rush in the 1880s. The hero of the story, Sean Courtney, is raised in cattle country and after a stint fighting Zulu tribes, Sean tries his luck in the goldfields, venturing on an impossible claim, which miraculously proves to be in his favour. It is an intriguing story, but the most dazzling scene in the whole book as far as I was concerned at the time, is when he takes a girl into a river and makes love to her. It was the most romantic thing I had ever imagined and I strongly recommended the book to all my friends.

At Marandellas High there was one particular boy who reminded me of Sean Courtney. He was popular, sporty, 'one of the boys' and seemed to like me a lot. In no time, Sean and I became an item. As often happens in small communities, our parents became good friends and when my mother and I moved out of our little house, his family invited us to live with them on their farm for a while until we found another suitable home to rent.

My mother and I fitted into their family as though we had always meant to be part of them. They were a big family of four sisters and two brothers. My boyfriend was somewhere in the middle. His younger sister, Emily, and I were three years apart and I adored her like she was my very own little sister. Those couple of months on the farm were the happiest times of my life.

It fulfilled my greatest yearning to belong to a 'normal' family. All I knew of a functional family, I learnt from them. Sure, they had their problems but they stuck together through thick and thin. There was never any doubt in anyone's mind that they wouldn't work things out and stay together—much like Wilbur Smith's fictional family, the Courtneys.

Life was fun and happy for the very first time since I could remember. We got up to lots of mischief in this small town. We sneaked into the local swimming pool one night, only to be arrested by my boyfriend's future brother-in-law. We rode horses and went fishing in the local dam. We played golf and tennis at the local club. We went to many parties and learnt how to drink and then later would throw up in the rose bushes. We would sneak out at night and meet to talk nonsense. We went to visit other youngsters on the neighbouring farms; we drove in the rain and got stuck in the mud, messing up my newly made dress, which my boyfriend's mother could whip up in less than a day. In short, I found a family who loved me and I adored them. I belonged. My prince on his white horse had rescued me and the future seemed bright.

My love affair with Sean helped to distract me from the strained relationship between my mother and me. I became very sceptical of her criticisms which were supposed to be for my 'own good'. She also developed double standards. She had a set for me and another set for my friend who came to stay. My mother became unduly fond of her and virtually adopted her.

This girlfriend was at boarding school in Marandellas. Her parents lived in the south of the country, and apparently sent her away because she was a so-called problem child. I instantly took pity on her for being all alone over weekends and decided to rescue her by inviting her to come and live with us. What I didn't bargain on was that she would become my brother's girlfriend and that she and my mother would also 'fall in love.'

My mum was forever telling me to "eat with your mouth closed"; "wash out the bath when you've finished" and "don't sit with your elbows on the table!" Well, this traitor-friend was guilty of all those things, which my mum didn't seem to mind in the least. I was starting to get very angry about this situation. Not only did she wear my clothes and share my bedroom; she took over the role that was rightfully mine—I was supposed to be the beloved daughter—not some stranger with despicable manners! I felt betrayed by them all, but mostly by her. She was invited home to be my friend and ally—not to strengthen the bond that I thought existed between my brother and my mother.

One afternoon while my traitor-friend was munching through a banana sandwich and attempting a conversation with me at the same time, I decided to interrupt her and give her a piece of my mind. "You eat like a pig!" I grumbled.

To my surprise she took this insult completely in her stride, almost like a real sister would have. Without missing a beat she started to exaggerate her chewing, opening her mouth even wider for me to see the slimy banana-and-bread mash while carrying on with the story she was telling me, purposely spraying spit and banana all over me.

I was not up for acknowledging this kind of intimacy with her at all and was determined to show her just how much she had hurt and disappointed me. I leapt up, grabbed the sandwich from her and smeared it all over her face. To my dismay, the open display of my hostility didn't move her in the slightest. I was gob-smacked—even I did not experience that level of security and acceptance of my place in the family home—how then could she?

There was a local pub in Marandellas called The Three Monkeys Inn, which my mother frequented. It was a far cry from the places she used to hang out at in Salisbury, and I knew at this point that my mum had lost her joy of life. When we lived in Salisbury, her life was very stylish. A night out on the weekend would have been to the 'Blue Room'—a very sophisticated venue where a pianist played all the romantic golden oldies from the Second World War.

It was very romantic. Even though Elvis Presley and rock 'n

roll was big, my mum loved the glamour of the forties with Marilyn Monroe and Zsa Zsa Gabor. We even had a white Persian cat called Zsa Zsa.

In those days, I would watch my mother while she dressed up to go out on the town. I even remember the beautiful midnight-blue, strapless taffeta dress, with its tiny little black tassels. My mother wore it with one single earring made of black and navy feathers that clipped onto her ear and curled over the top of her head like a petite evening hat. On these occasions my mother transformed before my very eyes into a gloriously beautiful and happy woman. I used to stare at her with such admiration, thinking: *When I grow up I want to be just like you.*

By the time we had moved to Marandellas, I had vowed: *When I grow up I will never be like you.* In hindsight, The Three Monkeys Inn is the very place where my mum gave up completely. She would join some of her drinking buddies and I would inevitably be carted along under the auspices of "spending quality time" with her.

In this infamous pub, time and time again my mother would get pickled, become loud and raucous and embarrass me. By that time I had already learnt to deal with my anger in a passive manner and she and I were already deeply involved in a typical power play. So, I would cast her a 'telling look'—a snide and disapproving glance. She would not hesitate to snap at me in front of her drinking buddies.

"What are you looking at?"

"Nothing ..." I would reply with feigned innocence and an apparently oblivious air about me.

I was fully aware of the fact that this little routine drove her crazy with rage and there was nothing she could do about it—I had done nothing wrong.

She would get me back. She knew I resented her drinking habit with every bone in my body, yet, every day when she came home from work, she would throw herself down on a chair, slip her shoes off and say with the same feigned innocence, "Caryl, would you please pour me a drink and light me a cigarette?" Had she known that I had started to smoke I knew for sure she would have gone ballistic. What's more, I was smoking 'OPs' as we called them—or Other People's cigarettes—hers included!

I was powerless to confront my mother's drinking habit with her and had no choice but to feed the demon inside her with brandy and ginger ale. Like clockwork, every single time that she had too much to drink, we would have a fight. In retrospect I realize that my mother was very lonely for the best part of my teenage years. She got herself involved with a married man when I was about eleven years old. The move to Marandellas was partly to get away from him as much as it was to get me off to a new start.

Her drinking decreased in the small community where everyone knew everyone else's business, but the affair continued. I adored this man and never lost hope that he would end his marriage and come to live with us and be a father to me. When I decided to be christened, at the age of seventeen, I asked him to be my godfather and he agreed. I had a spiritual hunger that was not nurtured in my home-life with my mother.

My grandmother and two aunts belonged to an organization called The Path of Truth. When I was little, I used to enjoy going to the toilet in my grandmother, nana's house, because that was where she used to keep little 'Path of Truth' booklets, and I would read them while on the loo. I suppose these 'toilet trips' constituted my spiritual awakening; and later when my mother and I lived on the farm with Sean's family some years later I would hear his mother praying with Emily at night. I would crave the spiritual direction and guidance from a loving and caring adult. Their intimacy would bring me to tears and eventually I would have to muffle the sobs where I was lying in the spare room so that they wouldn't hear me.

One Christmas Eve the 'Courtneys' invited me to join them for midnight mass. I had no idea how the service would be conducted, so I nervously followed everything everyone else did, including walking up to the front to take communion. Once the service was over and we were all gathered outside the church, someone asked me if I had been confirmed. *What the heck is that?* I thought, but I had already mastered the art of charming people by then and the manner in which I said 'no' had everyone in stitches.

"You're not allowed to take communion if you haven't been confirmed," was the reply, and although I had endeared myself to everyone present, I felt defeated. It was as if my every effort to draw nearer God was thwarted. *I had sinned again. I am somehow never quite good enough—not for my parents and not for God*, I pondered.

With all the turmoil in my mum's life, I suppose christening me was not a priority, let alone confirmation. So when I desired to follow a spiritual path, christening seemed the appropriate first step to take, and I selected my grandmother's pastor for the job. The ceremony took place on my mother's middle sister's farm in the beautiful district of Selous, a couple of hours' drive west of Salisbury. This aunt and I have a very special bond. She is my Earth Angel still and has been supportive of me throughout my life. She has given me unconditional love up until this day in spite of all my emotional turmoil and mistakes—just as she did for my mother.

My mother's eldest sister, on the other hand, did not attend my christening because she did not approve of my mother's relationship with a married man. This aunt always held strong opinions and I respected her for that.

The christening was a fairly informal procedure. I knelt down on the floor in front of the pastor, he placed his hands on my head and led me through an enactment in which I accepted

Jesus as Lord and repented of my sins. I cried when he prayed for me and truly felt I had committed to a new path. However, there was no follow-up or any further involvement offered to me, or asked of me. It amounted to nothing more than a nice little ritual, and even my newly appointed godfather disappeared from our lives the following year.

Just before I left high school, I pretty much stopped bothering about my salvation for the time being, and turned my attention to more exciting prospects. I entered a beauty pageant and came second. Sean was delighted, but it was his brother's girlfriend who won the competition and I think that irked him a bit especially since there was a rumour that her uncle had pulled strings to ensure her victory. Yes, even in the outback of Rhodesia I received my first taste of the conniving beauty industry.

ༀ

Sean and I finished school and the time came for our constant companionship to end. He was off to join the Air Force for his compulsory military service. At the time, Rhodesia was still governed by white minority rule, and the Bush War had not officially started, but we all knew that there was a guerrilla war pending and that all the young white men would be called upon to fight a losing battle. The whites were outnumbered twenty to one.

I, on the other hand, made the decision to go nursing straight after school. This way I could get out of the house immediately and away from my mother's control. We had lots of fights in my last year at school, which always escalated into verbal abuse from her where she would call me names and berate me. I wanted to get away from her, and get out into the big world, so I enrolled at the Salisbury General Hospital and I was hugely relieved when I was accepted.

Hairdressing was my real passion, but that choice of career was considered to be absolutely out of the question by my mother. Although, strangely, I was allowed to join a modelling agency to pursue a part-time modelling career after I left school, which was when my eating disorder kicked into full swing.

When I arrived late for class one day, our modelling instructor sarcastically said in front of the whole class, "Welcome the little hippo ..."

Of course, I was slender—not quite the skin and bone she wanted us to—but perfectly slim and trim. However, from that moment on, I stopped eating regular meals. Lettuce leaves, Marie biscuits and a small glass of milk became my constant diet. That was how I controlled my weight. In the meantime I started to enjoy nursing and felt it would be my career forever. I specifically wanted to do midwifery as my major, and I looked forward to a future as a qualified, professional woman.

Sean and I were seeing each other as often as we could. One weekend his eldest sister and her husband had to go away somewhere and they asked the two of us to look after their farm. They lived on a beautiful farm that was remote and without electricity. Emily, the one I had 'adopted' as my own, spent the weekend with us and it felt good to be trusted with all that grown-up responsibility. We rode horses and had a glorious free-spirited time together. The intimacy between the two of us was real. We loved each other and were certain of a future together.

That evening, after we settled his little sister into bed, I went to my bedroom while he went to switch off the generator. When I heard the generator go off and the deathly silence that followed, I remember clearly lying in bed and knowing with a calm resolve, "this is the night!" I was scared for a little while and then I saw him in the darkness, walking towards my bed. He said nothing but climbed into the bed next to me. He clearly had the same 'knowing' as I had.

Afterwards we were both very emotional. I could understand why I was tearful—it was a painful experience for me, but I couldn't understand why *he* was tearful. When we spoke about it later, he told me that he didn't think I was a virgin. The dreadful 'gangbang' story had made its way to Marandellas during one of the school's cricket outings! He hadn't known what to believe—the story, or my insistence to preserve my virginity during all those years of dating—up until that night. For once I felt vindicated—my innocence was indisputable and the proof was with an outspoken and courageous young man who would not hesitate to vouch for my virtue.

Not long after this, my mother quizzed me about my romantic relationship with Sean. My mother and I seemed to be on a different footing since I had left home and I was off her hands. She had even stopped calling me a "common hussy". However, when she found out that I had lost my virginity, albeit to the young man I had loved for all my teenage years despite the fact that we were both virgins, she refused to allow him into our home.

Even though I was certain that my own values were good and counted for something, her negative reaction to my well-timed rites of passage into womanhood left me with the feeling that I had done something horribly wrong. For the best part of my adult life, this tendency to shove my own truth aside and give authority to another person's value system has been my downfall time and time again.

I was hurt by my mum's attitude towards my first committed relationship, but Sean took her censure in his stride and soon surprised me with a charming little engagement ring with an aquamarine stone and two diamonds. The ring was a bit loose on my finger, and for fear of loosing it during my nursing duties I gave it to my mother to get the ring sized. That was the last time I saw my first engagement ring—it was stolen out of her bag and never replaced—not by her, not by him and not by me. I was angry with my mum for being so careless with something so precious. The engagement ring was, after all, the symbol of the commitment between Sean and me.

As always, I forced into the darkness of my soul the thing that I wanted to do most, but couldn't, which was to scream and scream and scream until I destroyed the rage inside me, before it destroyed me.

# One Flew Over the Cuckoo's Nest

The first year as a student nurse was great fun. The rules were strict though. We were only allowed out until 10 p.m. once a week. We had to sign ourselves out, and be back in the hostel at exactly ten o'clock, or earlier. If we were late, there would be serious repercussions, perhaps even expulsion.

It was common practice for the army guys to come to the nurses' home on a Friday night to find blind dates. Those who were keen sat dressed up to the nines in the lounge and waited for the guys to arrive. The nurses where known to be quite wild, as were the army guys, so they seemed to team up well together. Personally, I thought the whole 'sit-and-wait-for-a-date-ritual' was rather desperate, so I would team up with a small group of fellow nursing students who shared my point of view and we would go out without dates.

We would club together to afford a Rixi taxi 60666, and go into town to Le Coq d'Or—Salisbury's favourite nightspot that was always buzzing. We used to drink vodka, lime and lemonade, or Cinzano and lemonade and of course, there were quite a few drunk and disorderly evenings. The Bush War was pending and every young, able white male was in the army. So the 'fun fever' ran high and the scope of men in uniform was huge.

Sean was still considered to be my other half, even though there wasn't an engagement ring anymore. I asked him if we could date other people while he was doing his army service— nothing serious, just good, clean fun and an opportunity for both of us to experience the grown-up world of dating. I loved him, but I also enjoyed my newfound freedom and I didn't want to go out at night and have fun without his sanction. He was reluctant to agree at first, but eventually he consented.

After I had been nursing for about a year, my girlfriends and I went to a more exclusive nightspot called Bretts. The patrons were required to dress in cocktail wear and I thought the whole get-up was too glamorous for words.

One evening I decided to wear an outfit that I had designed myself. It was a long beautiful flowing white and gold skirt with a matching short top—made from an Indian sari, but without the customary sash draped around the waist and over the left shoulder. With this, I put on big earrings which had delicate chains attached to them. These I hooked into the combs that I put in my hair. My efforts impressed me so that I promptly decided to put a red dot on my forehead to round off the whole mystical look.

Soon after we arrived in the club, sat down and ordered our drinks, the maître d' called me to one side. (I think I should mention that with my long black hair and olive skin I was asking for trouble!)

"I'm sorry madam, but we can't serve you here ... this is a club for whites only." Suddenly my well-meaning intention to have a bit of fun turned sour. At first I tried to argue my case, but then my friends and I decided to leave. It was our first actual confrontation with the way things were for non-whites, and it was awkward for us as young white women to take a stance—our men were actively fighting a war to keep the country 'white'. Yet, we didn't really believe that it was the right thing to do.

The easiest way to deal with our dilemma was of course to simply ignore it and carry on having a good time. So, the next time my girl friends and I went to the club, I dressed appropriately as a 'whitey' and was even introduced to the owner of the club!

I instantly liked him. He was a typical Pommie with strawberry-blond hair and a fair skin. I felt charmed by him, but it was his friend that took my breath away. He was absolutely gorgeous—the proverbial god Apollo—tall, dark, handsome, sophisticated and much older than the young, regular army stock that we had to contend with.

Apollo and I connected immediately and when he asked if I would go out with him, I did not hesitate for a second. He collected me from the nurses' home the following week in his shiny red Alpha Romeo. I felt like a movie star. I suppose that in my heart-of-hearts I didn't believe that I was an attractive woman, which was why being dated by a handsome older man was so immensely flattering for me. And if I look back on my life, I realize that this has been my pattern all along.

The countless assurances I had been receiving over the years about my favourable physical appeal only caused my self-image to see-saw quite dramatically from 'ugly and awkward looking' to 'stunning and gorgeous'. It was as if I was incapable of reaching a well-grounded image of myself, and that someone else had to provide it for me.

Be that as it may, Apollo's attention was the first sign that the ugly duckling had swan potential, and I started dating him regularly. I didn't feel that I was being unfaithful to my fiancé because I wasn't in love with Apollo, and he never tried to consummate our liaison. In fact, he didn't put any pressure on me whatsoever. Instead, he spoilt me with flowers, bought me a gold bracelet and generally showed me such a good time that all my nursing friends were quite envious of me!

After Apollo and I dated for about three glorious months, I started night duty. It was difficult trying to go to sleep when everyone else was awake, so I went to the movies, had my hair done, did lots of window-shopping, and generally slept very little. Most days I went to sleep at about three in the afternoon, which is effectively the same as going to bed at three in the morning! As result, I was always tired and struggled to stay awake when I was on duty.

The first weekend I had off, Apollo invited me to his house, which he shared with the Pommie. The house was huge and beautifully furnished. The sheer sophistication that confronted me, made me feel a little out of my depth, but didn't raise my suspicion. Naïvety was still the order of my day.

On that weekend, Apollo told me that his father had built the well-known Polana Hotel in Lourenço Marques (now Maputo), and he wanted me to go with him to Mozambique for a short holiday to meet his family. I was thrilled to bits. For the next couple of days I was enveloped in a fantasy world where I would see myself lazing on the hotel's pool deck in a stylish white costume, sipping cocktails—just like the original Peter Stuyversant commercial.

৪১

Just before I was due to go on the short holiday, my nursing friends talked me into going with them to see the infamous Mrs. McGaskell, a clairvoyant. I didn't like the idea at all. I was still under the influence of my fiancé's Roman Catholic sentiments and felt that it was wrong—I was dabbling in the occult. Yet, I wasn't strong enough to withstand the pressure from my friends, so I obliged them.

Mrs. McGaskell lived in a little unkempt house just outside the city and there were funny little concrete gnomes all around her overgrown garden. She was the archetypal fortune-teller, and had the reputation of being 'spot on every time'.

One by one we went in for our tarot-card reading. We were childishly nervous and over-excited, each sharing the news of the things to come with the rest of the group. Soon it was my turn.

I was uncomfortable to begin with, but when I saw her mood suddenly change to one of doom and gloom, I wished I had followed my own heart and had never gone there at all.

She 'saw' that I was going to the sea on a holiday, but

warned me very specifically that it wasn't going to be a pleasant experience. She spoke of a hospital and "many tears". At that point I had heard enough. I stopped the reading and left.

I omitted to share the bad omen with the rest of the girls, especially as they all came away with the 'tall-dark-handsome-stranger stuff.'

For the next couple of days, I mulled over Mrs. McGaskell's predictions, and then decided to tell Apollo that I wouldn't be allowed to go unless my mother consented. In the meanwhile, I phoned my mother and told her about my visit to Mrs. McGaskell. She laughed it off as nonsense, but I was not convinced. I asked her to please tell Apollo that she was not at all happy with the idea of me going away with him, when he phoned to get her permission.

The next time that I saw Apollo I told him that I was unable to go. I didn't have enough money and my mother wouldn't give her permission. He predictably asked for my mother's telephone number. I quite confidently gave it to him.

He called me back the next day to say that everything was fine and I was allowed to go! When I asked him what my mother had said, he replied, "She said you are a big girl and you have left home. You are big enough to make your own decisions."

I felt betrayed. I might have been old enough, but I wasn't 'big' enough to make my own decisions—I still needed her help and support. If this was her way to spite me for moving out of home away from her control and losing my virginity, then she had succeeded.

My last line of defence was that my application for leave would be refused. Alas, it was granted and with this last 'sign' that Mrs. McGaskell spoke a lot of nonsense, I decided to push the fears and premonitions right out of my mind. To cheer me along, I bought myself the famous white bikini with the little white belt, which Ursula Andrews wore in the James Bond movie, and hoped like hell I was going to come out of the sea looking just like her. I also bought several pairs of hipster bellbottom jeans and some skimpy little tops. After all, I had to look the part. The following day, Apollo and I left for Mozambique by train.

During the three-day train trip, he was the perfect gentleman and I started to feel perfectly safe. When we arrived at his home, I was introduced to his Portuguese-speaking mother. She couldn't speak one word of English, but she was friendly and made a great effort to make me feel at home—offering me things to eat and drink while gesturing and babbling non-stop in her home language.

There was no sign of the successful hotel magnate father, but I liked his mother so much that I didn't dwell for too long on the obvious lie he'd told me.

The first few days we drove around sightseeing and went out to dinner at night. I was beginning to relax completely. He must have noticed this, because soon I let my guard down and he took me to a nightclub in the harbour. It was a sleazy, dark and dingy hole with dirty red carpets and low lights. A real flee-pit—quite unlike the places where we hung out together back home, or the classy club that his Pommie friend owned. What was even more disconcerting was that everyone greeted him as though he was someone of great importance. They even brought out the champagne to celebrate his arrival!

The waitresses in the club looked like prostitutes. They wore black stockings with excessively high-healed shoes, far too much make-up and skirts even shorter than my own! They kept staring at me and I would smile sheepishly back at them for lack of knowing what other response to give.

Apollo appeared to be in his element. He insisted on buying champagne for the waitresses and kept filling my glass. Fortunately I was sitting next to a huge pot plant and I started to pour my drinks into it without anyone noticing.

It was getting late and the club was filling up with rough-looking sailors—the 'deep-sea' types. My stomach went into a knot as Apollo greeted some of them with much familiarity.

I wanted to go back to the safety of his mother's apartment and started to complain that I was tired. He became irritated with me and delayed leaving for as long as he could. In fact, he started to walk around the club and chatted to everyone, leaving me by myself and terrified. Eventually, much to my relief, he said goodbye to everyone and we left.

We drove around the city for a while, looking at all the beautiful lights and the brightly coloured Chinese signs. I imagined that I was somewhere in the Far East and I started to relax again. But as we drove down to the beachfront, my stomach started to churn and I became quite nauseous with fear.

He parked the car, got out, and like the perfect gentleman, came round to open my door for us to go for a walk on the beach. He was being so nice to me that I thought my anxiety was silly and immature. After all, he was about ten years older than me, and I was only nineteen.

As we walked on the beach hand in hand, he suddenly pulled me around to face him and started to kiss me. He had kissed me before, but not like that. He was forcing himself on me and I could smell the alcohol on his breath. As I pulled away from him, he asked what was wrong. In an attempt to avoid a conflict, I replied, "Nothing". I said this without conviction, in the hope that it would exasperate him and that he would drop the whole idea of getting physical. Only this time, my old, tried and tested trick didn't work. He forced a kiss on me again and when I pulled away, he threw me down onto the sand and lay on top of me, forcing his tongue into my mouth. I started to push him off me, but the more I resisted the rougher he became.

With clenched teeth he said, "You are a cock teaser! Well you aren't going to tease me." He held my arms down with his knees while sitting on top of me. As he started to undo his fly, I began to whimper and beg, "No please don't."

He started to laugh at me, and just for a moment I considered letting him rape me—that way I reckoned he wouldn't hurt me. But survival instincts took over and I started to fight back. In the struggle, he rolled off me, grabbed huge chunks of my hair, and held my head in a tight grip and in a threatening tone he demanded, "Suck my cock!" I refused, pleading with him to stop.

"Suck my cock!" he screamed as he pushed my face down onto his crotch. "You bite me bitch, and I will fucking kill you!"

As I went down on him and smelled his sweat, I started to gag. He pushed me off him and rolled me onto my stomach, and in the same movement, he managed to pull my trousers down.

Screaming for help wasn't an option, the streets were empty and the roar of the sea was so loud that no one would hear me anyway. He tried to penetrate me from behind while still holding my hair in a tight grip, but I fought him off. He shouted at me to turn over, calling me "a fucking whore".

As he let go of his grip for just a moment, I managed to get up and started running down the beach. After a few yards of running and crying, I looked over my shoulder to see where he was. I saw him standing with his hands in his pockets, laughing at me. I kept running and crying for a while and when I turned around again, he was gone.

I don't know how long I stood on the beach completely bewildered, racking my brain for a plan of action. Eventually, I gathered myself, straightened my clothes and walked up to the road, but I had no idea what I would do if I saw a taxi or a car. I didn't know what his mother's apartment was called, or even where it was.

The angels must have been with me that night. Not only did I manage to avert being raped, but when I got to the road and looked up, I realized that I was standing right in front of the apartment!

I walked up the stairs and knocked on the door. His mother opened. She gave me one look and nearly burst into tears. She pulled me inside and hysterically asked, "Apollo? Apollo?"

I simply nodded. He wasn't home yet and she immediately took me to her bedroom where she made a bed for me on the floor. Then she sweetly wiped away my tears and gave me a warm cup of coffee made with condensed milk, to try and comfort me. For as long as I live, I will always associate the peculiar taste of that condensed-milk coffee with the anguish and powerlessness of the woman who realized that her beloved son was a misogynist. In my heart, and in spite of my own shock and pain, I felt true compassion for her.

Later on, as I started to doze off, I heard the front door open. Ma-Apollo, who was half the size of her disgraceful son, had been waiting for him. The minute he set foot in the apartment she started screaming at him like an express train. I didn't have to know Portuguese to catch her drift.

The following day I demanded to go home. Apollo assured me nonchalantly that the trains would be full. While he and I were quibbling, his mother screamed at him like a banshee in Portuguese. Her rebuke gave me the courage to stand my ground and I told him that I would wait on the station until there was an available train, no matter how long it took.

He didn't seem in the least bit put out by two embittered women having a go at him. He simply strutted around with a smug grin on his face, now and then shouting something back at his mother in Portuguese while haggling with me over my insistence on going home.

Eventually he agreed to take me to the station. When it was time to say goodbye to his mother, she hung onto my hand, looked me in the eye and said something to me in Portuguese. To this day I have no idea what the actual words meant, but her sincerity will stay with me forever.

Apollo reluctantly carried my suitcase into the station and

when we got to the ticket office, he purposely spoke in Portuguese so that I couldn't understand. Then he turned to me with a self-satisfied smirk and said, "You're too late; you've just missed the train!"

I dug my heels in and said with determination, "Then I will wait right here for the next one." My survival instincts had been triggered. I was perfectly prepared to sit on that platform right through the night if I had to. God knows I had enough adrenaline circulating in my system to keep me awake for several nights, let alone one!

To my surprise the ticket officer turned to address me, pointed towards the stationary train on the track, and in perfectly good English he said, "The train to Salisbury is about to leave. If you hurry, you can still catch it."

Without a moment's hesitation, I grabbed my case and ran down the platform. Apollo, of course did nothing to help me. He stood there with a snide grin, watching me writhing and wriggling with my heavy suitcase. The train was already beginning to pull away from the station when I reached it. A porter, who saw me coming, was holding a carriage door open and I handed him my case. He motioned me to get in at the next carriage door. With my last bit of willpower I reached for my salvation from Apollo. As I stumbled unto the train, I fell to the floor and sobbed for a good ten minutes. In spite of the sure knowledge that Apollo was in the wrong, I had escaped from my abuser with the nagging feeling that I had done something wrong, and that I was to blame for it all.

When I regained my composure and went to look for my suitcase, it was gone. I don't remember much else of the train trip back to Salisbury. When I arrived, I called Apollo's friend, the Pommie, to come and collect me from the station. He was the first and only person that came to mind and whom I thought I could confide in.

All the way back to his house, while I told him what had

happened, he was curiously quiet. When we arrived at his home, he took control and called the station to report my missing suitcase.

Then we sat in his lounge and he started to 'cross-examine' me. After a while he suddenly came over to where I was sitting, sat on the floor, put his head in my lap and started to cry. At first I thought he was crying in empathy for me, but then he looked up at me with his tear-stained face and said, "Caryl, don't you know that Apollo is my *lover* ... and that he's a *pimp?*" I had never even heard that word before and certainly had no idea what the Pommie was on about.

He then explained to me that Apollo made his money from the trade of white women from Africa who were shipped to the Far East and Egypt to become strippers, drug mules and prostitutes. Apollo was apparently going to 'introduce' me into the trade in Mozambique.

Then, with a slight irritation at my naïvety he asked me to recall an occasion when my friends and I had visited them in the middle of the night. We were on night duty at the time and we were supposedly having our 'lunch' break. We were sure of a welcome there even at that awkward hour. Apollo had insisted on making coffee for me even though I was not a regular coffee drinker. He'd stayed away for quite a while, but when he eventually brought the coffee I decided to be polite and have it. Sitting with this distraught Pommie in his lounge, I suddenly relived the moment when I'd taken the first sip of that coffee— it had tasted too disgusting for words ...

Then the Pommie explained that Apollo had put a witchdoctor's potion into my coffee that night. The potion was made with dry, crushed bones, sperm, burnt pubic hair and who-knows-what-else. It was supposed to break down my barriers so that I would perfunctorily walk into the life Apollo had planned for me.

In that short space of time while listening to the Pommie's

story, I suddenly grew up, or shall I say, I aged. It wasn't a good feeling—rather like something or someone had died. Life was suddenly without beauty and hope. All my pictures of a brilliant future disappeared. They were gone without a trace.

I left the Pommie's house in a state of shock. As I walked back to the nurses' home, down the jacaranda-lined street, I looked up towards the heavens and saw that the purple flowers had formed weirdly shaped, puffy clouds above my head, and it felt as though I was walking on a soft trampoline.

When I arrived at the nurses' home I was still not feeling any safer, so I phoned my fiancé, Sean. At that stage of the game, I still saw my destiny as a farmer's wife at Sean's side until death. There was no doubt in my mind that he viewed our future in the same way.

He came to the nurses' home immediately. The two of us sat in his little Mini Minor and the whole story, from beginning to end, just poured out of my mouth.

When I finished, he sat quietly for a few seconds, and then he said with much finality, "Wow! I can't deal with this. This is it! I can't do this. It's over between us."

&

I am not sure of the exact sequence of events from that point on. I am only able to recall a few flashes. I vaguely remember being in my hostel room and pulling the cupboard in front of the door. I can't remember what I used to slash my wrists, but I recall doing it with a purpose.

My father had moved back to Rhodesia by that time, and he came to visit me in hospital. He was visibly upset. As he sat down beside me, he took a folded-up piece of paper from his pocket and handed it to me. It was torn out of a *Reader's Digest*. At the top it said *Desiderata*. It clearly contained a message he wanted me to have, but couldn't express himself. I began reading it slowly to myself.

## Desiderata

*Go placidly amid the noise and the haste, and remember
what peace there may be in silence. As far as possible
without surrender be on good terms with all persons. Speak
your truth quietly and clearly; and listen to others, even to
the dull and the ignorant, they too have their story. Avoid
loud and aggressive persons; they are vexations to the spirit.*

The tears started to roll down my cheeks, and when I looked up
at my dad, I saw that he was crying too.

*If you compare yourself with others, you may become vain
or bitter; for always there will be greater and lesser persons
than yourself.*
*Enjoy your achievements as well as your plans. Keep
interested in your own career, however humble; it is a real
possession in the changing fortunes of time.*
*Exercise caution in your business affairs, for the world is
full of trickery. But let not this blind you to what virtue
there is, many persons strive for high ideals, and everywhere
life is full of heroism.*
*Be yourself.*
*Especially do not feign affection. Neither be cynical about
love; for in the face of all aridity and disenchantment it is
as perennial as the grass.*
*Take kindly the counsel of the years, gracefully surrendering
the things of youth. Nurture strength of spirit to shield you
in sudden misfortune. But do not distress yourself with dark
imaginings. Many fears are born of fatigue and loneliness.
Beyond a wholesome discipline, be gentle with yourself. You
are a child of the universe, no less than the trees and the*

*stars; you have a right to be here.*
*And whether or not it is clear to you, no doubt the universe*
*is unfolding as it should. Therefore, be at peace with God,*
*whatever you conceive Him to be. And whatever your labours*
*and aspirations in the noisy confusion of life, keep peace in*
*your soul. With all its sham, drudgery and broken dreams,*
*it is still a beautiful world. Be cheerful. Strive to be happy.*

'Desiderata' is the Latin for 'Things to be desired' and the poem became popular prose for the 'Make Peace, Not War' movement in the sixties, but at the time that my father found it and thought it appropriate to give to me, it was not at all well known in Rhodesia.

Since childhood I had turned my father into a hero. In my mind, he could do absolutely nothing wrong. When I visited him in Zambia at the age of seven, and came upon a *Playboy* magazine in the toilet, I completely denied the possibility that he could be debauched in any way, in spite of the evidence to the contrary. Hero-worshipping him was the only way I could deal with the overwhelming feeling of abandonment I suffered when he and my mother got divorced before marrying another woman and having four more children! Almost as if his marriage to my mother and the births of my brother and me were not meant to have happened at all.

However, while I was reading the poem, I instinctively knew he especially wanted me to believe the part that states that I have a right to be here. And coming from him, this made it very special—even to this day.

Then again, even if I were willing to embrace *Desiderata* with my whole heart and incorporate it into my worldview from that moment onwards, it was unfortunately not possible to accomplish a state of emotional health by simply reading a poem.

I tried to explain the trauma I had experienced in

Mozambique to both my parents. They were sympathetic, but dealt with it as they did with all uneasy situations—they ignored it. "It's over now. Let's not dwell on it."

Absolutely nobody talked to me about the situation. I was admitted to the hospital where I had worked as a student nurse and started to get the feeling that I was an embarrassment to the staff. My fellow students did not even visit me. It was as if I had done something seriously crazy or perhaps even evil.

Soon I was convinced that the whole debacle was entirely my fault and I spiralled into an even deeper depression. With the worsening of my mood, it was explained to me that I was going to be moved to a hospital where I would be a bit more 'private', where the hospital staff didn't know me.

With my mother's words still ringing in my ears, "You'll be fine", I was driven south to Bulawayo and admitted into the Nervous Disorders Hospital.

I suppose due to the fact that my parents had been divorced since I was three years old, there had been no combined, clearly thought-through strategy of how to deal with my problem, or shall I say, the problem that I had obviously become. It was literally a case of one flew east, one flew west, and 'one flew over the cuckoo's nest'. I was of course the latter.

On arrival there and to my horror, I realized that it was indeed a sanatorium for the mentally ill. My suspicions were correct—I was officially regarded as insane—cuckoo!

I couldn't believe my eyes. Most of the patients walked around the solemn, well-manicured garden in a trance-like state, totally 'cooked'. To the left was a man picking imaginary fluff off his well-washed hospital gown. To the right were a couple of women looking for things that they obviously never managed to find. Straight in front of me was someone having a tea party with make-believe friends! At first glance I could tell that I was going to be the youngest inmate there.

My treatment started almost immediately. The nursing staff

fixed me up with a weird-looking box that hung on a cord around my neck. The box had a gauge on it and two wires that came up the sides of my head and attached themselves to a device that was strapped to my forehead. The part that was in contact with my forehead had a sponge affixed to it. The sponge was saturated with cream and I was told that the reason for the cream was "to stop the burning".

Several of the patients who were lounging around had this 'thing' on. I asked one of the nurses what it was for and without missing a beat, almost as if she was bored, she replied flatly, "Shock treatment."

My appointment with the resident psychiatrist was disastrous. It felt as if I was a naughty child who was sent to the headmaster's office, rather than having an appointment with the compassionate and knowledgeable healer-type person I had hoped for. I so desperately tried to get the doctor to realize that I was not 'guilty'—that I was sane!

On the contrary, in the early hours of the first morning I was there, a team of nurses came into my room pushing a huge machine with many gauges all over it. They started to buzz around me like a swarm of busy little bees, strapping my arms and legs to the bed, preparing an injection, and giving each other congratulatory glances. I tried with all my might to object and to ask them what they were up to, but I was unable to move. I was obviously still under the influence of the heavy drugs I had been given the night before. Then they gave me an injection and I fell asleep.

For days afterwards I walked around like a zombie. When I finally came to my senses and made enquiries about the event, I was simply brushed off with the reply, "More shock treatment with Pentithol: the truth drug."

To my absolute horror I was informed that the psychiatrist would ask me questions while I was under the influence of this drug, and that I would be compelled to speak 'the truth'.

I felt violated. How could my parents have allowed this treatment? I bloody well only cut my wrists, for crying out loud! I wasn't a criminally insane person who had harmed another. *What the heck was wrong with these people!*

It reminded me of the time when I was sixteen years old and the doctor in Marandellas gave me an unauthorized internal examination, only to reach the conclusion that I needed my appendix out! When I reported this to my mum, she did not ask him why he had omitted to obtain her permission, or even bothered to enquire from me if there had been a female nurse present.

All these unwelcome intrusions of my privacy by older men, confirmed to me that men can do what they want with you and you mustn't complain.

To this day I will only see female doctors for gynaecological problems. At least I have a choice. The only way I could deal with the rage as a young woman was to deny it. Truth be told, I was angry with *both* my parents, but for the sake of my psychological survival, I needed at least one parent whom I could idolize. I chose my dad for this purpose. I saw little enough of him to risk disillusionment.

Even in my drug-induced state in that asylum, I began to realize that if I weren't crazy already, I certainly would be by the time they had finished with me so I started to scheme. We were not allowed to stay in our rooms and were encouraged to sit in the lounge and wait for out medication like programmed zombies. Medicine time was the highlight of the day. There was a bit of anticipation and organization because we actually had to line up for it. There was also a bit of chaos around medicine-time, and this was when I 'took the gap' to try and phone my mother from the call box.

Inmates got privileges according to progress or positive response to treatment, and I wasn't yet at the stage where I was allowed to make calls to the outside world, so I had to chance my luck and sneak a call.

After six weeks of no success, I decided to phone my mother's eldest brother. My luck was in and I shamelessly begged him to come visit me. This uncle of mine didn't like my mother. He was unmarried and had no children, so he had much to say about the way in which my mother raised her children. Of course, he vehemently disapproved of my mother's modus operandi regarding me.

Once he was with me, mingling among the other crazies in the hospital grounds, it didn't take much effort to convince him that I didn't belong there.

Two days later, I was released. The hospital staff did not support the decision and I was told in no uncertain terms that I would never be allowed back there again. On receiving this sentence I felt even more victorious!

಄

Soon after my release from the funny farm (which wasn't funny at all), at Joshua and Ruth's wedding I was asked to be the bridesmaid. I was apparently the only one in our family who had ever dealt with a personal crisis in the particular way that I did, so there was a bit of tension when we all got together at first. However, when my beloved aunt Angel laid eyes on me she broke the ice and said, "Come here, give me a hug!"

For a while I was kept busy with my bridesmaid duties and my mind was occupied with practical problems, rather than the nagging personal problems I obviously still had. During the wedding reception, however, the depression came back in full force and I slipped into one of the bedrooms to cry. I instinctively knew never to tell anyone in my family that I wasn't coping, for fear I would end up back in the asylum, but I didn't realize that I was being watched like a hawk. My mother soon appeared in the bedroom where I was and addressed me very firmly.

"Pull yourself together now. Stop ruining it for everybody else. This is nothing but attention-seeking behaviour."

And that was the very last word ever spoken about my 'untogetherness', the incarceration into an asylum or the set of circumstances that lead up to it.

Some years later, after I had already divorced my first husband, the movie *One Flew over the Cuckoo's Nest* was released and I went to see it. Within the first couple of minutes, I had to leave the theatre. It felt as if huge hands had grabbed me around the throat until I wanted to choke. I sat outside on the pavement, hyperventilating as I started to re-live the trauma of being incarcerated in an asylum against my will, of being sexually molested and then rejected by my fiancé who was clearly not mature enough to deal with my situation.

After the wedding, my plan was to go back to nursing. Before I was allowed to resume my training, I was to have an interview with the matron. She informed me that "theoretically speaking" I had done nothing wrong. However, the ward reports she had received from my time in training (before my attempted suicide) apparently stated that I got "too emotionally involved with the patients".

I wasn't sure how to take this criticism, or exactly what they were inferring. All I could think of was that I would often stay behind and read something out loud for a lonely and very sick patient after my shift was over. I would also be upset when one of 'my' patients was released the night before I came on duty, without my knowledge. That was of course my 'inner rescuer' running amok. But before I could object or discuss the matter, matron brought the interview to a close with a comment that was intended to hit hard.

"Perhaps you should rather stick to your modelling career."

She was referring to one particular evening when I went into the men's ward I was working in, with my hair all done up, to go out on a date. As I walked in, the men unanimously started to sing *The Girl from Ipanema*, and they were going full throttle when matron stormed into the ward. Needless to say, she strongly disapproved of any impulsiveness or disorder in 'her' wards.

Her insinuation that I was not dedicated to my career as a nurse and that I didn't quite have what it took, made me very, very angry. Unable to deal with my rage and the conflict, which would inevitably have ensued had I confronted her, I took flight.

My mother was then living in the tourist town of Kariba and she persuaded me to move there. She thought country life would be good for me, and she was right. I took a job as a tour guide and in no time I started to blossom again.

Kariba boasts one of the biggest man-made lakes in the world and I spent my days taking tour groups to visit the spectacular dam wall, telling them all about how it was built and everything else they wanted to know. In the afternoons we would visit the crocodile farm or go on a sunset booze-cruise.

Those were happy days. I went water-skiing almost every day and life was great. I even met a wonderful man and became quite smitten for a while. The only problem was that he wanted to dive for a living. As romantic as that might sound, I couldn't quite see myself sitting on the banks of a lake or beach for the rest of my life, waiting for him to come up from the depths of the lake, while I sat hoping like mad he hadn't been eaten by a croc or a shark! He also had an old flame still hanging on and I didn't want to stand in the way of a possible reconciliation.

Truth is, I wasn't nearly ready for a relationship. Even though I was happy, I was also plagued with out-of-control feelings every so often. I would become absent-minded and then experience a complete blackout for up to thirty seconds at a time. On other occasions I would hear a high-pitched sound in my ear, followed by a panic attack.

Eventually I was diagnosed with petit mal epilepsy and told that I would have to be on chronic medication for the rest of my life. The generous shock treatment I received in the asylum was pinpointed as the cause of the onset of these 'minor' fits.

The post-traumatic stress disorder, which I so clearly suffered from at that time, sadly remained untreated and I was aware of the fact that I had 'issues', but had no idea what to do about them. My suicide attempt was not the first show of self-destructive behaviour. Anorexia was—albeit that it went unnoticed by both my parents.

All I could think of doing to escape my emotional problems was to 'go away' and hoped that my problems would do the same. I teamed up with friends of mine who had plans of going overseas. The first stop would be South Africa where we would have the opportunity to make more money than in Rhodesia, and have a heap of fun in the process.

Despite appearances, I was on a downward spiral. In that lunatic asylum I had reached certain conclusions about life and my place in it that were pretty damning. Now I was off into the big wide world believing that I was not good enough and that I did not deserve any good that came my way.

But there was no turning around and facing the other direction. I was off to Johannesburg, come what may.

All said and done, while I was digging into the basement of my psyche to gather together all the information for this chapter and the previous one, I realized that we are indeed as sick as our deepest secrets. However, it is not the *details* of the secrets that make us sick, but the fact that we are keeping them in the dark, instead of bringing them to the light where they can be 'aired' and healed, most importantly—where we can let go of them altogether.

I was suddenly overcome by an intense desire to put my childhood to rest once and for all, and with this, a song came into my mind. It is a beautiful Zulu lullaby that goes: *"Thula thu thula nana thula sana. Thula umama uzobuya ekuseni,"* which means *"Quiet, quiet child".* The song ends with the promise *"Quiet mother will return tomorrow."*

Now, my relationship with my mother was admittedly almost completely without this kind of trust, and it was certainly devoid of closeness. The only intimate time I shared with her was the moment when she died. But, believe me, that single instance was so profound and meaningful to me that it made up for all the lost time.

And what's more, I firmly believe that by being there with her in that crucial moment, we broke an ancient cycle that had been passed on from generation to generation, and changed the course of the mother-daughter relationships in our lineage of women, for all the generations to come.

My mother went to a strict colonial-style school in Burma, where her father served in the British Army, during her formative years. Then she was sent to a boarding school in England while her parents remained in India. She hardly ever saw her parents and there certainly was no closeness, or even regular communication with her mother. I don't believe her mother even knew that she felt abandoned and unloved.

It is no small wonder that she drank in order to 'loosen up' and feel comfortable in her own skin. Or that she escaped into long periods of silence when she was unable to process something, or deal with conflict. Or that she was hypercritical and seldom saw any good in anyone, including my brother and me. She was simply not equipped to deal with relationships. Absolutely no one could ever give her the one thing she needed most—self-acceptance.

My heart filled with gratitude towards my mum, as I understood that by me being there at the intimate moment of her death, and with her 'allowing' this, the buck stopped with her and me. No longer will my three beautiful daughters, or their daughters, and their daughters' daughters—long after I have gone—have to suffer the aloofness of a mother who simply doesn't know how to love. Surely that constitutes two women's lives well spent.

My father—well, perhaps he *did* pay maintenance and my mother "drank it all away" as his wife assured me when I phoned her after his death to find out what had happened to his estate. The fact is, my brother and I enjoyed no financial benefits from him at any stage of our lives. Judging by the date on my parent's marriage certificate and my brother's birth date, he probably *was* 'forced' into a marriage with her. None of this can alter the reality that he was still our dearly beloved father.

The last time I saw him, we spent many hours talking about his youth. He seemed to believe that he had somehow let his family down, and most of all, that he had disappointed his parents. After his parents had passed away, very little of the family heirlooms were handed down to my father. Most of them went to his sisters, and he mentioned to me, with evident bitterness and sarcasm that "a few crystal glasses would have been good".

When I was 18 years old, my father, after a heavy drinking session with his buddies, lost a leg in a near-fatal car accident. He wore prosthesis and was able to walk without a limp. In my eyes, my father was an absolute gentleman. He spoke beautifully and dressed with authentic British class. I was so enormously proud to have him as *my* father. Yet, he went to his grave with his childhood wound of believing that he was not good enough.

Despite my parents' circumstances and shortcomings, I was finally able to remember only the wisdom and the love. Yes, I would forgive and forget all the ugliness. I no longer needed to hang onto those memories and nurture them anymore. Surely my parents had done the best they knew how.

But parental wounds are not the only wounds inflicted upon me. My peers played a role there too. My very first boyfriend in primary school, to save himself from being teased by his friends, threw a bar of soap at me, hitting me on the head. He then said out loud that he hated me. At the time I told him that he would regret doing that. I wasn't sure what I had in mind, but many years later when I was modelling we bumped into each other again. The look on his face when he saw me told me he found me very attractive. We made small talk for a while and then he asked if he could have my phone number. I smiled calculatedly and reminded him of the soap incident, and then declined to give him my number.

The point of this little story is to prove that I'm no stranger to the bittersweet taste of revenge. But time had come to "Thula, thula mtwana" and to let go of all the resentments that I had secretly been harbouring all those years. Freedom would not be total if I hung onto even *one* of those painful experiences.

It was with this calm resolve about my childhood that I decided to pay my aunt Angel a visit. She had moved back to England after Zimbabwean independence and was nearing her eighty-fourth year. I wanted her to see that after all that had happened in my childhood, as well as all the disastrous choices I had made since then, at the age of fifty-six, I was okay.

The simple truth had dawned and I finally grasped the awesome life lesson that the events of my childhood were meant to teach me—*I am a child of the universe, no less than the trees and the stars; I have a right to be here. And whether or not it is clear to me, no doubt the universe is unfolding as it should.*

Top left: My mum and dad on their wedding day.
Top right: My first day of school
Above: My brother and me.

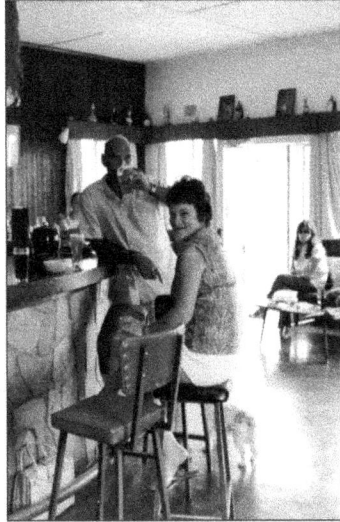

Top left: Stepfather one.
Top right: Stepfather two.
Above left: Nursing.
Above right: The crocodile farm in Kariba.

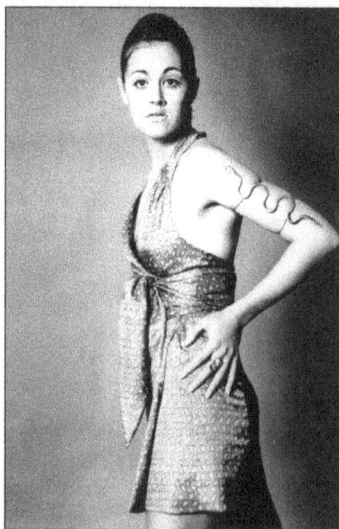

My modelling days.

Top left: Pregnant with Sunshine. This was taken in Maseru.
Top right: Anorexic.
Above left: Just before I divorced Andy. / Above right: Trying to cope after
my divorce from Andy-the harbour looked inviting.

Top left: Early days of my bulimia.
Top right: My escape overseas.
Above: Me and my forever friend.
Right: My earth angel aunt.

Top: Joshua and Ruth on their wedding day.
Above: My father and me, during my bible-school days.

Top left: "Out of the Wilderness" days, married to Danny.
Top right: Taken when I first met Babe.
Above: Our first holiday to Mauritius. When we returned I was told the relationship was over.

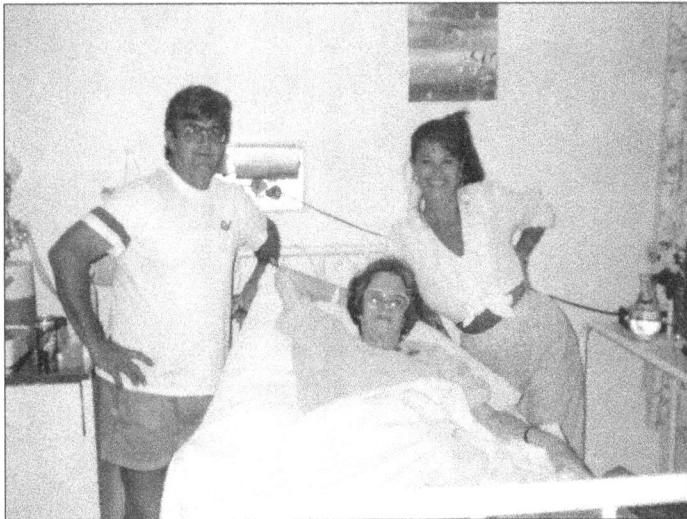

Top: On the way to see my dying mother. My daughter said she could see Nana dancing n the sky.
Above: My brother and me with my mother during her last days.

Some of my paintings. I
'purged' a lot of emotion
through my paintings and
journaling.

Top left: Cape Town – before I married Babe the first time.
Top right: Second marriage to Babe.
Above left: Our honeymoon in Thailand.
Above right: Breakfast in Thailand.

143

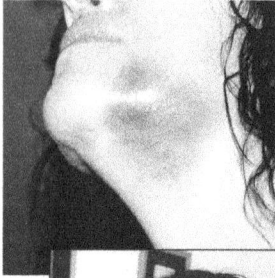

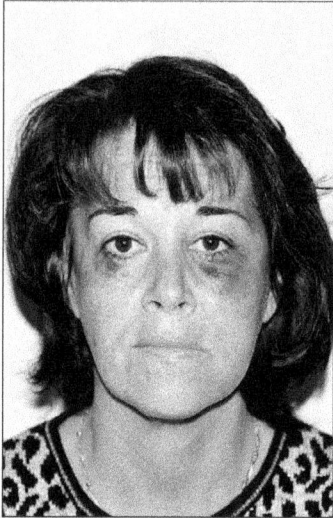

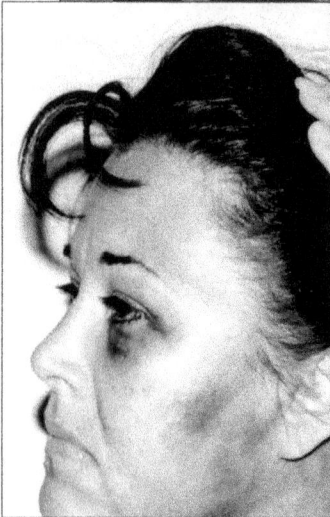

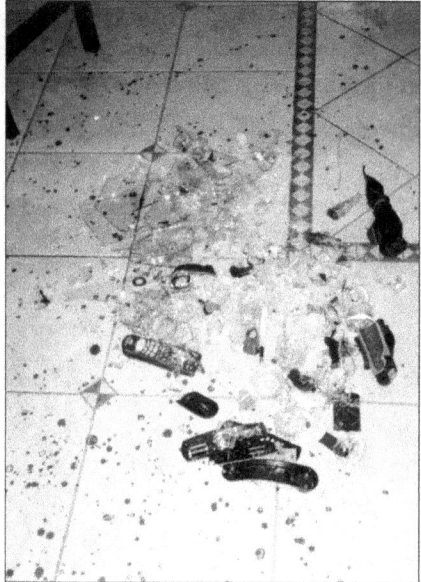

Not much explanation needed, these were some of the photos I would take after being beaten – and when I re-decorated the house.

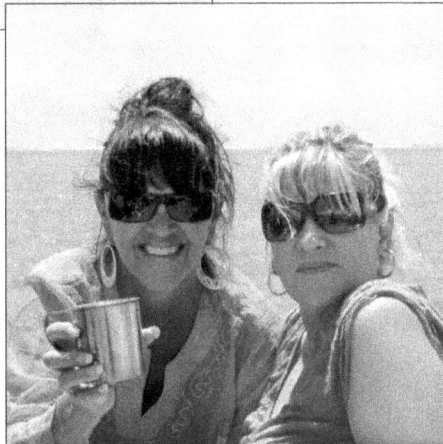

Above: Babe and me in Argentina. Our holiday ended in Cape Town where the 'tsunami' hit.

Right: My forever friend and me in Mauritius after my divorce, 2006.

145

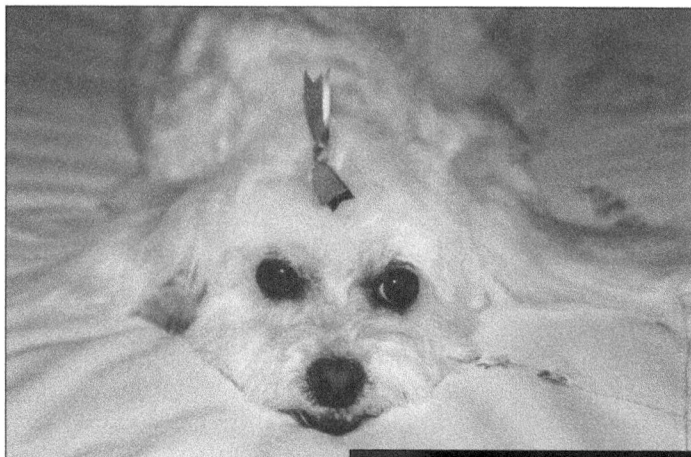

Above: My beloved Sushi.
Right: Sushi and Harley.
Below: 2007, snowing in London.

I GOT THE TEE SHIRT!!!

I have always believed that god is god & we are bad.

I have served god and felt great peace & I have rebelled & felt such fear.

I have been loved and missed my children so much I couldn't breath.

NEVER be remembered as I believe in the past one!! I will always survive the blues.

I have been blessed & cursed so many times but I know the difference.

An extract from my journal, 2005.

147

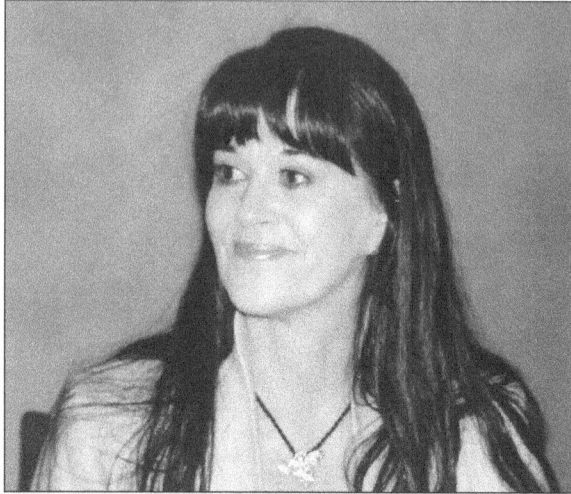

Top: Holding it together at a birthday dinner my daughters organized with all the Lunch Club ladies.
Above left: At home writing this book.
Above right: My Zen garden.

# *Transformed*

It was snowing when I arrived in London to visit my mother's two older sisters. Strange as it may seem, especially when one considers all the travelling I had done with my bountiful third husband, I had never witnessed snow before. This new experience made me feel as if something huge was about to happen. I wasn't wrong.

My beloved aunt and Earth-Angel, whom I remembered fondly under the majestic African skies and vast open plains on the farm where she lived in her hey-day, now lived in a tiny little apartment in Bracknell, in southwest England. The sight of her old and frail frame in this grey and rather depressing town contrasted with my memory of her in the colourful gardens and acres of rolling lawns that surrounded the manor house on the farm in the erstwhile Rhodesia, made me very, very sad. After a short visit I decided to bid them both farewell, realizing this might very well be the last time I would see them.

While I was preparing to go back to London, I glumly pondered the undeniable fact that no matter what we accomplish or own in this life, we are born alone and we die alone. Suddenly it felt as if the lights had come on and a new thought entered my mind: *If this is so—that we are born alone and die alone, and go from dust to dust—then why do we create such despair in the middle?*

I wanted to cry and laugh at the same time. I was tingling all over. I started to look bewilderedly around the hotel room. It felt as if I had forgotten or lost something. Then I realized with a mixture of amusement and relief that it was my anger that was gone! It took me a while to assimilate that. After all, anger had been my faithful companion for the best part of my life. In that sobering moment I was suddenly without anger—even towards both my violent ex-husbands!

That was huge. For nearly thirty years I had been at war. At different times I had been victim, victor, the one who declared war, the one who called for peace. I had been the aggressor, I had been the defender and everything in between. Now, without anger as my ally, I surrendered to the forces and left the battlefield altogether! *Is this what forgiveness is all about?* I wondered.

Back in London, I walked in the snow, which was great fun and went straight to Kensington Palace. In my opinion, Princess Diana had been a kindred spirit, fighting the same losing battle as I and so many other women had been doing for eons—trying every trick in the book to make our princes meet all our needs and fulfil all our desires. I don't know where I learnt to give my power away to another so freely. Such surrender of personal power simply has to lead to abuse—no human being can handle this amount of power, because it is said: "Absolute power corrupts absolutely". In spite of this knowledge and its logic, many women, myself included, stood in awe of Princess Diana, the archetypical 'Damsel in distress in need of rescue'. And when her dream was tarnished, we got angry with the prince—exactly the way it happens in our own lives today!

A few years before my visit to Kensington Palace, when I was still completely in denial and going through the trauma of being shoved into jail by my third husband (more about this later), and Princes Diana was doing her secretive (and desperate) late-night television interview about the breakdown of her marriage, I had a dream about Princess Diana and me:

She and I were very good friends. We were sitting on the floor in Kensington Palace, drinking a bottle of wine and discussing our heartbreak over our failed marriages. We encouraged each other, and told each other that we would "pull through", no matter what. When I woke up, I was laughing heartily with her!

Well after her untimely death and my inevitable divorce, walking through the palace rooms where Princess Diana and I had shared our courage and hope in spirit, believing that it was 'us against them', I came to the sudden insight that we *all* have the same dreams and longings, hopes and fears. Yes, *all* of us— men too, and with that I include both my violent ex-husbands.

Then, just for a moment, time stood still and I glimpsed the bigger picture. W*e are joined together in relationships for the sheer purpose of spiritual growth—nothing else. We are each other's teachers and keepers. The lessons we teach and the roles we play may not always be pleasant, but they are compulsory for the evolution of our souls.*

Over the next couple of days, reflecting back on this insight, I became a bit rebellious. I was okay with the idea that my soul mate or any of my romantic relationships for that matter, were not meant to deliver my happiness on a platter and that I indeed had many lessons to learn. But *why*, I wanted to know, was it necessary to suffer in order to learn?

*"... Because you weren't ready to learn in any other way,"* came the answer. Then I grasped it—the only way I could have been reached by God, was through pain and suffering. And when I look back on how my conscious walk with God began, it is clear to me that I needed another soul to torment me to such a degree that I would become ready to surrender.

You may recall the mention of my first husband in an earlier chapter—the charming Andy Gibb lookalike musician whom I met when I came to South Africa after my 'flight over the cuckoo's nest'. I had fallen pregnant with his child and after a failed attempt to rescue myself from his clutches, I married him, remember? Well, it was through *his* shenanigans that I was eventually led to an irrevocable spiritual awakening. Let me explain ...

ॐ

The year was 1973 and my beautiful daughter, Sunshine, was about to be born. Andy and I were living in Maseru, the capital of the Basotho people of Lesotho. He had a contract as resident musician for the Holiday Inn. Maseru is a typical African— street vendors, open markets, trading stores and donkey carts as the primary means of transport. It was also on the border of apartheid South Africa, and having just escaped the Bush War in Rhodesia, I was petrified of the so-called 'black-on-white' vengeance.

I didn't want to give birth in Maseru, mainly because of the passport problems it would cause for my child later in life. But, let truth be told—I was raised and brainwashed into believing that there was a difference between black and white people. Having a black doctor examining me was an absolute no-no. So, we would dash across the border to the nearest South African town, Ladybrand, and there a white doctor attend to me instead. I harboured serious doubts about his professional ability to safely deliver my baby, but I had no other option at the time.

It was the middle of winter. Lesotho is the only country in the world with all its territory above one thousand metres, and it is situated at the highest rim of the Drakensberg escarpment. I am telling you this because I want you to believe me when I say it was *cold.* I had no clothes for my soon-to-be-born baby and was fervently knitting booties and little jerseys at night while Andy was working.

A week before she was born, we went to one of the local African trading stores and bought nappies and vests. I could hardly contain my excitement when I handled these little items. *I am going to have a baby!* A few days later my spirits were dampened by the worrying news from the doctor that I might have to have a Caesarean section due to the appearance of genital warts. Initially I didn't realize that it was a sexually transmitted disease I had contracted from my husband, and naïvely thought it was some or the other pregnancy problem.

To my utter humiliation and embarrassment, Andy had to paint medicine on the warts while I lay on my back with my legs in the air. I was so shy in those days I didn't even sleep naked, but I couldn't manoeuvre past my big belly, so he had to do the job!

When my contractions started, he took me to hospital and sat by my side reading *Monty Python and the Holy Grail* out loud to cheer me up. *Heavens, what was he thinking!* From what I can remember, it generally spoofs the legends of King Arthur's quest to find the Holy Grail, and every so often he would pause for effect after a line like, "Arthur, this is the Holy Grail. Look well Arthur, for this is your sacred task to seek this Grail. This is your purpose, Arthur." During his dramatic pauses, I would fake laughter. I was scared that if I didn't he would abandon me in my hour of need.

The town of Ladybrand was apparently named after the mother of Sir John Brand, President of the Orange Free State in the mid-nineteenth century, but let me assure you—one century later when I arrived there, respect for motherhood was non-existent. I was absolutely terrified of the impending birth, but I dared not complain. According to the doctor and my husband, having a baby was the easiest thing in the world—women have been doing it for centuries. (It is this sort of attitude that makes me hope, my Christian sentiments notwithstanding, that there is reincarnation after all. I would love to see them both reincarnated as a woman and go through fourteen hours of labour as I did with my firstborn.)

Anyway, after a major production with forceps, suction, episiotomies and finally twenty-six stitches, I managed to burst all the blood vessels in my eyes and the veins all over my chest and delivered my beloved daughter, Sunshine, safe and sound and healthy as could be. Soon after giving birth, it was so sore 'down there' it felt as if I was sitting on razor wire.

I woke up one morning and found to my horror that my milk

had dried up overnight. I was devastated and very worried about the effect it could have on my baby's health.

My chauvinistic husband showed little concern for our baby. In fact, he seemed jealous of her and wouldn't allow me to console her when she cried, for fear of spoiling her! Having had two children from his previous marriage, he claimed to be an expert. In response to my breasts rapidly changing from a size thirty-eight to a meagre thirty-two, he started calling me 'Teabag Tits'. In retrospect I realize that my milk dried up because I was anorexic.

While I was writing about this part of my life, I couldn't recall eating one single meal in those weeks after the birth. I must have been too pre-occupied with my new 'toy', and my husband sure as hell would not have cooked me a meal. When Sunshine was four months old, Andy got a job in Cape Town.

ॐ

When she was a year old, I took a job as a model for a company that imported clothes for various boutiques around the country. It was a wonderful job. I loved the work and my employer seemed to be very fond of me.

Soon, Andy's jealousy was out of control. He constantly checked up on me at work, and at home he started to dish out one vicious beating after the next. One morning when I arrived at work with visible bruises around my throat and swollen eyes, my employer sent me straight home to pack my bags so that I could go back to the safety of my family in Rhodesia. He paid my full salary, helped me to get an emergency passport for my daughter, and sure enough, I was at the airport, ready to fly out by late afternoon that same day. I phoned Andy from the airport and told him that I wouldn't be at home when he got there. I said that I was at the airport and that I was going back home.

His voice was cold as he replied, "I will see you at home."

And with that he put the phone down on me. Truth be told, he actually exercised such a reign of terror over me that those words could easily have turned me around in my tracks. It was only the fear of knowing that I would certainly have my face punched in when I got home that made me stick to my plans.

I arrived in Rhodesia feeling happy and free. I went to stay with the wonderful Courtney family on their farm. My first love, Sean, had just met the girl whom he was to later marry, which freed the two of us to bond in a platonic way. At first I felt a bit awkward about my obvious bad choice in a marriage partner, but he genuinely admired my baby and that made me feel so intensely proud.

The farm was close to Salisbury and I soon found a job working for a radio station, typing scripts. I loved the job and it started to look as if I might have a future in the world of radio. The producers and presenters of the radio show liked me a lot. To crown that, they were friends of my mother's and it felt as if I had once more become part of one big, happy family. Life was beginning to show me its magic again, so much so that I did not even give the practicalities of getting a divorce from Andy a second thought.

Andy managed to track me down. He proceeded to break down all my defences by sending me flowers, writing letters, telling me how much he loved me and how sorry he was for treating me so badly. I can't remember which of his ploys persuaded me to go back to him, but that's what I did. Now, I used to believe that it was at this point that I made another big mistake. I had a chance, right there, to send my life into a different and happier direction. However, in the light of the realization I'd come to on my recent visit to England, I know that I had to take this particular road to get to where I eventually needed to be.

ಐ

For a short period of time after my return to South Africa, Andy and I experienced the happiest time of our eight-year marriage. During this deluded period, I decided that I wanted another child with him. I became pregnant and we moved from Cape Town to a beach town north of Durban, called Umhloti, because Andy got a job there. He also worked as a musician in a nightclub, and little did I know it at the time, but in the midst of the calm, life was brewing a hurricane that was going to blow me apart.

Our lives became one party after the next. 'Friends' came to our beach house every single weekend to drink excessively and to make merry. I soon began to resent this routine—I was the one who spent the entire day barefoot and pregnant in the kitchen, making salads, keeping the glasses filled and sweeping beach sand out of our home. Come Sunday night I was completely exhausted.

My two-year-old daughter, Sunshine, and I were getting very excited about the arrival of the new baby. Sunshine started to live every moment of my pregnancy with me. She used to tell anyone who cared to listen, that she was having a baby and then she would lift her little dress up and proudly expose her plump little tummy. I eventually became a bit concerned about this and sought the advice of the paediatrician. He assured me that she would spontaneously get over it.

One night, she had a terrible tummy ache and when I asked her what was wrong, she cried, "The baby is biting me!" After that night of discomfort and pain she was no longer having a baby.

With Moonie's birth, I had an unusual experience. When the doctor put her on my chest, I heard a voice say, *"She is not yours, she is mine."* I immediately thought of Kahil Gibran's verse in *The Prophet*:

*Your children are not your children.*
*They are the sons and daughters of Life's longing for itself.*
*They come through you but not from you,*
*And though they are with you, yet they belong not to you.*

*You may give them your love but not your thoughts,*
*For they have their own thoughts.*
*You may house their bodies but not their souls,*
*For their souls dwell in the house of to-morrow, which you cannot visit,*
*Not even in your dreams.*

*You may strive to be like them, but seek not to make them like you.*
*For life goes not backward nor tarries with yesterday...*

My husband dismissed this experience as an 'emotional trauma' after giving birth. But I had already made acquaintance with the awe-inspiring sound of that Voice. And true enough, my second child is a gentle soul. The only problems I had with her as a child were health related.

On one occasion she became very ill with Herpes Simplex. The blisters were around her mouth, down her chin onto her chest and even down her little throat. I used to lie on the floor next to her camp cot, gently rocking her night after night. For six whole days she did not even consume one teaspoon of food, or sleep for more than a couple of minutes. Eventually I was so sleep-deprived and desperate that I had her admitted into hospital.

Andy was furious and shouted at me, "What kind of a mother are you that you can't even look after your own child?"

Now, I could take his beatings and verbal abuse, live with the outings with his friends until the early hours of the morning—but criticizing my motherly instincts and questioning my unconditional love and concern for my child was too much for me. He had finally crossed a line of no return. I began to plan my escape from this man once and for all. The first part of my plan was finding a job. I instinctively knew that in doing this, Andy would go out and stay away from home even more, out of sheer spite. I nevertheless decided to seal our fate.

I started working for a pharmaceutical company as a promotions co-ordinator. The job entailed calling on pharmacies all over Natal. They supplied me with a company car, and I earned a good salary. The other part of my escape plan was to start praying in earnest for a way out of my hellhole.

One evening Andy came home with a Herb Alpert cassette and urged me to listen to one track in particular, *Rise*. I loved this tune so much that I started playing it in my car every single day. Soon after this, I heard a rumour that he was having an affair. He apparently even had the nerve to take her along on a visit to the home of one of our friends.

One evening after I had put the children to bed, I decided to play a wild card. I told him that I knew he was having an affair and I knew where she worked. Then I announced that I wanted a divorce. Without missing a beat, he said, "I will count to ten, whatever you can take in that time, you can have." I knew he was about to get violent any second, so I ran into the children's bedroom, grabbed each one under my arm and ran out of the house down the driveway as fast as I could.

A little way off, I heard a gun shot but I didn't dare turn around and see if it was him shooting at me.

I wasn't sure where I was going so I ran to the neighbour, but they weren't in. Then I ran to the next house. It so happened that the owner was a local policeman. There was a look of absolute horror on his face when he saw me standing in his doorway in my pyjamas with two crying children under my arms. He hurried me inside and his wife covered me with a dressing gown. I explained my situation and the policeman decided to confront Andy.

Apparently when he arrived Andy was standing in the doorway with his hands in his dressing gown pockets as if he was waiting for him. Of course, Andy denied that he had fired a shot after me or even that he owned a gun. Unlike these days, not many South Africans used to carry guns at that time, but my beloved Andy had a gun. Of that I am very sure—I even had it stuck under my nose once when he was upset with me, and he used to take me to target practice with him at an indoor shooting range.

When I eventually managed to calm the children down, I phoned a friend who immediately came to fetch us. I never went back to my home to live there again. The following day, I collected a few things from the house, but I stayed with my friend and started the divorce proceedings immediately.

∞

A couple of weeks later I was out to dinner with friends and that's when I was told who Andy was having an affair with and where she worked as a showgirl. Not too surprisingly, she worked at the same nightclub where Andy had worked as a musician for a few months. God's angels were a step ahead of me—before I even asked it was given to me!

I decided to go to the club to see what she looked like and to speak to her. When I arrived, the man at reception seemed surprised to see a woman arriving at the nightclub alone. He asked me if I was to meet friends there. I was still feeling completely in control at that stage and replied, "No. Is Lola here?" He told me that he expected her to arrive any minute and asked if he could give her a message.

"Yes. Tell her that her boyfriend's *wife* is in the bar and I would like to speak to her." I was quite calm when I spoke to him, but as soon as I got to the bar, I ordered a Southern

Comfort on the rocks. Considering that I was a non-drinker at the time, this was a stiff drink for me. Yet, it did nothing to calm my nerves. By the time the lights went off and a drum roll announced that the show was about to begin I was shaking.

A spotlight came on and the curtains opened. In the middle of the stage was a black motorbike with shining chrome. Across the seat of the bike lay an attractive, slim and petite girl with long blond hair to her waist. She was wearing a skimpy, black-leather dominatrix suit that barely covered her perfect little figure. Without being told I knew it was Lola. My heart almost stopped beating.

The second number she danced to, slowly and sensually, was the very same Herb Albert tune that Andy had given me and that I had listened to every day in my car! The room started to spin and I thought I was going to be sick. All I wanted to do was to run from the club, but I couldn't without making a complete spectacle of myself. I had no other choice but to endure the entire show, gulping back tears that made my throat hurt.

When the show was finally over, I sat as if frozen on my barstool. The next thing I knew she was walking towards me with a pretty smile and exaggerated stage make-up still on her face. She stood in front of me and said, "I believe you want to see me?"

I was so shocked by her chutzpah that I grabbed my bag, jumped off my stool, looked her straight in the eyes and said, "I have changed my mind. I have nothing to say to you."

I so desperately wanted to come out with a line that would have embarrassed her or left her speechless. She was the 'other woman' for goodness sake! But alas, that night, I realized that my self-esteem had been completely eroded by the abuse in my relationship with Andy. She effortlessly stood her ground with me, and as I walked out of the club I could feel her eyes burning a hole in my back. I wanted to die.

When I got to my car I decided to drive to the house where Andy and I had lived together. It was pouring with rain and I was sobbing loudly, not paying much attention to the speed limit and hoping that a bridge would jump in my path.

Lola had obviously phoned to let him know I had been at the club because when I arrived at the house, Andy was waiting for me at the door. As I walked up to him, I asked through my sobs, "How could you do this to me and the children?" For once he was quiet and simply pulled me inside the house. We didn't talk about his infidelities, or about Lola. I lay across his lap and sobbed for hours. Eventually I got up and left. He called me once after that and asked me to reconsider, but as far as I was concerned, it was finally over—for good.

Lola was, of course, the answer to my earnest prayers. Only, at the time, I couldn't accept it. I hated her. I started tormenting myself with the belief that she was now living the dream that was actually meant for me. I began to doubt my decision to leave him, thinking that our problems could have been worked out if it hadn't been for this 'other woman'.

The final time I went to the house to get the rest of my belongings, Lola opened the door, wearing one of *my* T-shirts! She had clearly just woken up, and suddenly the thought of my husband making passionate love to this adulteress, filled my heart with pure acid. Without being able to contain my hatred, I said to her, "That T-shirt looked better on me, but you can have it." She stared at me with a puzzled look on her face, as if to say: *What makes you think you have any right to be here?* I was livid. I asked for my things and left.

∞

Moving on with my life was not easy. My hellish marriage was over, but the pain of abandonment and rejection was about to begin, and it would nearly kill me.

I had moved with my children into a very pretty apartment with all the amenities to make my life comfortable—a crèche, a little shop to buy bread and milk and friendly neighbours—but I had sunk into a deep depression that simply wouldn't lift. I had a constant pain in my gut and genuinely wondered if I was going to die from a broken heart.

What made it worse was that I couldn't understand why I was feeling such angst, since it was after all *I* who had wanted out of the marriage. I would try and reason with myself, but alas, no amount of logic could get rid of the constant pain. It seemed to get worse instead of better as the days passed. I couldn't function properly and started to miss work.

Eventually I decided to move in with my brother and his wife shortly before Christmas. They lived in Pinetown. It was going to be the first Christmas since Andy and I had met that we would be apart. Although my children were with me, and my mother came down from Rhodesia, I felt desperately sad and couldn't stop crying. In front of my two little girls though, I acted as if I was cheerful. I dressed them up as angels to perform a nativity play for my mother—just the way my cousins and I had done when we were growing up—but not even that could lift my mood.

Andy and Lola came to visit on Christmas Day to bring gifts for the children. I feigned a friendly response and invited them in for tea. Lola was heavily pregnant and quite frankly, I wanted to put my hands around her throat and strangle the life out of her. Once they left, I went into the bathroom where my children couldn't see or hear me, and I wept inconsolably.

℘

After the Christmas season was over, I moved into a quaint little house that I thought would finally make me happy. Of course it didn't, so I tried to fill every minute of the day and night with activity. My daughters were six and three years old respectively and I started to entertain regularly at home. I used to throw 'chicken-and-chick' parties—the ladies had to bring the chicken and the men brought their chicks. I became well known among my friends for my famous marinade. As soon as my guests arrived, the chickens would go into a pot with orange juice, and when they were almost cooked, I would put them into the 'secret-recipe' marinade.

I was innovative and made sure that I was fun to be with, but the instant I was alone, the inexplicable pain crept into every crevice of my soul. I had nowhere to hide from it and in desperation I started to eat compulsively. Food seemed to be the only thing that filled the hole in my soul, albeit only temporarily. In no time I had developed a hunger that consumed me so completely that I would slip out of the house in the middle of the night and go to a roadhouse, buy two hamburgers and gulp them down like a ravenous dog.

I could feel the excess weight pounding into my body. I was constantly bloated and uncomfortable, but I couldn't stop. I went from fifty-eight kilograms to seventy-two kilograms in less than four months! Even my skin didn't get enough time to stretch to accommodate this 'new body'. When I bent down I couldn't sit on my haunches because my knees felt as though they would burst and I could feel the rolls of fat around my waist. My face puffed out and I lost the once-chiselled cheeks I used to have as a professional model. In plain and simple terms I looked like 'Porky the Pig'.

My life was spiralling out of control again. I felt helpless. The more weight I put on the more suicidal I became. One Friday night I went out to dinner with friends. A well-known Natal rugby player was part of the group. He was playing a big game the following day and the mood was very festive. I watched him scoffing down his food as though there was a time limit. When he finished, I discreetly asked him how it worked that he could eat so much when he was going to play a big game the following day. He leaned forward and confidentially whispered in my ear, "I go home and put my finger down my throat."

*Now that seems like a pretty smart thing to do* was my immediate reaction. So the minute I got home, I did the same. I was caught by surprise as I experienced complete euphoria when I saw my dinner in the toilet bowl.

Needless to say, it became a habit, and my eating disorder developed into full-blown bulimia. I literally thought of food every moment of my waking hours. The binge-purge routine resulted in a constant sour, bitter taste in my mouth. I also knew it made my breath smell, so I started carrying a toothbrush and toothpaste in my bag as well as breath freshener. Because I didn't want anyone to see or hear me gargle and spit so often, I took to drinking the breath freshener, knowing full well that it contained alcohol. So, apart from the euphoria from purging, I now added *getting high on breath freshener* to my list of 'sins'! And while I'm at it, I may as well confess that I was horribly addicted to slimming tablets as well, taking up to ten barbiturates-type tablets a day.

As my debts began to mount, I realized I was eating my salary away. Soon I couldn't pay my full rent and started to fall behind. I became so desperate that I decided to sell some of my furniture. Some of the goods I parted with were very valuable and dear to me, like a beautiful stinkwood bed and an antique monk's bench.

When Andy came to fetch the children for his weekend with them, he walked past my bedroom and saw the mattress on the floor. When I told him that I sold my bed, he picked the kids up into his arms, looked at me with utter contempt and walked out of the house without saying another word. Once they were gone, I flopped onto my mattress and started to cry. I felt like a real 'Orphan Annie'. Clearly no one was going to rescue me.

৪১

What happened next is still so painful that I could hardly bear to write about it. It made me realize that some emotional wounds are so deep that they probably never heal. And I wonder if they should. Perhaps we are meant to honour and grieve over them, rather than try to heal them and pretend they don't still hurt every single time we recall them.

After Lola had given birth to her baby—making my ex-husband a father for the *fifth* time—I plucked up the courage to confess to Andy that the wheels were falling off and I couldn't fake it any longer. I felt that I needed time out to pull myself together and asked him to take care of our two daughters for a while. He agreed, and I was surprised at the unusual sympathetic response, especially coming from him.

However, a couple of months later he moved his family to Johannesburg and took my children along—without telling me! My baby, Moonie was in her cutest stage and my eldest, Sunshine, had just started school. The moment I realized what had happened, the downward spiral happened at the speed of light.

One morning shortly after I discovered my children had been taken to Johannesburg, I woke up in the morning with the strangest feeling, or should I say lack of feeling in my face. I got up to see myself in the mirror and was horrified to see the whole of the right side of my face was paralyzed. When I tried to smile only the left side moved upward in an awful grimace. After an urgent visit to the doctor I was diagnosed with Belspalsy. The long-term prognosis at its worst would mean that my face could be disfigured for life. The only thing I felt I had left to protect me was my face and it looked like it was melting down the side of my neck. I worked with people all day and felt my appearance was vital; I needed to be well dressed and sophisticated. I was off work for several weeks and it was this turn of events that influenced me to quit my job. In no time I found myself in a huge black pit of despair. (I was one of the fortunate ones; my face finally returned to normal after about four months.)

In order to at least try and keep myself financially stable, I started to work at a restaurant in the evenings. I soon packed up my day job. I convinced myself that I preferred the informal atmosphere of the hospitality industry to the corporate world, and that I might even be able to make more money that way, but you probably have guessed the truth already—the restaurant job gave me an opportunity to feed my addiction (pun intended). I ate everything and anything that came my way, even leftover food off the patrons' dirty plates!

One night in my rush to get rid of the contents in my stomach, I dashed to the toilet, put my finger down my throat and vomited up the whole day's food. There was so much debris in the toilet that when I pulled the chain it wouldn't flush. The toilet filled up with water and threatened to spill the entire contents all over the clean floors. In a panic, I started to scoop up the contents, layer by layer and threw it all into the bin. Somehow I managed to avoid blocking the restaurant drains, but from that day on I carried plastic bags in my handbag.

I had learnt a new trick the hard way—first put the plastic bag like a container into the toilet bowl, *then* puke. Afterwards, tie a neat little knot in the bag and throw it into the nearest bin.

I had it sorted. However, sometimes this proved to be a problem. One evening at a friend's home, I went to the toilet to do the 'dirty deed' as usual after dinner. Once I had placed the contents in the plastic bag, I couldn't find a bin to dispose of it, so I had no option but to tuck it into my handbag! To this day I have no doubt that everyone sitting around that dinner table could smell it.

Be that as it may, no amount of shame could stop me. The pattern was always the same, pain-binge-purge-euphoria-pain-binge ... on and on it went. It never varied.

On top of that, I was so hooked on slimming tablets that when I tried to come off them over a weekend, I fell into a deep sleep on the Friday evening, and when I finally woke up and switched the television on, I realized it was already Sunday night!

At the restaurant I worked with a girl who was much younger than me. She was saving like crazy to go overseas, and this gave me the idea that if I could just get away for a few months, I would be able to pull myself together. With that thought, and realizing that I would never get my children back unless I got a grip on my life, I booked a ticket to London and sold off more of my furniture to cover the costs of the trip.

I also cut my long hair short, and traded my smart, sexy business suits for jeans, T-shirts, caftans and sandals. I didn't realize it at the time, but I was making myself appear as unattractive as possible to men in a futile attempt to avoid more pain and disappointment. I was thirty-two years old at the time.

ॐ

In London I met some friends from Durban and I had to sleep doubled-up with someone most of the time. I was with them, but I wasn't there ... if you get what I mean.

After a while, I went to meet a cousin of mine who was also living in London, to spend some time with her and her boyfriend. They stayed in a bed-sit that had a communal kitchen and lounge. A couple of 'druggies' were staying in the same building, and one night we all met in the communal lounge for a 'jamming session'. We each had a different instrument and proceeded to make music together. It was different!

The next minute one of the guys opened a square silver foil. Neatly in the middle of it was something that looked just like an Oxo cube. I have never seen hash before, let alone the 'ritual' of rolling and smoking a joint, so I watched with wide eyes as he crushed it, then mixed it with something else and rolled it all into a joint.

After this procedure, it was generously passed around, and rather than acting like a total nerd, I took a few deep drags. Within a matter of seconds I was hopelessly stoned. After a while I began to lose control and the next thing, paranoia set in. There was nothing else to do but to go to bed.

Once in bed, I started to hallucinate. I had a vision so beautiful that I have retained it till this day. The visuals were animated, as in Walt Disney movies, and the colours were unusually bright and sharp:

*I was standing in heaven. There was a rainbow and a river winding though the foliage. The flowers were huge and so were the butterflies. I was happy. In front of me was a huge archway and a very bright light was beckoning me to walk through the arch. For a while I was bathed in this glorious light of hopefulness.*

℘

The following day, when I recorded this episode in my journal, I knew the solution to my problems was to walk towards this Light, in other words, to follow God—but I wasn't sure how I would accomplish this. After the 'trip' I decided to go on a real one and joined a six-week camping tour of Europe. It was a wonderful experience, but I was constantly aware of the emptiness inside. All over Europe, no matter where we travelled, I was magnetically drawn to the churches. I would go into a church and sit there alone for hours on end, looking at the artwork and choking back tears.

Occasionally I joined in the nightly drinking sessions with the other tour members, but I never felt part of the fun. Instead, I tried to reach high into the heavens and find answers to my life's pressing problems. For whatever reason the answers were not forthcoming.

The day before I went overseas, while I was in Durban, a friend talked me into going to see a clairvoyant. My friend went in first and then I followed. Just as it was many years before in Rhodesia she received good news, and I didn't. The clairvoyant told me that she could 'see' that I was going over water to a foreign land but that I should be extremely careful because someone was going to try to kill me. This time I really did not believe her. Once I started the European tour, I forgot about this warning until there was an unpleasant incident.

&

We were in Brindisi, in the south of Italy and we were playing games in the pub, like 'boat-racing' whereby two teams compete and race to the bar, down a drink and place the empty glass on their heads. They then race back to their team and the next member of the team repeats the cycle. It was great fun. Part of my team was a married couple that were so ugly that the rest of the group actually gossiped about them, saying things like, "Just goes to show, there's a lid for every pot." I was quietly convinced that they were both slightly retarded.

The night of the 'boat-race' game, the wife became extremely drunk. After the game, she got onto a table and started to dance. All the guys encouraged her, shouting, "Take it off, take it off!" The husband looked very concerned but stood by and said nothing. As she started to take her blouse off, I pulled her off the table and helped her to button up. The guys protested, "Leave her, she's enjoying herself!" But I knew she was going to be very embarrassed the next day if she continued the striptease, so I wouldn't allow her.

The next thing I knew, the tour guide tried to pull her away from my protective grip. I held onto her and reprimanded him,

169

saying that it was not funny. Without warning, he slapped me across the face so hard that I fell backward onto the floor. After this incident I remembered the clairvoyant's warning and the thought crossed my mind that if I had to report this incident to the tour operators, he might actually kill me rather than face the consequences of what he had done. I soon decided to put that stupid thought out of my mind. *After all,* I thought, *we were all drunk and acting out of character that night anyway.*

Our next stop was Greece. We stayed in Athens for a day or two and then went to Mykonos by ferry. It was Easter, and the atmosphere was very festive on the island. On the Friday night everyone walked through the streets, carrying flowers, candles and large, gold religious symbols. I was standing on the first-floor balcony of a building, all by myself, looking at the glorious processions below. The other tour members had gone to eat in a restaurant and I opted to stay behind to enjoy the religious spectacle.

After a while I became aware of a man who had appeared next to me. He was a good-looking Greek and he leaned against the wall as if he knew this. Eventually he started making small talk in broken English. We chatted for about two hours, until well after midnight, and all the while he was very friendly. He told me interesting details about their religious customs.

After midnight, he invited me for a cup of coffee in a nearby restaurant. There were still lots of people in the streets, so I wasn't afraid. While we were sitting drinking Ouzo and coffee, he excused himself. I thought he was going to the toilet and thought nothing of it. But he took ages to come back. I started to get nervous because I had left my wallet back at the villa where we were staying and I had no money to pay for the coffee. Eventually he returned and apologized for staying away so long, but he was acting very strangely. He would tell me a story and then suddenly stop in mid-sentence. I thought he might be on drugs. When I encouraged him to carry on with the story, he would get irritated with me and rudely say, "Carry on what?"

This happened several times until eventually I said that I needed to get back to my villa or my friends would start to worry. The streets had become quite deserted by then and I was beginning to get scared. The path back to the villa was up a steep cliff. Down below I could hear the waves crashing on the rocks.

While we were walking he suddenly became very cocky and said things like, "Why do you tourists come here just to play with the local boys?" I tried to protest and keep the peace, but then he grabbed me and swung me around, manoeuvring us towards the edge of the cliff. With this he said, "I can throw you off this cliff!"

I managed to break free from his grip, but I was very scared and confused. I had just escaped from an abusive marriage where I had feared for my life on a daily basis. *First it was the tour guide, and now this. What in the name of hell was going on with me?* Then I remembered the vision I had had when I realized that there was a better future waiting for me. Drug-induced or not, the thought of that beckoning Light I had seen in the vision gave me hope that night.

෴

Before I returned to South Africa, I went to Scotland and visited my father. He lived in Inverness with his wife and children. It was good to see him, but I couldn't open up and share my extraordinary longing for my two girls with him, in spite of the fact *he*, of all people, would have understood. He'd abandoned my brother and me. I was only three at the time and my brother was in primary school. My childhood situation was similar to the situation my own beloved kids found themselves in. History sure has a way of repeating itself—until we finally get wise to it.

ನಿ

When I arrived back in Durban I felt strangely disconnected from all my old friends. I had no desire to see anyone and became quite reclusive. I took accommodation in a cottage at the back of a big house that was shared by seven professional men.

They used to hold open-house parties over weekends, but I had no desire to join in. Instead, I would stay in my room, watch television—and eat. Yes, I'm afraid to tell you that the curse of bulimia was still with me, and hiding my eating disorder had become nigh impossible.

On one occasion, late into the night, I tiptoed into the main kitchen to forage around for food. To my utter shame, I was caught red-handed by one of the men as I was stealing food from the fridge and scoffing it into my mouth. He rebuked me most severely for not buying my own food. Little did he know that I did, and lots of it—biscuits, chocolates and cakes which I hid away in my cottage for my solitary feasts.

The longing for my two daughters began to consume me like a cancer. After a particularly bad binge, I took all my wedding photographs and stabbed them hundreds of times with a knife, making sure to destroy each and every one of them. I felt totally betrayed, abandoned and angry.

I can't remember what I used to slice deep into my wrists, but one thing is for sure, I felt no pain at all. As I watched the blood drain away, I became drowsy. Then I climbed into bed and waited for death.

One of the seven men apparently found me, and I woke up in St. Augustine's hospital in central Durban. When I saw my bandaged wrists, I felt a deep sense of failure. Nothing I did seemed to work. This was the same hospital where I gave birth to my second daughter, Moonie, and remembering the Voice that commanded me moments after her birth, and my spontaneous link to Kahil Gibran's wisdoms, didn't make me feel any better:

*You are the bows from which your children as living arrows*
*are sent forth.*
*The Archer sees the mark upon the path of the infinite,*
*And He bends you with His might that His arrows may go*
*swift and far.*
*Let your bending in the Archer's hand be for gladness*
*For even as He loves the arrow that flies,*
*So He also loves the bow that is stable.*

I was no 'stable bow'. Of that I was painfully sure. Yet, in the depths of my depression in that hospital, I had a strange visitor. It was an elderly lady with a warm, kind face. She quietly appeared out of nowhere one fine day, sat next to my bed and held my hand. After a while she spoke softly.

"I just had to come and see you." I didn't ask her who she was. I couldn't care less. As she was about to leave, she squeezed my hand and said with much conviction, "God loves you." I doubted that very much. When I saw that she had left some Christian tracts behind, I had to force myself not to throw them in the bin.

She visited a couple more times, bringing me fruit and cold drinks. Little did she know that it was like giving heroin to a drug addict! But, at least I began to look forward to her visits—the hospital wasn't giving me nearly enough food. On the last day of my stay in hospital, she asked for my telephone number. I was becoming a bit suspicious of her, and finally decided to ask her what her name was.

"Irene," she said, and then calmly added, "I am Lola's

mother."

*Well, blow me over with a feather!* I thought.

I wanted to scream at her to leave me alone, but I was so shocked that I said nothing. Her final words to me before she left were, "Caryl, I am not happy with what Lola has done, but she is my daughter and I love her. I am here for you if you need me. I can be your spiritual mother if you let me." I allowed the tears to roll freely. When she hugged me to say goodbye, I saw that she too had tears in her eyes.

The weeks passed by slowly, bulimia controlling every minute of every day. I had mastered the binge-purge routine—I no longer had to put my finger down my throat, tickle my epiglottis and dig out the food. I simply bent over the toilet and it came out like an undigested sausage. I was impressed with this 'progress' in a weird way, but I had developed legitimate fears of my teeth falling out, or the acid in my stomach burning a hole right through the lining. And of course, my finances did not improve.

I attempted suicide again, this time by taking an overdose of sleeping pills. It was the same story, but this time I was sent to the psychiatric ward at Addington hospital, near the beachfront in Durban. I shared the ward with a number of other patients who were decidedly more 'disturbed' than I was. There was one patient in particular who caught my attention. She lay on her bed, staring at the roof, refusing to eat. I soon gathered that the doctors were getting more and more concerned about her.

One day I walked over to her bed, sat down next to her and asked her name. She ignored me. Instead of leaving, and much to my own surprise, I heard myself saying, "You are going to be just fine. God loves you." With this I put the Christian literature that Irene had given me about two months previously (even though I hadn't read any of it myself) next to her bed and left her alone.

The days passed without any change in her stubborn refusal

to eat. Then suddenly I noticed one of the little books I had given her was opened and turned face down. She clearly had been reading it. Soon after that, she started to respond. At first with a weak smile, then she would signal with her forefinger for me to come to her. However, when I got to her side, she would ignore me. I would simply sit down and speak to her anyway.

A few days later she and I both took the option of skipping the occupational therapy session. All the wards were empty and as usual, I went and sat next to her bed, chatting away more or less to myself. Suddenly she turned her head to look at me, and after a while of staring at me intensely, she said, "Do you know, God will never forgive me."

"Why? What did you do?" I insisted.

Then she quietly told me her story—why she had tried to commit suicide.

She was from Mauritius and had two children. She had caught her husband having an affair. He was an abusive man and told her he wanted to be with the other woman rather than with her. Soon thereafter they got divorced. After her attempted suicide, she was flown to South Africa where her sister lived.

"The problem is," she continued, "I am a Catholic. Divorce and suicide are unforgivable sins." I immediately protested, telling her that God loved her unconditionally and would forgive any sin. I told her that Jesus died on the cross for her sins. At that moment the nursing staff came down the passage and she immediately ignored me and returned her gaze to the roof. I was surprised to hear myself talk about God's love with such conviction. *I* certainly didn't feel very loved by Him at the time.

Sadly, another opportunity to speak to her didn't happen. Soon after that incident, I overheard the medical staff talking about transferring her to a mental institution in Pietermaritzburg, the capital of KwaZulu-Natal. They were discussing her refusal to speak, eat, bath or change her clothes.

On hearing this, I impulsively walked over to where they were standing. I came to a halt directly in front of the psychiatrist, fixed my eyes on her and said, "She is *not* crazy. She *does* talk. Please don't take her away." The doctor dismissed my pleas and ordered me back to my bed and to mind my own business.

"Please! You have to listen to me; she is talking ... She spoke to me!" I started to cry, and without any further ado, I was led back to my bed and told sternly to stop causing a scene.

Within the hour, the orderlies had strapped her onto a stretcher and had taken her to the ambulance. I was very upset, but something positive had come from the situation—I had inadvertently stumbled upon the cure for self-pity and depression: *Reach out to another person who is worse off than you are.*

The following day I was high-spirited enough to sign myself out. As before, when I was admitted into a mental institution as a young woman nineteen years of age, I was told that I would never be allowed back to that hospital as a patient again. And again, I didn't mind that in the least. I had no intention of going back there anyway.

৪৩

Once I was back in the real world I experienced a curious surge of creativity. I moved into a flat in the suburbs of Durban. I came up with the innovative idea of making little gift packs consisting of clay frogs in matchboxes with an encouraging message. I sold hundreds of these to gift shops in and around Durban, and working from home as hard as I did, kept me far away from everyone and anyone who could hurt me.

Irene (Lola's mother) kept in touch, though. Like the proverbial faithful servant of God, she would phone me every Monday and invite me to church with her the following Sunday. I would promise to meet her, the following Sunday, but on the day, I would find an excuse not to pitch up.

Church was not my thing. Yet, Irene never gave up on me. Come Monday, she would phone as if it were only the first time I had let her down and say, "I missed you on Sunday. Please come next week." Like clockwork, I would agree, but not pitch up. This ritual repeated itself for months on end.

One weekend I went up the north coast to stay with friends. I had flu that had developed into bronchitis and I needed the sea air to clear my chest. By lunchtime that Sunday, I guiltily started thinking about Irene. By the time I arrived home, it was pouring with rain, and that gave me just the excuse I wanted not to meet Irene at church as I had promised. I climbed into bed and switched on the TV for a cosy night in.

It was around 6 p.m. and a blond-haired man was preaching. After a while I got the strange compulsion to get dressed and dash down town to the spot where I had agreed to meet Irene.

When I arrived, I found her standing, alone and under an umbrella in the rain, faithfully waiting for me. I cringed with guilt as I wondered how often she must have done that. She practically beamed as I walked up to her, and gave me a huge hug. Then she said, without a hint of resentment, "I am so glad you came." We hurried inside the city hall where the church service was in progress. The hall was packed to the brim with people. We shuffled our way though to some empty seats, and when I eventually looked up at the preacher, I saw, to my utter surprise, that it was the very same blond-haired man I had been watching on TV minutes ago. I felt a chill run down my spine.

After the service the preacher asked those in need of healing, to come to the front of the hall. I had no intention of doing that, especially as there might be someone in the hall who might recognize me. Eventually the front of the hall became so full of people that the preacher suggested that those who could not find space in the front simply stand up from their seats and let the people nearest to them lay hands on them and pray.

Irene elbowed me to stand up. I sat glued. In my mind, faith healing was for the 'big stuff' like cancer and blindness. Again she gave me an encouraging little shove, but this time she said assertively, "Stand!" For fear of attracting attention from the other parishioners, I stood up. Then, as the preacher started to pray, it felt as though someone had broken an egg on my head. This curiously warm feeling passed over my head and ran down my whole body, and with it came the certain 'knowing' that I was healed. And true enough—in that moment the bronchitis and flu symptoms were gone!

Soon after this I realized that my addiction to barbiturates was also miraculously cured. There was no turning back for me after that dramatic experience. My conscious walk with God had officially begun.

About a year later I drove to Pietermaritzburg and went to the hospital where I knew the woman from Mauritius had been sent for treatment. I found her there, well on her way to recovery—and most important of all—a committed, happy and smiling Christian. I was ecstatic. There and then I understood that I had inspired my fellow man with the awesome grace of God—the very 'lesson' I was about to learn myself. I felt blessed when I realized that even in my weakest state, God 'had use' for me.

In the meanwhile, I had joined the Invisible Church. I'm not sure why it was called that, but I remember thinking to myself: *Hopefully going to a church with a name like that, no one will notice me.*

Although I was committed, I was very shy about my status as a re-born Christian. It felt as if surrendering to God's will and going to a church was publicly admitting that I was not coping—as if *that* wasn't perfectly visible to all around me!

Be that as it may, I made some very good friends at the Invisible Church. One of them was to become my mentor and 'Forever-Friend'. Nearly twenty-five years later, she stood by me in Cape Town when the emotional tsunami hit and when I came out of the denial of the lies I had told myself about my third marriage.

Yes, little did she and I know at the time that the journey forward was not going to be all smooth-sailing simply because we were 'saved'? In fact, had I known at the time exactly what I was committing to when I committed to my spiritual journey, I might not have been so quick to do so! 'To thine own self be true,' is no easy task. On the contrary, it is an arduous, but sacred process. And this damsel in distress, in need of rescue, had only taken the first step on the journey inwards.

# Choose Life

Suicidal thoughts started to creep back. To die meant nothing could ever hurt me again. I didn't want to die, I wanted to stop the pain, but life and pain went hand in hand as far as I could tell.

The months dragged by and things didn't get any better. I moved into a flat on the esplanade in Durban with a beautiful harbour view, but nothing seemed to lift my depression. The more I heard that God was pruning me and preparing me for greatness, the angrier I became. *How much more pruning did He need to do before I would be good enough? And anyway, pruning for what?*

I continued to eat myself into a coma. I had borrowed a large sum of money from a friend to sort out my debt, and ate it instead. I don't mean literally, but I may as well have. The minute I received the money, I drove to a cake shop and bought two-dozen cakes, telling the shop owner I was buying cakes for the office. I started eating them in the car and continued eating all the way into my flat and I did not stop eating until they were finished. It took an hour or two, and of course, you know exactly what followed—the purging and the flood of tears—and more cake!

My mentor and Forever-Friend, answered my desperation with the well-known quote from Scripture, "Seek ye first the kingdom of God and His righteousness and all these things will be added unto you." I had no idea what this actually meant. I thought the kingdom of God was in 'heaven' and I thought seeking it meant, go to church, read the Word, pray and mix with other Christians on a daily basis.

I was fast beginning to fall into the trap of making an idol of my religion. As weird as this may sound, the truth is, one can indeed become obsessive about being perfect at all costs through a life that has no blemish—the perfect family, perfect home, perfect career—in order to please God or to find favour with God. A totally absurd and impossible prospect yet it is one that many re-born Christians attempt to attain.

I was of course 'manipulating God' into loving me, the same way I was used to manipulating people. I didn't believe I was worth being loved the way I was, so I set out to earn love by putting my best foot forward. I never missed a Sunday church service or Bible study during the week. I became involved with every church activity that would have me. I attended church camps; worked the soup kitchens—you name it and I was there. The only problem was, when God didn't do things my way, I would be hurt and become resentful—the same way I would react with people.

I was working for a cosmetics company at the time, and one day as I was walking down the street the heel of my one shoe caught in the crevice between the paving stones. I looked down and I saw a pair of fancy men's boots hovering a little too close to me. They belonged to a good-looking, dark-haired stranger, who stood right in front of me, ready to charm me. I shyly dodged out of his way and rushed past him. When I got back to my car he was sitting on the bonnet with a bunch of flowers in his hands.

"You are the most beautiful woman I have seen all day," he said as he handed me his business card and added, "I know if I ask you for your number, you won't give it to me. So, you phone me when you have time. Please, I want to take you for coffee." I took the card, jumped into my car and left.

Admittedly, I felt good for several days after the encounter but I had no plans of phoning him. I was not going down the familiar garden path with a charmer again. However, on the day I bumped into him, he must have noticed the point-of-sale material on the back seat of my car, because a week or two later, a beautiful orchid was delivered to my work. The accompanying card said, "I am still waiting for your call." When I told the girls in the office the story behind this romantic gesture, they all encouraged me to call him.

After a couple of dates with him, his agenda became very apparent. I was determined to stand by my newly found Christian values and explained this to him in no uncertain terms. He invited me to his home for breakfast the following day.

At breakfast, as if he was trying to be vulgar on purpose, he downed a shooter and then offered me one. When I declined, he took me into his lounge rather determinedly, sat me down and then he made me listen to a tape. I couldn't quite work out what the tape was all about and when I looked at him in a puzzled way, he switched it off with an exaggerated gesture and asked me in a dramatic tone, "Do you know what that is?" Naturally I said that I didn't. With that he put his face a couple of inches from mine, and spelled out the words as if he was talking to an idiot.

"That is *brainwashing* from the communist army in Mozambique. Your church is *brainwashing* you!"

Truth be told, I was privately worried about this possibility. There was much publicity at the time about the hold that various cults had on their followers. To crown it my ex-husband had called me 'fanatical'. In retrospect, he was not entirely wrong. Some of the literature I have on my shelves today I was 'ordered' by the church to burn in those days! Yet, at that stage of my life when this man accused me of being brainwashed, I enjoyed the continued *experience* of the presence of God. No outside opinion could deny that. And what was more, I desperately *needed* that constant feeling of being supported by a Power greater than myself.

So I jumped up from the chair and said straight back, "Well, all I can tell you is that I hope you never need God like I do." I left his place in tears and swore never to mix with 'non-Christians' again. Little did I know, the two of us were to meet again some years later, and the situation would be quite different.

&

In spite of the many joyous spiritual experiences I had in those years, my life still seemed to be going nowhere. I tried everything in my own power to get my children back. I prayed and I begged. Every time I made the request, I was met with a response like, "Hell will freeze over before you get them back!" or "I would rather put nails in your coffin than give the kids back to you!" This response obviously came from my ex-husband and not from God, although, at the time I couldn't really tell the difference—Andy still had the power to keep or to give me my beloved children.

During this time I had read an article in the newspaper about a man who had driven into the sea from a specific point in the harbour that I knew well. He had succeeded in killing himself. My immediate response was: *Now that's a good idea.* As I started to fantasize and scheme about doing the same, I received an out-of-the-blue phone call, from my cousin Ruth in Zimbabwe. She was in a panic.

"Caryl I don't know what is going on with you, but Joshua and I were praying this morning and God showed us you are in trouble. We want you to come to Zim. immediately. Your life depends on it."

Ruth had done all the right things with her life. She was the darling of the family and married a man of integrity—Joshua. He had played rugby for the erstwhile Rhodesia and his morals and family values were very strong. They were devoted Christians and of course they were spot on about me being in trouble.

ೊ

The next day I drove from Durban to Borrowdale in Harare, in one go—eighteen hours, non-stop. My brother and his wife sorted out my flat in Durban while I stayed in Zimbabwe for almost a year.

During that year, I went to a Christian counsellor for inner healing. She took me back to my childhood (through prayer) and asked the Holy Spirit to reveal those times in my life that had caused so much emotional damage. Some of the incidents that were revealed to me had happened when I was still a baby. When I mentioned them to my mother she confirmed their occurrence much to her shock and surprise.

I slowly started to feel better through these spiritual-healing sessions. However, I hadn't told anyone about my bulimia. I was far too ashamed. And, of course, as long as I kept silent, it had power over me.

Ruth and Joshua nurtured and cared for me as though I was a convalescing patient. I found out later that one of Joshua's sisters had committed suicide after her divorce and they had been warned that I might do the same. That was why they had sent for me so urgently. I also found out later that they used to hear me crying myself to sleep at night.

One morning after a particularly lonely night, Ruth empathetically said to me, "God has a big plan for you." I wasn't ready to hear that at the time and cynically thought to myself: *That's a nice way of saying I don't know how to help you. Just tell someone God has a big plan for you.*

Yet, this wasn't a cheap shot. Ruth and Joshua's whole life genuinely centred round God. There was an amazing feeling of consistent peace in their home. They did very little without the Lord, and by that I mean we prayed about everything.

After almost a year of being with them it was time for me to return to South Africa. It was my absolute desire to be re-united with my children and to go to Bible School. Having lived with mature Christians like Ruth and Joshua, I had learnt how to pray; I started to pray to God with an expectation that He would answer. As far as Bible School was concerned, He did answer. The pastor of the church and his wife offered to sponsor me through Bible School. They specifically told me that they had received instruction from the Holy Spirit to do so. I was thrilled.

I had no idea of how I was going to get back to South Africa, but trusted the process of prayer and then simply phoned a travel agency to enquire about airfares. During my conversation with the travel agent I mentioned that I was going to Bible School. To this the agent replied, "Which one? Because I'm also going!" Believe it or not—we were booked to go to the exact same college. With this news she suggested that we drive down together. I accepted and in the process I made a close friend.

We shared a caravan that was parked on the Bible School property. We prayed together for everything, from money for food, to passing our exams, and when we had to give up the caravan, we simply prayed for another 'nest' and found one effortlessly and easily with a woman who specifically wanted "to open her home to Bible School students". She generously also opened her home to my two girls who visited me over weekends.

One day, while I was at Bible School, I received a vision about my ex-husband's marriage to Lola. I decided to phone him in spite of the fact that there had been absolutely no closeness between us for years. I opened the conversation with a congenial warning like, "Are you sitting or standing?"

He was immediately suspicious, but I pressed on and he transferred my call to the privacy of his office.

"Is there a problem?" he asked.

"No, but I need to tell you, God has shown me that if you don't pay attention to your marriage, Lola will leave you."

There was a long silence and when he finally uttered the words, "Well thanks for that ..." I could hear by the tone in his voice he thought I had finally lost the plot all together. A short while later, I heard that Lola had left him that very same night while he was at a meeting.

And not long after that, I had another supernatural experience. It was three years after my encounter with the man who accused me of being brainwashed by the church.

I was driving home with two of my fellow students after a particularly wonderful day at Bible School. Suddenly I got the urge to make a phone call to this man. My friends were puzzled, but we stopped at the first roadside café with a pay phone. (Those were the days long before cell phones.) First I phoned his work. He had apparently not worked there in a while, but I was given the forwarding number he had left with them. That number was also bogus.

We drove home, but I was immensely anxious and at the same time, I had no idea why it was so urgent—I just knew I had to track him down. Well, I eventually did find him through someone who knew him. He had been admitted to the cardiac unit of the Johannesburg General Hospital after having suffered several heart attacks.

When I arrived there, I had to persuade both the doctor and his mother to allow me to see him. I would never have recognized him, but there he was, pale and thin—very unlike the proud and good-looking man I had previously met. I gathered the courage and asked him if he remembered the last words I had said to him during our earlier encounter, "I hope you'll never need God like I did." He nodded and a tear rolled down his cheek. He was too weak to talk. Then I asked, "Can I pray with you?" Again he simply nodded. He closed his eyes and holding his hand I said the Sinner's Prayer:

"... I ask you Lord to come into my heart and my life. Lord forgive me my sins, wash me in your blood and make me brand new. Father, I forgive all those who have sinned against me and I accept that you are Lord of my life, in Jesus' name. Amen."

Soon after my visit he was transferred to Cape Town to await a heart transplant. When I phoned to enquire after his well-being, I was told that he had passed away.

I was nearing the end of my training at Bible School and it was time for me to move on. I was thirty-four years old and afraid of a future without the day-and-night security and comfort of being surrounded by faithful Christians. My heart's desire was to be reunited with my children and I realized that for this to happen, I would first have to find a job and move into a 'proper' home of my own.

In the interim I stayed with a well-known South African actor and his wife who were members of the church I belonged to. It was like living in a halfway house while I was preparing my re-entry into the big wide world.

I managed to find a suitable job very quickly, but I needed a car. I prayed. Very soon after this, the actor's wife unceremoniously came to me and said, "We want to help you buy a car." I bought a little Mazda and moved into my own house. So far every single one of my prayers had been answered, except the most important one. I was beginning to get desperate about my children. *Why was God not answering this prayer?* The pain of being without them was eroding my faith. It felt as if I was taking one step forwards and two steps back.

৪০

Then one weekend when it was time to say goodbye to my kids after their visit, I surrendered. In the forefront of my mind was the Biblical story where God asks Abraham to lay his son Isaac on the altar and sacrifice him. As far as I was concerned the fight for my children was over. My life had been on hold for almost three years and I was ready to accept that if it were

God's will that they never live with me again, I would have to accept it.

I sat my two little girls down on the floor and held their hands. Then I prayed, "Lord if you want me to let go of my children, I will. You know that I want my children, but if this is not Your will for our lives, then I will let go and move forward without them sharing a home with me."

The following day I phoned Andy and I knew in my heart it would be the last time I ever asked the question again, "Please will you let the children come and live with me?"

That time round, he was quiet for a moment and then he said, "Call me this afternoon." Later that day, when I phoned back he said without any stipulation, "Okay, you can have them." At first his words sounded too simplistic to be true, but I had no intention of challenging him, or God's mercy for that matter.

Two months later, kids by my side, I resigned from my job and we moved to KwaZulu-Natal to be near to my family. My brother and my mother had moved to a town called Mtubatuba and I wanted my two girls to get to know their cousins and grandmother. I was happy and thought life couldn't be better.

The kids and I settled into a home in St Lucia. I made close friends with a delightful woman who still seemed to live in the hippy era (I could tell by the way she dressed and the music she listened to). My hippy friend had recently got divorced, and had two small children who lived with their father and who only visited her over weekends. She missed her kids and, having just been down that road myself, I was only too happy for the two of us to spend every single moment of the weekend with our kids. We had lots of fun amusing our children; we dressed up and made pancakes. The children bonded like brothers and sisters from the start.

In the meanwhile, my ex-husband didn't miss a beat. Straight after Lola had left him, he promptly started to date one female celebrity after the other. I was angry that life seemed so kind to him when all my attempts at romance had failed. One night I jokingly told Hippy that I wanted to meet a man, 'make' him fall in love with me, and then treat him in the same way I had been treated—*Love him and leave him.* To this Hippy said she knew just the man—a local guy who was known in the community for being a 'player'.

ℰ

In no time, the stage was set and I met the Player. He was a professional fisherman, good looking and charming. We met for a couple of evenings, and then, one beautiful moonlit evening after a party, we ended up on the beach. I had not had a sexual relationship in five years at that stage.

I met him three more times, but the guilt started to get the better of me. I was a Christian, driving around with the symbol of a fish on the boot of my car. *What would the people say?* I felt like a hypocrite and a fake. My relations with this man had to stop! But before I had a chance to officially break off my relations with the handsome fisherman, I woke up one Sunday morning feeling 'someone' sitting down at the end of my bed. Thinking it was Hippy, I sleepily lifted my head from the pillow, but when I looked towards the end of the bed, there was nobody there—only a very bright light that was shining into the room. It practically blinded me. Then the familiar Voice spoke to me.

"Why are you doing this? Don't you know that I love you? This is not the solution. Stop it!"

I started to sob and cry out to God, "How long do You want me to be alone?" I received no answer, but in that moment, I knew I was pregnant.

I went to see Hippy as soon as I could and told her what had happened, but I could see she didn't believe me. She smiled faintly and said, "That's wonderful."

Later that month, I did a home pregnancy test at the back of the shop where Hippy worked, and sure enough—I was pregnant. She was so happy and so were our children but I was numb. *What the hell have you done?* I silently asked.

The weeks passed into months and my initial shock turned into depression. All the while Hippy tried to get me to see things as a blessing. Eventually she asked me if I was prepared to see an artist friend of hers. This woman was apparently deeply spiritual, but not a Christian as such and Hippy believed that meeting her would do me the world of good. I was very reluctant because I thought she might persuade me to have an abortion and justify why God would understand such a move.

When I met Hippy's artist friend, I liked her immediately. After we had spent some time getting to know each other, she asked me why I was so distraught about being pregnant. I explained how long I had been separated from my two daughters and that I "owed them some quality time". The new baby would interfere with this. Then I added that I had asked God why He had allowed this pregnancy. Why would He do this to me? Because I had not received any clear answers, I figured it was punishment for having had a sexual relationship outside of marriage.

The Artist smiled silently while I rambled on. When she spoke, it was with serenity that I will remember for as long as I live. She said, "Do you know what puzzles me the most?" Before I could answer she continued, "You are such a committed Christian, don't you know that your God created the heavens and the universe and only *He* creates life. *He knew you from the foundations of the earth and called you by name.*" This 'non-Christian' artist was quoting truths from the Bible. She was beginning to get my full attention.

"He also created your baby. *You* might be totally shocked, but He isn't! This is part of His plan for your life. Consider this a blessing."

That night I prayed, "Lord, help me. I can't do this by myself." In that very instant I was cured of bulimia.

Needless to say, the fisherman denied paternity and I had no intention of having blood tests done. I was on my own and happy about it—for once there was no father to interfere with my way of mothering my baby.

ഏ

Four months into my pregnancy I was asked to open a restaurant in the village. My boss and his wife were very supportive and said I could work for as long as I wanted. Sometime during this period, Hippy mentioned that she wanted to introduce me to her ex-husband. I was amused, "Why would you want to do that? If you didn't want him, why would I?"

She was adamant, "I just think you two would suit each other." Then I tried to encourage her to reconsider her own situation and perhaps get back together with him herself. After all, she had never complained that he drank too much or beat her up, or even had an affair. But she said, "I don't have those kinds of feelings for Danny anymore, it just wouldn't work."

He was living and working in Richard's Bay, about an hour's drive from St Lucia. Hippy arranged for him to phone me while I was at work in the restaurant. From our first phone conversation we spent many nights chatting away on the phone when the restaurant was quiet. He seemed like a really nice guy and when the time came to bring the telephone romance into 'reality', I asked him the inevitable question, "How will you explain to everyone that you are dating someone who is pregnant with another man's child?" He responded to that calmly and with certainty, "That's got nothing to do with anyone else."

Our first meeting went well. He was kind and seemed very

concerned about my unborn child. After a short courtship, he asked me to marry him. I was never madly and passionately in love with him, but he was just the kindest and most gentle man I had ever known, and I agreed to marry him after my baby was born. From the very start I didn't want to hide the fact that he was not the father of my unborn child.

Suddenly, my pregnancy became a wonderful experience. Both my daughters, as well as Hippy and Danny's two children (who were my soon-to-be step children) were excited. To crown that, Danny had asked me if he could register his name on my baby's birth certificate. I had enough experience with men at that stage of my life to know that my unborn child could do a lot worse than have Danny as a father, and agreed.

The birth went without a hitch and Danny was with me throughout the delivery. After the birth he registered himself as her father on her birth certificate—just the way we both wanted it. This officially turned all of us—Hippy included—into one big, happy, 'hippy' family!

Shortly after the birth, Danny and I moved to Johannesburg with my two children, his two children and Star—the baby we 'shared'. We had a small wedding at Mount Grace with all the children being part of the procession. Hippy came up for the wedding with her new boyfriend, and my ex-husband was there with his new girlfriend. Everyone seemed to be happy and set to live happily ever after.

We were living a very simple life in a small mining town near Johannesburg. The marriage was sound or so I thought. Danny worked on the mines and I was a stay-at-home mother for the five children we had between the two of us—aged thirteen, ten, eight, five and the newborn baby.

Danny didn't earn a good salary and we struggled terribly. To help, I designed and tailored a clothing range called 'Out of the Wilderness', hoping that the money I earned from this effort would bring us out of our financial wilderness! Danny and I sat up many nights until the wee hours of the morning, dying metres and metres of calico fabric in my washing machine, ready for me to cut and sew the next day.

I also gave sewing lessons, taught embroidery and candle-wicking, and made duvets and cushions to order. During the holidays I looked after other people's kids, arranged face-painting and dress-up sessions and gave art classes. All these efforts contributed a few very necessary extra rands.

I also served on the committee at the kids' school where Moonie was a prefect and ran the soup kitchen in aid of the children whose parents couldn't afford to give them lunch. My own kids, in spite of all my efforts, would go into the soup kitchen line on occasion (except Moonie who was far too embarrassed about our financial predicament). But it seemed that no matter how hard Danny and I tried, we just couldn't make ends meet. Was life, after all, simply a struggle from the cradle to the grave?

The other struggle we had was with my eldest daughter, Sunshine, who was going through puberty. Being the eldest, she distanced herself from the rest of the children. At first I did not pay much attention to her because I thought that she was appropriately rebellious for her age. But then she started to bunk school and began sneaking out of our home at night. On one occasion she left the door wide open, which put the whole family in danger.

Given her childhood history, she was understandably turning into a difficult young girl. What I didn't bargain for was that our relationship would become as strained as it did. Suddenly I did not have the wherewithal to cope with her.

ॐ

In the meanwhile I had received good news from my father who was living in Scotland. He had decided to come to South Africa for a long visit to see my brother and me, and all the grandchildren. He was going to spend two months with each of us, starting with me. The even better part of the news was his wife was not going to join him. She had never made an effort to befriend my brother and me or to accommodate our relationship with our father.

Danny and I, with the five children lived in a tiny three-bedroom house. We slept in the main bedroom, my two daughters, Sunshine and Moonie, slept in the second bedroom and the baby, Star, slept in a camp cot next to their bed. Danny's two kids, a pigeon pair, slept in the third bedroom. So where was I to put my father? It was proving to be a big problem. We were already doubled-up and tripled-up! But I was not going to be deterred and eventually found a spot for my Dad in my sewing room.

We were packed like sardines in our modest home yet those two months were easily the happiest of my whole life up until that point. We were like the American sit-com family of old, *The Brady Bunch*. Even Sunshine took part in the fun.

One evening my father asked me, "Do you and Danny always talk to each other like that?"

"Like what?" I wanted to know.

"You are very expressive and direct with each other. You talk about things that I wouldn't dream of talking to my wife about!"

It turned out that my dad and his wife communicated only about day-to-day things and hardly ever expressed their feelings. He seemed a little uncomfortable with the level of honesty and openness in my home!

Soon after that conversation, I broached the subject of spirituality and aired my strong Christian views. He was touchy about the subject and said that he thought religion was private. I was not about to be fobbed off. I pushed for at least an opinion on the matter and eventually he shared his views.

"Religion in my opinion is like looking at a lamp with a shade made of stained glass. The lampshade has many different colours and different shapes, but when we look through each piece of glass individually, we all see the same light."

I was not about to challenge this profoundly tolerant viewpoint. At the same time, he voluntarily joined us every Sunday for church. Ours was a charismatic church—people raised their hands in the air and tears freely rolled down cheeks. My father found 'the freedom of worship'—interesting.

One Sunday the pastor made an alter call at the end of the service, asking all who wanted to give their lives to the Lord and be born again, to raise their hands or come to the front. Quite unexpectedly my father raised his hand. I was so proud of him and felt *"a peace that passeth all understanding"* come over me. My beloved father and I could now share our walk with God.

This idea eased the discomfort I had been feeling about not seeing him for so many years. I had such a great love for this man, but at times over the years I had even begun to wonder if my brother and I were included in his family tree. But after he gave his life to the Lord it felt as if I had reclaimed the special bond my beloved father and I used to share.

A few days later my father left to visit my brother in KwaZulu-Natal. The plan was that he would come back to us for another short visit before returning home to Scotland. I was ecstatic about this. I thought the extra time would cement our freshly rekindled bond, and that I would have time to discuss the few niggling questions I had. I wanted to know why he was born in China. And why his marriage with my mother ended when I was only three. Did he have an affair with the woman he married next? And why did he allow her to hinder his relationship with my brother and me?

As I waved my father goodbye at the airport, I shouted after him, "Goodbye dad, I love you!" Little did I know that those spontaneous, childlike words would be the last I would ever say to him? Early in the morning on the day before he was due to visit me and before his return trip to Scotland, I received a phone call from my brother.

"Caryl, I am so sorry ... Dad passed away this morning."

On the one hand I was devastated. I didn't expect him to suddenly abandon me again. And this time for good! I felt angry, in fact I was furious. There were still so many unanswered questions but it was too late—I would never know.

On the other hand, although it was such a very sad time for both my brother and me, he came 'home' to die with us—his two unrecognized children. This knowledge made his unexpected death more bearable. My brother gave the eulogy at his memorial service and all my father's faithful friends from Zimbabwe attended his funeral.

જી

In the four years Danny and I were married we had moments of fun amidst the hardship. Danny was the kind of guy who would play practical jokes and had no qualms about making an ass out of himself. The two of us were often in cahoots, especially when it came to entertaining the kids.

I remember one day while we were still dating and I was in the final stages of my pregnancy, living happily in St Lucia, I dressed up like a big, fat Afrikaans man with khaki shorts and a comb in my long socks. I wore a checked shirt, which did not completely cover my pregnant tummy. I used brown eye shadow to create a five o'clock shadow on my chin and cheeks and I let a cigarette hang out of my mouth. Danny in turn put pretty coloured bows in his hair. He fashioned a nappy for himself and put a huge dummy in his mouth. Then we told the kids we were going to the beach and watched them get into a panic as they tried to block our path and push us back into the house.

We had many laughs like that with the kids, but the struggle with money—that was never quite enough—was wearing me down. At the same time, I had the strong, yet curious feeling that I was at the right place at the right time. This was confirmed and strengthened by a peculiar happening.

Danny and I were sitting in the lounge one evening when he decided to do the accounts. He went to fetch a file, and when he brought it back I glanced at the writing on the side of the file. 'Services Unlimited', it read. A chill ran down my spine.

"Where did you get that file from?" I asked him, and he nonchalantly explained that he got it from his ex-wife, Hippy. Then he added, "It belonged to her mother, Paddy. She had a small business called Services Unlimited."

But I knew that already, because when I was nineteen years old and living in Rhodesia, I had a temporary job as a receptionist for Services Unlimited. Paddy was my boss, and moreover—the writing on the side of the file was mine! It felt as if God was telling me to hang in there—especially for what was about to happen next.

One evening while Danny and I were watching TV, his eight-year-old daughter stormed into the lounge in tears. She was closely followed by my teenager, Sunshine, who was giving an unsolicited explanation of what had happened. I calmly raised my hand to silence them both and explained that I would first listen to the youngest and then hear the other side of the story. But Sunshine burst into tears and screamed, "Why is everything always my fault?"

Danny and I tried to calm her down, but she was inconsolable. She stood in the middle of the room sobbing and grabbing chunks of her hair on either side of her head. Then Danny held her firmly on both shoulders and shouted, "Calm down! We will listen to the whole story." But by then she had already lost all self-control. He tried to hold her and ducking under his arm he caught her in a headlock and they struggled.

The next thing she ran back into one of the bedrooms with Danny short on her heels, trying his absolute best to calm her down. As she threw herself on the bed, Danny tried to reach her and steady her, but she started to kick him. The more he tried to hold her down, the worse the situation became. Eventually all four of the other kids were crying and the whole situation got completely out of control.

I was standing behind Sunshine and shouted at Danny, "Just leave her!" As he backed off from her, she ran out of the house. He was concerned for her safety and wanted to run after her, but I stopped him. I thought she had gone into the garden to cry and that it would be best to leave her until she had calmed down. When she didn't come back inside after a short while, I searched the garden for her but she was nowhere to be found.

My first thought was that she had gone to a friend's house down the road, and I was fine with that. I thought she needed someone outside the family circle to talk to. But when she hadn't returned after about half an hour we were ready to go to the police—Sunshine had beaten us to it. The next thing we knew, two policemen arrived to arrest Danny! When I asked on what grounds they were making the arrest, I was told in no uncertain terms, "Child abuse."

Danny was arrested and spent the night in jail. He was let out on bail the next day. Sunshine was placed in safe care at first and then she went to live with her father.

I was absolutely confident that the trial would go well and that once I had a chance to explain the whole scenario, the case would be dropped and we would return to being one happy family again. Sadly, this was not what happened. Even though I testified and said my husband was definitely not a violent man and had certainly not hit or abused my daughter, Danny was found guilty of child abuse and received a suspended sentence! The law did not condone the physical restraint Danny had exercised on Sunshine by attempting to hold her down when she was hysterical.

It has taken twenty years for Sunshine to tell me her side of the story and that is, that in the scuffle, Danny grabbed her so hard around her throat she couldn't breathe. She was terrified that he was going to kill her. The next day her throat was bruised and sore. None of this came out in court and I didn't know how serious it was. Surely I must have seen what was happening? But I didn't. It all happened so quickly.

It's important to note that twenty years later, when Danny wanted to emigrate from South Africa, Sunshine wrote him the most beautiful letter to absolve him from all guilt. In this letter she explained that she had witnessed male-on-female violence and abuse since birth, and when he tried to hold her to calm her down, she was certain he wanted to harm her. Danny now lives happily in the country of his choice with his third wife.

⌘

Way back then, straight after the ordeal and his undeserved criminal record, our marriage suffered irrevocable damage. I hasten to add that this was not to say it was my daughter's fault—our relationship was far too open and honest for that. It was something else. Eastern religions make it so easy with the philosophy of 'karma'. That one little word explains so much and spreads the responsibility for any situation equally and evenly without affording blame and guilt to any one party involved.

I'm not sure how to explain my choice to break up this marriage. Yes, of course I know the Bible states God hates divorce. And yes, I did take the regular 'for richer for poorer, until death do us part' marriage vows. Yet, I can only tell you my truth: I knew I could not fix the marriage. I had the same calm resolve come over me when I saw my own handwriting on

Danny's file. I simply knew that the time had come for me to move on.

It was also purely a practical matter of survival. Even with my eldest daughter out of our home, it had become clear to me that Danny's salary was never going to be enough to meet our financial needs. I was forced to get a full-time job and the prospect of having to work full-time, raise five children, cook and do the housework, was too much for me to bear. I felt I could carry that kind of weight with my own children on board, but not with Danny and his two children as well. I was holding out some hope that Sunshine would come home, but once she went to live with her father he put her in boarding school and there was nothing I could do about it.

I now realize that this marriage and divorce was a lesson in humility in the midst of my obsession with religious perfection. Sadly, I must admit that I was not yet ready to learn it at the time. I pretty much swept it under the carpet and persisted with self-righteous anger towards my first husband for breaking his marriage vows, for treating me so badly and for having had an affair. In fact, I actually totally blamed my ex-husband, Andy, for the mess my life was in.

I firmly believed that had he not done the things he did, my children and I would not have had to go through the ordeal of another family break-up! After the marriage to Danny I entered a period of respite. It was as if I was gathering strength before continuing my journey. And oh boy was I going to need strength!

There's a Sufi prayer I once heard that goes, "God, please send me the one that will so completely shatter my heart, that when I rebuild it, I may build a chamber just for you." This prayer is the damsel in distress's worst nightmare! We so desperately want to believe in the fantasy that there is a knight in shining armour that will adore us unconditionally and never leave us.

I definitely didn't pray this prayer, I assure you, yet this was exactly what happened to me with my third husband. He broke my heart so completely and guess what? I survived!

You have read in the earlier chapters detail about my years of addiction to Hitler-Babe. And I have no doubt it is clear to you that I made an idol of him and of the so-called soul-mate relationship—just the way all damsels do.

Well, I have since learned one of life's most painful lessons: every single idol I have made and worshipped had clay feet—be that money, security or a public image. They *had* to fall so that the fantasy could be brought to the Truth.

The last couple of years of my ferocious determination to hold onto my fantasies are worth recording just in case there is a reader or two in the same situation as I was in, who still believes there is an excuse for abuse and that a violently abusive relationship can or must be saved.

I have come to realize that most people in these abusive relationships have a very short memory. We only remember the *passion*—the glorious, magnificent passion. I know. I've been there.

# Happy Birthday

The year was 2000 and I had been married to my millionaire third husband who alternated on and off between the personas of Hitler and Babe for ten crazy years. The pressure cooker was boiling. I was taking more and more tranquillizers and struggling to cope with my life.

My husband was ignoring the fact that my fiftieth birthday was due within a few weeks. The millennium was after all, a momentous occasion for all and we could've thrown a party. He was clearly not going to offer me the money to have a celebration of my choice. The only way that I could keep my intense disappointment at bay was to start planning something myself. All along, I quietly prayed that my husband would at least show an interest.

When that did not happen I frantically organized a champagne breakfast for myself. I invited, even though I did not know them well, the wives of my husband's Round Table friends, so as not to annoy him.

Of course, it didn't work. On the contrary, it was a sad and humiliating experience for me. The only thing that made the day memorable was the precious birthday gift from my three daughters. It was a framed picture consisting of photographs of my three daughters and an accompanying poem which they had found and then adapted the words to suit the occasion:

*Here are all your children in one place,*
*Placed behind some glass within a frame,*
*Symbolic of a much more complex grace,*
*Years of memories lie behind each face,*
*A wild sea no blessing can contain*
*Years of love, of joy, and pain*

*Of mysteries no heart can hope to trace,*
*Here are all the objects of your love,*
*A frozen section cut away from time,*
*A summit between dreams and memories,*
*Which you need only to look this way to climb;*
*An icon for domestic reveries*
*Through which a thousand answered prayers move.*

*—Happy Birthday Mom, we love you!*

*Oh thank God! I still have their support*, I thought when I read it. If I doubted they could still love me, this beautiful gift proved otherwise.

My husband took me to Mauritius for my fiftieth birthday. God in heaven! We could go on holiday anywhere, at any time, for any reason. What made him think that I would want to go away without my children for my fiftieth birthday? Even a dinner at home with all the kids and my close friends would have been better than this trip. We had been on so many holidays around the world—always without my two older children. I was a rich man's wife, and my own children were the poor relations. Even the elaborate diamond ring he gave me left a bitter taste in my mouth.

He spent every waking moment reading Richard Branson's autobiography, while I sipped cocktails and cried quietly under my sunglasses. I had every material thing any woman's heart could desire, but it felt as though I was losing the most important thing in my life—the respect of my children. And the worst part of it all was that I didn't know how to turn things around. In spite of my growing awareness that 'it takes two to tango', I was too fervently engaged in the co-dependant dance to stop. So I simply carried on.

Determined to pay my husband back for the injury he had done to me on *my* birthday, I decided to ignore *his* birthday. He was going to turn forty, four months after I had turned fifty.

I needn't have bothered to plan revenge—I received a phone call from his secretary a couple of weeks before his birthday, asking me if I wanted to invite anyone. I had no idea until that moment that he had simply assigned it to his secretary to organize the event. When I asked her what he was going to do for his birthday, she was quite taken aback and said, "Oh didn't you know? He has invited a hundred people to his birthday at the Country Club at R200 per head. There will even be a live band." He sure knew how to out-manoeuvre me!

My next move to spite him was to be noticeably absent from his birthday party. I could not be there and pretend that we were a happily married couple.

On the night of his birthday I asked a friend if she would spend the evening with me. We went out to dinner, but neither of us enjoyed it. I was riddled with guilt and kept obsessing with the idea of arriving at the party, even if I was somewhat late. I started to struggle with my conscience. Which would be more truthful: to be there or not to be there—that was the question?

Eventually, fear of his reaction prevented me from going. I was certain that he would publicly humiliate me, or say something under his breath and hurt me so badly that I would be unable to control the tears and make a fool of myself.

Still, I wanted to do something to salvage the situation. It occurred to me that he or his secretary might not have remembered to organize a birthday cake. So I ordered a beautiful and expensive cake from Franco (a well-known baker) to be delivered to his party.

The following day the cake was delivered back to the house, completely untouched. I gave it away to an orphanage and the two of us didn't speak to each other at all the whole day. I knew by his silence that he would get his revenge, and he did in a grand style at my daughter's wedding. He took over the speeches and annoyed my daughter's father so much that he left the wedding and went home with his wife. Then he proceeded to ignore me for the rest of the evening.

The weeks that followed became more and more stressful. I had been to see an attorney to start divorce proceedings, and told my husband so. Yet, I was doing this for effect only. What I really wanted was for him to fight for me and try and make amends. But it soon became clear that this was not going to happen.

In sheer desperation, I made an appointment with a member of the Round Table. My husband served on the committee. At our meeting I poured my heart out to the Round Tabler. I told him that my husband and I had a very volatile relationship and that I was feeling at the end of my tether.

Then I said, "Round Table raises funds for charities, right? Would Round Table help women who are trapped in domestic violence?"

He became uneasy and looked at me as if to say, *Where are you going with this?*

Then I added, "I want to show you something," and I passed him the photographs of my bruised body and face. I watched his expression as he glanced through the photographs. He didn't show an ounce of shock—let alone compassion. So, I challenged him and asked why a reputable organization such as the Round Table would tolerate a man like my husband on their committee, who physically abuses his wife. There was no reply.

Then I started to plead with this man to talk to my husband. "Perhaps if you do, and he becomes aware of the consequences of his actions, he might stop!"

As it turned out, the man definitely did address the issue with my husband because I received a letter from him warning me that "threatening to ruin his reputation" was akin to blackmail. He sent a copy of his letter to both our attorneys.

ℰᴑ

In the meanwhile I had been seeing a therapist who recommended that I go on an anti-depressant. Due to nasty side-effects I experienced from the medication, the doctor switched my medication from one 'cocktail' to the other. In no time I had accumulated half-full containers of so many different schedule-six drugs that I could have opened a pharmacy and dispensed them myself! Yet, nothing seemed to have the power to calm my shattered nerves and chronic lack of sleep. A loss of appetite didn't help the situation either.

At the same time (I already knew the signs so well from past experience) I was slipping into the abyss of depression and there was no way out. I had gone too far down that road and there seemed to be no other option open to me anymore.

One evening as I sat in the lounge, drinking wine, I felt exhausted from lack of sleep. I hoped that the wine would make me drowsy enough to fall asleep. Then I decided to take some tranquillizers with the wine, and started to pick pills from the many half-full containers. "Eeny, meeny, myni, mo!" I said as I made my choice.

I can vaguely recall getting into my car and driving off after I had swallowed a handful of tranquillizers. My regular routine, when I was severely upset, was to get in my sport's car, turn up the music and go for a ride on the highway that circles the city. Round and round I'd go, until I had comforted and calmed myself and gathered sufficient courage to face the adversity in my own home again.

This time, however, I didn't get further than the security gate at the entrance of the estate where we lived. I drove straight into it! The security guard did me the favour of calling my husband. I can't remember exactly how I got home, but I do remember my husband dropping me as he carried me up the stairs, because I fell on my face and broke my nose in the process. Then he simply threw me onto the bed.

Eventually I managed to get myself into the bed, and that's where I stayed comatose for several days until my housekeeper became concerned that I was not showing much sign of life. I believe that my husband was hoping I would die. She called my daughters and I have a hazy yet very tender memory of my two daughters helping me downstairs, into their car and driving me to a private clinic. I was admitted and spent the next two weeks there, heavily sedated.

For Mother's Day, my wonderful three daughters arranged for us to have a picnic in a quiet spot on the hospital grounds. They had packed a basket fit for a princess, but I felt like a complete failure. The obvious lack of concern from my husband's two children rubbed salt into my wound, as they did not come to see me. They had come to live with us when his son was seven years old and his daughter was five—the same age as my youngest daughter, Star, at the time.

It had been my heart's desire to be a full-time mother and homemaker, just as my two aunts had been. That, to me, was the true symbol of success—not the money, the jewellery, the car or the house. But it seemed that the one thing I yearned for most had eluded me. I was fifty years old already and my children were coming to home-leaving age. Playing 'happy families' was clearly a dying dream.

I came home to an icy atmosphere. In the meanwhile, I had run out of chronic medication I had been taking for petit mal epilepsy since I was a young adult. It was no secret to my husband that omitting to take this medication could have dire consequences. Yet, when I asked him for money to buy my medication, his response was outright, "Go and get a job."

Within days the withdrawal from the hospital drugs as well as my regular medication began to take its toll. In addition to that I discovered my husband had re-established a relationship with an ex-girlfriend—visiting her as a 'friend', I was walking on eggshells around him and feeling as if I was living on borrowed time in my own home.

ॐ

One evening both the teenage girls (his and mine) went off to a nearby casino and entertainment complex. I was trying to relax and ease the disorientating symptoms I was experiencing from drug withdrawal, when I received a call from my husband to say he had met his daughter and was not coming home for some time. When I asked him where *my* daughter was, he replied spitefully, "That's not my problem." Had he forgotten the numerous times I had fetched and carried his children from their sporting activities and from their friends' parties in the middle of the night?

In my foggy state, I had completely forgotten that she had made arrangements to go to a friend's house after her trip to the casino complex and I went into a blind panic. My husband's apparent indifference to her safety only added fuel to the fire.

Suddenly in a trance-like state, I picked the TV remote up from the coffee table and threw it at our big-screen television. Through my dazed confusion it sounded as though the screen had smashed into smithereens.

Then, as if hypnotized by the sound of breaking glass, I walked around the living room sweeping everything onto the floor. I ripped the glasses from the bar shelves with a vengeance, getting more and more demented as I thought of the role alcohol played in our marital problems; of the heavy drinkers we had become and of the way he and his friends would go out and get smashed night after night.

When my blind rage subsided I sat down at the dining-room table and looked at the devastation I had caused around me. Somewhere in my wild rage I had cut myself. The combination of blood and glass was most dramatic in the bar. I felt no remorse at all.

Without my knowing, my stepson who was in his bedroom with a friend had phoned my husband the instant he realized I was losing it. The next thing I knew, my husband walked into the house and perused the devastated scene. He started to shake his head in a patronizing manner and with a sarcastic grin on his face, he said, "You have done exactly what I wanted you to do." Then he fetched my camera and started to take photographs like a forensic detective, laughing to himself with every click of the camera.

This taunting drove me back into my frenzy and I lunged towards him, grabbed the camera out of his hands and smashed it to pieces against the wall.

After this, he walked out the room, and within no time a police van arrived. I remained seated at the dining-room table. When they started their questioning, I fetched an envelope that contained the photographs of the numerous beatings I had been subjected to throughout our marriage. I showed the policemen the photos and pleaded with them, "Please look at these pictures of what he does to me. Can you see one mark on him right now? I have broken *things*, not bones!"

While the policemen were standing around looking very uneasy, Lawyer-Cousin and his smiling wife arrived on the scene. At first I naïvely hoped that their intention was to help and to resolve the situation. They had, after all, been witness to many of the fights between my husband and me.

Instead they watched without empathy as the policemen ordered me to get into the back of their van while they "speak to my husband and his lawyer".

It was shortly after midnight on a particularly cold winter's night, but I couldn't feel the cold. I wondered whose thoughtful gesture it was to get me a jersey—I doubted that it was my husband's or his cousin's—but the policemen came out of the house with a jersey for me and without any further explanation, they locked me in the back of the van and we drove off. I was under the impression that I was going to the police station to make a statement and so I was calm, but quite resolute.

When we got to the police station, the sergeant unceremoniously took my fingerprints and told me that I was under arrest for malicious damage to property. I was gob-smacked. How was that possible, we were married, glasses and ornaments belonged to both of us. I sat in the charge office in a complete daze.

The next moment, the sergeant started to make arrangements to take me to a hospital and only then did I notice the deep cut on my hand.

On our way to the hospital I had to sit in the front of a small van in between the two policemen. Suddenly the driver pulled over in a secluded spot. I am ashamed to admit, but the thought that they might be taking me there to rape me, raced through my mind. Instead of my worst fear coming true, the driver got out of the vehicle and had an innocent pee behind the back of the van.

As we drove off again, he asked me, "Why do you stay with a man who can do this to you? He is not a good man if he does this to you. You are just a *woman*." He shook his head and added, "You must believe that Jesus can look after you."

I felt severely chastised by that simple statement of truth. The reason I was in this situation was not because my husband did not love me, it was a lack of *faith* that I would be taken care of if I had to leave him. I started to weep and to my surprise the two policemen comforted me.

We arrived at the hospital in Hillbrow, the Sodom and Gomorrah of Johannesburg and, in the midst of stab-wound patients, beaten-up prostitutes and overdosed drug addicts, I was taken into theatre where an over-worked and very unsympathetic doctor stitched my hand.

Back at the local police station, I was taken into a holding cell. I had always thought that the clanging sound of cell doors opening and closing in the movies was exaggerated—believe me, when you are the one going through the gate, it is that loud!

The cell was filthy and stank of urine and sweat. I once read that a person tends to sweat more when afraid, and judging by the pungent smell lingering in the cell, the other three prisoners were as scared as me!

There was no furniture of any description in the cell and the other three prisoners were huddled together in a corner under a grey prison blanket, their big white eyes on their black faces staring at me. The cell had a cold cement floor and in the other corner was a stinking, dirty toilet—*à la* open plan.

I badly needed to use the toilet, but couldn't face the prospect of being stared at by the other women. There was nothing else to do but to sit down on the floor in my imported leather pants, suede boots, my genuine diamond jewellery and my mother's jersey. Yes, ironically the jersey the police officers brought for me as I rode in the back of the police van was one that belonged to my deceased mother. My dear, dear mother who had whispered to me on her deathbed that my husband was such a nice man!

I was lonely and very afraid. When the other prisoners fell asleep I tried to use the toilet. It didn't have a seat and was filled to the brim with used toilet paper and faeces. The walls on either side were smeared with the same gruesome contents, so I couldn't even lean against the wall to keep my balance.

I gave up the challenge and took a blanket from the pile to lie down. These blankets clearly hadn't been washed in months. I couldn't decide whether they stank of sweat or urine, but I finally fell asleep praying and clutching my mother's jersey. In the end I had indirectly presented her with an opportunity to comfort me. I could even smell her perfume.

The next morning, around six o'clock, the steel door of the cell slid open and we were led out into a courtyard where dozens of convicts were shackled and handcuffed together. The women prisoners were taken to prison vans and we headed for the courts.

When we arrived there we were packed into the holding cells like sardines. Finally, around nine o'clock a man made his appearance and summoned me, "I am your appointed attorney. Your divorce attorneys have appointed me. You will have to wait until they call your name."

I was still stupefied and made no attempt to reply. The room was ice cold and I was freezing. I wrapped my mother's jersey tightly around me and waited.

Lunchtime came and all the prisoners were ushered through to a hall. On the way I asked the warden if I might use the toilet. By this time my bladder was practically bursting. Alas, the toilet door was broken and left a huge gap when I tried to close it. People walking past could see in, and I simply couldn't get myself so far as to use that particular toilet. It had been over fifteen hours since I had been to a toilet!

I joined the other prisoners for lunch. Trust me—it wasn't crayfish thermidor at R1 000 a tail and Moët Champagne, as I was accustomed to. It was 'bunny chow'—hollowed out bread filled with who-knows-what and tea in an enamel mug. I declined lunch and they locked me in a separate cell with all the others who refused to eat.

A long hour passed and we were led back to the holding cells. It was Friday afternoon around four o'clock and the courts were about to close. An Indian lady who had been looking in my direction every so often throughout the day, came to my side and asked politely, "If you don't mind me asking, why are you in here?"

I told her with some sarcasm that I had "redecorated my home and my husband didn't like it". She showed some appreciation for my black sense of humour, but warned me that if my case were not heard that afternoon I would be kept in jail for the whole weekend. One look at my face on receiving this news and she took charge of my dire situation and asked the policeman to call my attorney.

I was shocked when I saw my two eldest daughters alongside my attorney. The lost and devastated look on their faces cut right through me and all three of us burst into tears.

The attorney explained to me that there seemed to be a problem with my case. The court had lost the docket. How convenient! My husband and Lawyer-Cousin came instantly to mind. I had been privy to their lack of scruples around the law many a time. I presumed they had paid someone to lose my docket.

When I mentioned this possibility to my attorney it was as if a light bulb went on in his head. He then promised me that even if he had to "give someone a blowjob" He would do what ever it would take to find my docket and get me out of jail for the weekend. He had apparently already asked my daughters during the course of the day to source as much cash as they could. They phoned my husband, but he, not surprisingly, refused to help. Clearly he was still in his infamous Hitler persona and wanted to see me in jail the whole weekend.

They did, however, manage to procure a handsome amount of cash from a friend of mine who was in the habit of keeping money stored under her mattress. God bless her! An hour later my attorney returned and when I saw the look on his face I knew he had been successful in offering a counter-bribe. I was released.

ɞ

Believe it or not, my husband and I were reconciled as if nothing had happened. Soon he was sending me text messages on my cell phone to tune into this or the other radio station and listen to the love song that was playing, like Garth Taylor's song which says: "Why is it when I'm sad I always think about you. Why is it when I'm lonely I just can't do without you?" or Shania Twain crooning: "They thought we wouldn't make it, look how far we've come my baby ..."

For as long as I had known him, this habit of calling my attention to a special song was his 'love language'. In retrospect, of course, I realize that our relationship was as sentimental as it was brutal.

Shortly after our reconciliation, my husband and I took a trip to Bali. It was decidedly the worst holiday we had been on together. Except for the New Year's party when we ended up fully clothed in the hotel pool, together with a whole bunch of the other drunk and disorderly guests, the two of us were in separate worlds.

For some time our spiritual beliefs had diverged. He had become convinced in reincarnation and this ideology went against my Christian belief. However, he believed: "We were soul mates in a previous life and we have issues which we need to resolve in this lifetime." In my desperation to keep him I was willing to shelve my own beliefs and agree with his.

But as the saying goes: "You take yourself wherever you go," Bali was not the idyllic island holiday I had hoped for.

One evening after we had an argument I couldn't fall sleep. I remembered reading at reception about a show in the restaurant that night. I decided to go and see it and left my husband asleep in bed. When I got there I positioned myself quite close to the front of the stage. Initially I was enthralled with the show, totally mesmerized by the Balinese costumes and exotic make-up. The music was mystical and enchanting.

However, I soon started to feel uncomfortable. I realized that the general theme of the show was good versus evil. There is certainly nothing original about that, but I was becoming increasingly disturbed by the shenanigans on stage.

I wanted to leave, but I had such a prominent front row seat that I would have disturbed the performance if I did. Then the thought occurred to me that perhaps there was a special message for me contained in that event—a reason for my being there.

When the show ended I decided to stay up for a while longer to fathom what the Holy Spirit was trying to say to me. While I was sitting in the hotel lounge, I suddenly heard the sounds of familiar Christian music. At first I thought I was dreaming. But when I looked around, I saw that a group of local Balinese musicians had set up their instruments just outside the pub, and sure enough they where playing all the songs I had learnt when I first became a Christian!

I was in awe—a million miles from home, while questioning my spirituality, here was a band in Bali, playing familiar charismatic Christian music, reminding me of my spiritual home. It was as if God was touching me personally and saying in that recognizable still, quiet voice: *"Wherever you are, I am with you always even until the end of time."*

My relationship with God had sustained me through the most trying times, but that night I had to admit to myself and to God that I had neglected my part in the relationship—actually, I had *replaced* it altogether with my obsession for my so-called soul-mate relationship. I had begun to worship a false god—looking to my husband for material and emotional sustenance instead of looking to God. Suddenly if felt as if I was back on track!

The following day, I read that the show was considered to be such an emotional burden on the cast that a priest had to pray for them before and after every show in order to dispel the evil spirits. This bit of news served as a confirmation that I was not imagining the intensely personal responses to the show I had experienced the previous night.

I told my husband about my joyous and unusual experience, but we were not on the same page anymore. The separation of our souls had begun. It was simply a matter of time.

ം

Four years earlier, at the age of forty-seven I had picked up a paintbrush for the first time in my life and started to express myself on canvas. I had also taken up a three-year course in graphology, or handwriting analysis, which had been a long-standing interest of mine. The subtle step of deciding to use my God-given talents to follow my passions started to gradually bolster my self-esteem. This, together with my renewed connection with God began to give me strength and courage to begin to stand my ground with my violent husband. But there was one more trial to go though before my inevitable freedom from this macabre dance.

I had put a parcel of dog poo on the floor next to my husband's bed in a moment of extreme anger. You may recall the story from a previous chapter—I had done this after he told my daughter to clean up after the dog, to make the point that it was *his* dog that was messing all over our new house. Then I had stormed past him on the way to my art studio and snapped, "Clean up after your own damn dog. Star is not doing it." But I never told you what happened next.

As I sat in my studio, livid, Hitler walked in. (It was about a month before my daughter's wedding.) His eyes were glazed with anger. He walked straight up to me and grabbed me by the hair. He lifted me up off the chair by my hair and threw me over the desk on which contained all my art tools. As the paints, inks and brushes went crashing to the floor he screamed, "Don't you dare fuck with me!"

Every time I tried to get up from the floor he would kick me in the chest and I would fall back onto the floor. This happened several times and he kept screaming, "Who the fuck do you think you are, you fucking bitch!"

Eventually I decided to simply remain on the floor, but as I lay there staring him in the eye, my eyes glared at him with sheer hatred. Then he put his foot on my chest and, with his finger pointing at me and frothing at the mouth like an absolute demon, he said "Don't mess with me. I will fucking kill you."

In that moment the thought flashed through my mind that the relationship between us would never change—but *I* could.

I didn't know it at the time, but as it turned out, that was indeed the last time I would allow a man to physically abuse me. And the last time in my life that I would find an excuse for abuse. Never again would I cover the bruises with special make-up to protect my abuser from being identified by the outside world. Never again would I justify his behaviour to myself or to others. Never again would I expect my children and my close friends to look the other way when I went back to him after a beating. No! This was the last time I would allow the creation of God within me to be disgraced in that particular way.

It was soon after this incident and my daughter's wedding that we went on holiday to Argentina and Cape Town and I came out of denial with the absurd little message from his lover on his cell phone, which he did nothing to cover-up or deny.

I'd be lying if I told you that I wanted to divorce this man. Even after all the pain and humiliation that had gone down over the years, and every inch of knowledge I had gathered about the nature of abusive relationships such as ours, even with the dire 'prognosis' for our marriage from several therapists—I was *still* prepared to hang in there. I did not want to get divorced.

On that very same fateful holiday in Cape Town, just days before the emotional 'tsunami' hit me and drowned our marriage once and for all; my husband asked me a very pertinent question. "How does one know the difference between greed and ambition?"

I knew without a doubt that he had been severely challenged

by this issue and I was not going to let a chance to influence him go by, so I said, "Greed is when you are prepared to sacrifice your family for success. It is when a man says that he loves his wife and that the sex is still good, but he is screwing around like a jackrabbit, unable to get enough. It is when a man is so driven to make money that he is prepared to lose his family in the process."

Naturally, I wanted to make the point that his greed for money, success and other women on the one hand, and his lack of ambition for a happy marriage and family on the other, were morally wrong as far as I was concerned. And even to the bitter end I was hoping for a miraculous change in his values. I was grasping at straws. According to telephone records, that very same day he was still sending his lover messages. My message had clearly fallen on deaf ears.

But of course, I knew the truth in my own heart—I was less concerned with the way he behaved than the possibility that he might leave me. I had stayed in this violently abusive marriage with him much longer than I would have had I not feared loneliness and poverty as much as I did. I don't want to be misunderstood with this admission. I did not stay with him because of his money. I put up with the abuse because I feared being alone and poor *more* than I feared the occasional broken bone. That was the exact size of my fear of abandonment and poverty.

Predictably, life was going to give me a chance to face my greatest fear: my soul mate and sole source of financial security decided to divorce me. Or shall I say—I was retrenched. That's exactly what it felt like. Not only was I ten years older than this man, he also, all through the marriage, treated me as if he was my boss and somehow 'owned' me. His business was a huge success, his children were about to leave the nest, the maid had learnt to cook, and suddenly my services were no longer required. I was offered a severance package and I was free to go. It was time for young blood. The new victim was a few years older than my daughter. Was I bitter? Yes of course I was.

# False Friends and True Enemies

I had always been under the impression that a university degree qualified the person to speak into my life. Over the years I have happily given my power over with a confident heart to these so-called professionals. Some of these are genuine earth angels; others, I dare say, have little concern for the human soul.

Some weeks before the nervous breakdown when I 're-decorated' the house I had consulted a top divorce attorney. I even took a friend of mine along for moral support. A few days after this consultation he phoned me with the following advice: "I have given your matter some thought and I doubt you will get the settlement you want. You will be wasting your time and money fighting for it."

I was standing in a shop at the time of his call, and I remember clearly walking outside the shop to avoid drawing attention to myself. I was very upset with his sudden change of heart and started to raise my voice.

"Can't you see what's going on? Can't you help me?"

He had proof of the domestic violence in my marriage but in spite of this he simply replied that I would be fighting a losing battle. We argued for about ten minutes as I tried to convince him to take my case and get me a fair settlement.

Eventually I threw in the towel, said goodbye and stormed off to my car. As I got into the car I burst into tears feeling powerless and frustrated. *What now?* A short while later I received a call from my husband.

"Are you prepared to settle?" he calmly enquired. Before I could answer he smugly continued, "You're wasting your time, you don't have the money to fight me and you don't have a leg to stand on."

When I asked him how he had come to this conclusion, he

said, "I was sitting in your attorney's office when he phoned you and I heard exactly what he said to you."

℘

Now, if you think unethical behaviour like this is typical of the legal profession, let me tell you about the therapist I saw in the last year of my marriage.

My husband and I went to see her together. She suggested that we attend a few sessions together to begin with, and that I should see her separately as well. I could tell from the onset that she liked my husband a lot, perhaps even fancied him. This disturbed me but I went against my better judgement and continued the sessions with her.

A short time into our therapy it became perfectly clear that she could no longer discern between the lies he was telling and the truth. In one of the sessions, while my husband was holding the floor, I became so incensed with his perpetual lying that I got up to leave. She commanded me not to leave so I confronted her, "How can we get anywhere if my husband is incapable of speaking the truth?"

She looked quite surprised but failed to take control of the situation.

"I can't do this," I said and walked out.

According to my husband, after I left she said to him, "I don't know how you have put up with this for so long!" I was offended by this blatant betrayal. I had been vulnerable and honest with this woman. She had seen the photographs of my battered and bruised body. She knew my fears and hopes and I was furious that she had turned into my husband's personal cheerleader!

So I decided to see her one more time and to take my youngest daughter along with me, as she was witness to the violence in our home. I thought that a qualified therapist should have no problem detecting the truth after listening to the testimony of a traumatized child.

She told us that we were 'overreacting' and implied that we had a very comfortable life with my husband. We should be thankful instead of complaining! Then she added for my benefit that many couples work out their differences after an affair and sometimes it even strengthened the relationship. *Who said anything about an affair?* I wondered. We were consulting her to help us deal with the conflict in our marriage.

On second thought, I should thank these two 'professionals', because without them my story would have ended quite differently. They cured my naïvety about university graduates and taught me to use discernment with anyone who claims to be able to speak into my life. When the time finally came for my divorce, and I was ready to enter the dark night of the soul, I chose angels without university degrees to support me.

∞

A very dear friend of mine spoke to me on several occasions on the success of her therapy with a particular traumatologist. I was stubbornly resisting the idea of engaging in counselling again and felt caught between a rock and a hard place. On the one side I was determined not to waste another cent on pointless therapy and on the other I was in dire need of emotional guidance and support for the traumatic divorce battle I still had to face. So when the opportunity came (through another dear friend of mine who also needed counselling) I convinced her to make an appointment with this traumatologist, Dr. T, and offered to accompany her.

Dr. T was kind and friendly, and completely honest. I listened intently as she told my friend, "I am a results-driven psychologist. I don't like to waste my client's or my own time so when I don't see any change by the time I expect it, I may refer you to someone else."

These no-nonsense words made a great impression on me. I was struck by the notion that she wanted to be effective and see results. It was then that I realized that this doctor was probably my last chance at sanity.

At the time I was staying in a tiny one-bedroom townhouse, situated next to the main security gate which clanked open and shut at all hours of the day and night like prison doors. My husband had been ordered to provide my teenage daughter, Star, and me with accommodation since the night he and his Cocky Friend had provoked me to such an extent that I called the police (thus playing right into his hands that I had deserted the matrimonial home).

At first Star and I stayed with my newly wedded daughter, sleeping in her lounge on the floor, and from there we found a haven with a friend for a while. Then we moved into a B&B, until I ended up in the townhouse, which was too small to house both Star and me. She had to stay with my newly wedded daughter without most of her clothes and matric schoolbooks. She and I had with us only the few possessions we were able to take the night we left home. My husband locked everything else we owned in storage the following day.

Star was in her final year of school and I am mortified to think that neither my husband nor I could shelve our private agendas for her sake. Of course I know that Star, like my other two daughters, has her own journey to make and how she responds to adversity will be up to her. Yet, I am a mother, the *life-giver* and I will always feel remorse for the way in which I was unable to put my children before me at the various stages of my life.

Be that as it may, the time of living on my own in that little townhouse was one of the scariest and most depressing of them all. During my time there, I had a very disturbing dream one night:

My husband and I were still living together in our dream home. He was in his 'Hitler-mode'—dressed immaculately in his designer men's wear, eating cereal while walking around, holding the bowl in his hand. (This was a regular occurrence in real life.) He would habitually address me in this patronizing manner, eating his cereal, dressed up to the nines while I looked my very worst. He would usually start the conversation with, "What's upsetting you so much?"

In the dream, he was staring at me over the top of the bowl as he scooped a mouthful of cereal. With food swishing around in his mouth, he told me quite casually that he never wanted me back in his life again. "This time it really is over." I was absolutely crushed in the dream.

Then he ordered me to eat the dog food out of my Maltese poodle, Sushi's, bowl. I got down on all fours and ate the food like a dog. It was absolutely disgusting and I wanted to throw up.

ᘓ

When I woke up I was crying and I was left with the devastating feeling that I would never see my darling dog, Sushi, again. And true enough—a few days later I received a text message on my phone callously informing me that Sushi was dead. She had been run over.

During the troubled marriage, for the best part of six years, Sushi and I spent many hours together. I would lie with her on the bed when I cried, and then she would put her little ears back and tenderly lick my face. We were inseparable. After I left home, I begged my husband to let me have her. He refused, except once. While I was staying at my friend's home for a short time, he allowed Sushi and me a weekend's visit.

My friend had cats, so Sushi and I spent most of the

weekend in the bedroom. It didn't matter—we were overjoyed to be together once more. As it turned out, that weekend was our last together.

After I received the news of her death, I drove straight to the vet. I spent an hour with her little dead body in the vet's surgery. I was inconsolable. Eventually I took her body home. Once I was home, I sat with this furry little dog on my lap and cried uncontrollably the entire evening. Then I wrapped her in a blanket and took her to bed with me.

This reaction to a dead pet may sound macabre to those who have not been blessed by the unconditional love of an animal friend. But let me assure you, lying in my bed that freezing cold night, in the lonesome one-bedroom townhouse, which felt like a prison, remembering Sushi's absolute unreserved and unrestrained love for me stopped me from putting an end to my life.

For weeks I had not been able to sleep and when I did, I had the most dreadful nightmares. I had no appetite and my usually shiny long black hair was falling out in handfuls.

In the morning I was calm. I dropped her body off at the vet to be cremated, but I knew I was living on borrowed time. I phoned Dr. T and asked her if she would take me on as a client. She agreed.

I was still mainly living out of the overnight bag I'd grabbed and filled with a few things on the night Star and I had left home. My married daughter had fetched a few more bits and pieces, but I couldn't even put a matching set of pyjamas together from the assortment I had with me. My journals, art materials and other intensely personal belongings, which I held dear and which gave me comfort, were all locked in storage.

I did, however, have the photographs showing the injuries I'd received at the hands of my husband. I used to carry them around like an identity document and would show them to whomever I thought might be able to help. Of course, this strategy was useless—it simply made me look crazy! In fact, I had begun to fear the worst myself. Although I knew I was far from insane, I could not deny that I was mentally and emotionally unwell.

I had seen so many therapists over the years and all along my situation had steadily worsened instead of improved. It was certainly not for a lack of trying from my side.

At our first appointment, I wanted Dr. T to tell me something, *anything* that would make my marriage 'work'. I had come out of denial about my husband's infidelities, but I still believed there was some sort of cure that would make him mine again. In fact, I *expected* her to produce the miracle. Of course, she did quite the opposite.

"Do you think anything can save this marriage?" She wanted the verdict to come from my own mouth.

Reluctantly I shook my head slowly from side to side. I knew that once I had made this admission, I would be held accountable for it.

And true enough every time I slipped back into denial, there she was, kindly but firmly reminding me of the truth. *My marriage was over.*

Soon after the first session with Dr. T, my husband invited me to lunch. He told me that he was willing to try again and I instantly decided to fight for this marriage right until the bitter end. I was not at this stage going to allow anyone else to decide when my marriage was over and I persuaded him to come with me for therapy.

At our very first session with Dr. T, it became clear that my husband had a private agenda for agreeing to see her. He was going to prove once and for all that I was emotionally unstable—crazy in fact.

Initially it looked as if his plan was going to succeed, but then Dr. T started to probe a little deeper. The atmosphere suddenly became very tense and my husband started to lie about many of the questions she asked. When I couldn't take it anymore I put my hand on his shoulder and, as he turned to look at me, I asked him, "Why are you lying?"

In response to this he shook his head from side to side as if to say, "There you go again."

I looked at him with complete exasperation and asked again, "Why are you lying like this? We will never get anywhere in therapy if you can't be honest about anything."

But he refused to tell the truth. This upset me and I started to cry. He looked at Dr. T and raised his eyebrows, giving her the message that this was the kind of 'madness' he had to put up with—exactly as he'd played all the previous therapists.

When he eventually got up to leave, Dr. T gestured for me to stay behind. I suppose she noticed my total frustration because she attempted to give me moral support. But I felt completely defeated—it was his word against mine and as far as I was concerned I had come to the end of the road. I wasn't even sure if I could trust Dr. T anymore. I sat there and quietly contemplated admitting myself into the 'funny farm'.

However, as God would have it, on the way home I listened to a voice message that was left on my phone. It was from my husband. He admitted tearfully that he had lied and said how sorry he was.

Although I was terrified I would delete it by mistake, I managed to forward the message to Dr. T. She could hear for herself—I was not insanely imagining things!

I needed her witness so badly. I had begun to doubt myself... Did I read the message on his phone correctly, 'No I'm not horny but when are you due home?' Was I the only one who noticed his shameless flirting with Moonie's best friend, in the garden at her kitchen tea? Did I really see him cut and paste a client's signature onto another document? And did I hear him instructing his secretary to do the same?

I knew after the exposure of his lies there was no turning

back. Dr. T didn't have to put the words into my mouth, my inner voice was practically screaming day and night, *Caryl, you have done everything you possibly could—it's time to switch the machines off.*

From that day onwards my husband and I saw Dr. T separately. I would drive away from my sessions with her, crying so much that I could barely see the traffic. I knew only I could make the final decision. She couldn't help me. I had to say, "It's brain dead. Today I'll switch this machine of my marriage off." But, I simply couldn't do it. My head accepted that it was over but my heart reversed away from the truth. I was hoping against all hope. Until death do us part? I feared this time it might be just that. I had been a nurse and seen people come back to life and enjoy a full recovery after the physician had declared there was no hope. I also wanted a miracle. *Why was it not forthcoming?*

Dr. T had commenced my therapy by explaining the cycle of abuse and the way in which the victim becomes abusive by being *passively aggressive*. I had of course been told about my passive-aggressive behaviour in the past, but I had always managed to rationalize and justify that stone-walling my abuser was better than screaming or shouting or provoking him even more. But Dr. T would hear nothing of it—passive-aggressive behaviour made me an *abuser* along with the person whom I had accused of abuse. I was not the defenceless and innocent victim that I had perceived and projected myself to be.

At this early point in the therapy with Dr. T, I instinctively knew the dark night of the soul had begun and for this I at once loved and hated her. With my co-operation she started to probe deeper into my psyche to find the reasons why I had landed myself in such a mess in the first place. "When was the first time you felt that you had to rescue someone or that you are responsible for another's happiness?" she asked.

More and more questions like these came my way, and she

eventually proved to me that I was co-dependent—that I had developed a pattern of believing my right to exist depended on helping or rescuing others. *Caryl, the human being, is not good enough simply to be.*

I suddenly understood my complete self-rejection since childhood. *Caryl, by herself, has no value.* I thought. For as long as I could remember my validation had to come from others. Now Dr. T was challenging me to believe that "… simply by being here," she continued, "sitting here today in front of me, stretch marks and all, without having to do anything, or to perform and achieve anything in life—makes you good enough. The fact that God thought it well to create Caryl makes you good enough!"

Over and over she would confirm, "You do not need other people to justify your existence. You are good enough as you are. You don't need their pain and their problems to give you a reason to exist. You are good enough."

Although I was beginning to see the light, the therapy was becoming tougher. The diagnosis of co-dependency was a pretty nasty label I thought; and if I accepted it, I had to admit that I was manipulative. *Did I rescue others in order to control them?*

I resisted this notion with all my might. I argued that a woman was required to submit to her husband and be a little bit of a doormat—*it even says so in my Bible.* This was not being manipulative. I saw nothing wrong with the way I acted and I was quite prepared to continue doing it. The only thing I was objecting to in my marriage was the domestic violence and adultery—everything else was 'fine'.

I was tempted at this point to stop seeing Dr. T altogether, and then my husband asked me to meet him for coffee. We met at an open-plan coffee shop. I was very cautious, knowing that I was extremely vulnerable and he had manipulated me so many times in the past.

I could sense he was up to something, but nothing prepared

me for the 'sale's pitch' he launched into while sitting in that uninspiring and unromantic place.

"You know you're very special to me. You know I want to be with no one but you." And then the clincher, "Babe would you consider reconciliation?"

He seemed so sincere. He added that we could continue therapy. He suggested we live separately while we resolved our problems in therapy and offered that I move into my favourite of the many houses we owned—a beautiful, thatched, double-storey with an art studio in the garden. *Well, blow me over with a feather.* He also mentioned that we should replace our ante-nuptial contract with a new agreement so that the house I was going to live in would be in my name.

Then I told him that a friend of mine was going to Scotland. She was also in a very troubled marriage and she had decided to take some time out. To this he replied, "Why don't you go with her?" and he offered to pay for the plane ticket! He did.

I was in seventh heaven by the time we left the coffee shop. In the car park he hesitated for a moment and said, "I have something to tell you ..." But then he thought better of it and said he would rather phone me from his car. Of course I asked him why he couldn't tell me there and then, and he replied he was scared of my reaction.

When the call came he said that he wanted me to know he was planning to go to Dubai with another woman that coming Friday. However, the following day he took me to buy new kitchen appliances and a bed, just the way he promised. He also assured me that he would have all my goods that were in storage delivered to the house.

All I could think of was my daughter and I would be in our home and I would get my art materials back. It was as if I had gone completely blank about my past experiences with this man. I had forgotten about the time he had dropped me for his blonde colleague on the very day I was about to move in with him. All she could say was, "Sorry Caryl, I know this must be hard for you, but we have been seeing each other all along. He's been very confused about whom he wants, but now he has decided, and it's not you".

I had also forgotten about the time he invited me to get my Christmas gift, made love to me and then went off to Thailand with another woman. Most importantly, I had forgotten about the time he seduced me into believing he wanted a reconciliation only to get me to sign consent for a divorce. All this and more I had totally forgotten!

ℰℴ

In the meanwhile I had inadvertently met a group of earth angels through a friend. There were six earth angels in the group, all of whom were either in the throes of divorce or already divorced. Yet, they each displayed an obvious sense of self-worth. I, on the other hand, felt completely stripped of my power. Fixing my troubled marriage had been my full-time occupation and it validated me—it provided me with a reason to exist. I had felt, at first, intimidated by these women who looked ever so glamorous and in control of their lives compared to me, who was struggling to keep Humpty Dumpty together.

As the conversations progressed and each of us started to share our stories, I began to feel the connection. One of the women, Veronica, and I shared a special bond—she was also born and bred in Zimbabwe and was going through a divorce. She was married to a narcissistic attorney who proved to be a very difficult man. As it turned out, we had even appointed the same divorce attorney! I was beginning to feel at ease and started to enjoy myself more than I had in years. *These are 'real' women,* I thought.

The one thing that made the biggest impression on me was the way in which we were able to laugh at our fears and our pain and yet have so much empathy while we were together. We were united. I was clearly not the only one to realize this because from that day onwards we decided to meet once a month for lunch.

The date with the Lunch Club ladies became the highlight of my month through the long, dark season of my divorce. At the first Lunch Club date (after my husband's offer to reconcile, change our ante-nuptial contract and go for therapy) I told the earth angels of my husband and my plan. Before I was even finished speaking, the one sitting next to me looked as if she was going to have a stroke. "Are you absolutely out of your mind? Can't you see he is manipulating you, again?"

"You, his wife, will be set up in a house while he goes away with Miss Dubai. Are you crazy?" Unbeknown to me at the time, he had already spoken to her about marriage.

They all challenged me about my decision. They believed I was being set up again and that all he was trying to do was get me to sign an early settlement. They reminded me that he was going to Dubai with another woman.

Of course I could see all that—I was not stupid. But, unfortunately, I had stubbornly gone into complete denial again. Intelligence and common sense are no match for the force of denial. I had even convinced myself that the other woman was only a client of his! *After all, why would he want to be reconciled if he was romantically involved with someone else?* I argued quietly in my own baffled head.

Before I had any more time to think things over, my husband had the furniture collected from the one-bedroom townhouse and moved to the thatched house the following day without any further discussion with me.

ಐ

On the same Friday he was leaving with Miss Dubai, the sex

therapist, he also scheduled a meeting for me with the conveyancing attorney who was handling the new agreement— replacing our original ante-nuptial contract with the new one. He offered some lame reason why Lawyer-Cousin, who handled *all* his legal work, was not handling this contract.

At our meeting I told the conveyancing lawyer that I wanted to show the document to my attorneys before I signed. However, she had unpleasant news for me. "Your husband has instructed me not to hand over the keys of the house unless you sign the new agreement. And in addition to this, he will deduct the airfare to Scotland from your next maintenance cheque if you fail to do so."

*Absolutely all my belongings were locked up in the house. The townhouse (where I had been staying until that morning) was completely empty, except for a bed. He would be away for two weeks in Dubai.*

I was played for a fool again. Betrayed and messed with— the penalty for denial. I was so angry that I stormed out of the office and said, "I will be back!"

I went back to see the conveyancing lawyer again a little while later, with my friend in tow. This particular friend knew my husband well. Ironically, when I first met her, I was a bit scared of her—she appeared to be very confident and outspoken. As it turned out, she had proved to be a real friend.

I explained to her the trick he had played on me and begged her to help me convince the lawyer to hand me the keys to the house. She wasted no time.

"You listen to me!" she protested in my defence, "You have no idea who this poor woman is dealing with. He has no intention of honouring his commitment to Caryl and has never had any such intention. All he is doing is forcing her to agree to a settlement that is much lower than she is entitled to. He is nothing more than a lying, adulterous bastard!"

This avalanche of fury from my friend took the lawyer by

surprise, but she nevertheless, stood her ground. She firmly believed we were both wrong. She had spoken to my husband on the phone and as far as she was concerned, his intentions were honourable. Then she concluded, "All I am telling you is that your husband, as we speak, is on his way to the airport and has forbidden me to hand over the keys for the house unless you sign the new agreement."

Hysterically I grabbed the document from her and signed it. I cried uncontrollably all the way home. *How could I love this man who was proving to be such a callous man?* I wondered. I was behaving just like a child—putting a hand repeatedly on a hot plate and then crying when it hurt. I never seemed to learn my lesson. I just didn't get it.

ɞ

With this in mind, I recalled one Father's Day when I had organized a private striptease show for my husband in a desperate attempt to stop him from going to strip clubs! And as if that wasn't enough to set myself up for unnecessary hurt, the striptease artist coincidently danced to the tune of our favourite song and of course, I felt completely gutted while he smiled like a cat that'd got the bowl of cream. "That's why I love you so much—you would do anything to please me," he said.

Clearly I didn't need any enemies—I was doing a good-enough job of taunting and thrashing my own soul by myself!

My attorneys despaired when I told them what I had done by signing the new agreement. I was at breaking point and I told them to accept my husband's offer. Even though I knew in my heart I was doing the wrong thing, there was no fight left in me.

My attorney on the other hand was only beginning to warm up for the battle. "Absolutely not!" was the response. "We will fight this on the grounds that he got you to sign under duress."

On my husband's return from holiday with Miss Dubai he

came to see me and gave me a bottle of my favourite Coco Channel perfume he had bought from the duty-free shop. *What does he say to these women when he buys perfume and then doesn't give it to them?* I wondered. *Or is he so skilful at this game that all these years he has been doing it to me as well without my noticing?*

He had already received the news that my lawyer and I were contesting the new agreement, and he asked me to attend a meeting with the conveyance lawyer. He was going to prove that his intentions were indeed beyond reproach.

In the meantime, my divorce attorney passed away unexpectedly. His two sons took over all his cases but at this stage I had not yet built a relationship with them. So when it was time to meet my husband and the conveyancing attorney, Dr T came with me (at my request).

I arrived for the meeting at the same time as my husband. As I got out of my car we stood in front of each other.

"Do you even love me anymore?" I asked him.

"No," he answered without much hesitation before adding, "but we can still work this out."

I had never heard him say that to me before. Less than two months before, when he convinced me to go on holiday with him to Argentina and Cape Town, he told me that he loved me more than anything in the world and no amount of money could ever replace me. Which was the truth: did he love me or didn't he?

Once we were in the meeting and while he was explaining this crazy idea that he and I would stay married but change our marriage contract to include certain assets in my name and thereby absolve him from any future claims I might have against his estate, it finally dawned on me that he was manipulating all three of us: the conveyancing lawyer, Dr. T and me. I suddenly realized he was buying time so that he could move or hide his assets before he divorced me. Then I lost it. I exploded. "Do you really think I am that bloody stupid? I *know* you!"

"But you agreed," he protested.

Then I let him have it. I screamed at him that he was a pathological liar, a manipulator, and up to one of his no-good tricks again. I didn't care that everyone down the passage could hear me, in fact I took advantage of the situation by giving him a piece of my mind while I was in the relative safety of a lawyer and a psychologist!

When I was done spewing my venom, he calculatedly got up and walked to his car. I was beside myself and looked towards the other two women for reassurance and support, but there seemed to be none.

Then my husband came back into the office with a book that he pushed across the desk to Dr. T, while giving her a knowing look. The suggestive title of the book made my blood boil. Clearly, it seemed to me, they had a little secret between them—a private pact of sorts. *Sold out again,* I thought. *Was there no woman on God's earth who could resist this man's charm?*

However, when he got up to go, to my utmost relief, I could tell from the expression on Dr. T's face that my husband had done something that revealed his true colours to her. I didn't know exactly how or why or what it was, I simply knew—he had blown his cover. That day, Dr. T committed to stand by my side through the process of my divorce from Hitler.

I read somewhere that a person's soul is like a ragged army on the march—some aspects move ahead, while others lag behind. My attorney's offices were in Pretoria. Every time I drove into the city from Johannesburg, I would have an anxiety attack. At first I put it down to the enormous stress I was under with the divorce. But then an incident I had suppressed many years before came back to me.

My first husband, Andy, had a part-time gig in a ladies' bar in a hotel in Pretoria. I was already pregnant with my first child, although I didn't know it at the time, Andy expected me to come along so that I could watch him adoringly all night long, and of course, so that he could keep an eye on me. I was never allowed to talk to anyone.

However, on one particular evening while I was sitting at the far end of the bar minding my own business, a man came and sat one seat away from me. He ordered a double Scotch and downed it in one gulp. He didn't even look in my direction. Only after his third or fourth drink did he look at me sideways and then asked rather absentmindedly, "What would you do if you wanted to marry someone who is going to die?"

This was the kind of question I simply couldn't ignore. I asked him what he exactly meant. Then he explained. "My girlfriend has cancer and I want to marry her, but she has refused. She says she doesn't want me to be a widower at my age. Must I leave her and go and find a new girlfriend? What would you do if you were me?"

I was extremely aware of Andy's hawk-eyes on me, but at the same time I felt sympathetic towards this stranger. I told him that his girlfriend was still young and had a very good chance of beating cancer. "Definitely don't give up on her. Be patient with her." I argued that she might come around and accept that he knew what he was letting himself in for.

While I shared my pearls of wisdom, I kept looking in Andy's direction. Suddenly I noticed that he was glaring back at me and I ended my conversation with the heart-broken stranger immediately. I was about to leave my seat at the bar when Andy grabbed me by the arm and, marching me into the reception of the hotel, he threatened me viciously under his breath. "Wait until we get home ..."

Once we were inside our hotel room he threw me on the bed, took out his gun and held it under my nose. "You fucking bitch! What the hell were you doing chatting up that guy at the bar?"

I tried to explain the stranger's unusual situation as best I could as I stared down the barrel of a loaded gun, but Andy wouldn't hear any of it. "Don't talk rubbish! I saw you looking at me hoping that I wouldn't notice you flirting with him!"

ꙮ

I will never forget his finger on that trigger, trembling with uncontrollable rage. I was certain that I was going to be killed that night. Every time I drove through to Pretoria to see my attorneys I subconsciously re-lived the incident with Andy and it would trigger my fear of not surviving—no matter what the eventual divorce settlement might be, I knew that it would be finite. The day would come when there would be no more money.

Added to this was the realization that I didn't know how to work with money. I had been married to a man who was the sole breadwinner and handled all the financial matters without ever involving me. He provided me with pocket money and that money I was solely responsible for. Yes, of course I also had a fear of being alone after the divorce, but it was the fear of being incapable of surviving on my own that drove me into a near-frenzy.

It had also become perfectly clear that my husband was planning to wipe the floor with me in the divorce. There was going to be no special clemency for the years of keeping a home together while he was following his ambitions and making a lot of money. When I had met this man, he lived with his parents, drove a Mazda 323 and had very little else, except for huge ambition and immense potential. By the time we got divorced, he had accumulated great wealth yet he was unwilling to settle fairly.

Dr. T's cure for the ensuing chaos in my life was to focus my attention almost exclusively on my 'inner life'. I started to tune into TBN, the gospel channel on television, every single morning. I prayed and meditated regularly and started reading my Bible again—sometimes on an hourly basis; I kept a journal and let rip in it—I pasted pictures and painted memories on those pages in order to be purged from my pain.

Slowly but surely, I started to accept that God had a plan for me other than spending my life fixing my marriage. Dr. T also gave me homework, as she called it. There was one exercise in particular that helped me tremendously. I was to affirm myself regularly. *I acknowledge, accept and express God's creation within me fully.*

My subconscious seemed to have bought into these words, and I gave myself the right to exist without needing outside validation. *I* was going to decide what I was worth—*nobody else*. And that also applied to the divorce settlement I rightfully deserved.

Most of my friends who knew my husband well advised me to "accept his offer no matter what and move on with my life". Yet, with all the pro-activity and my ever-increasing faith in God's healing power, I was quickly gathering strength and courage to go the distance and to fight my Goliath.

In addition to this, the firm of attorneys I had appointed employed a woman who took over my case. We developed a very close relationship in a short span of time. She gave me her phone number and said I could phone her any time I needed— even at night or over weekends.

She became like a mother to me. Many a time I simply dropped my head onto her shoulder and we cried.

After about three months of dealing with her, she told me that she was semi-retired and didn't have to work. However, when she was asked to come in and help them out after the old man's death, even though she didn't want to, she knew God wanted her to be there. "If you were the reason I had to come here, then it was worth it," she said.

I didn't know it at the time but she had cancer and left the firm before my divorce was finalized. Yet, she gave me her phone number so that I could consult her or call for moral support whenever I wanted to.

I leaned on this remarkable woman's strength and wisdom until her daughter phoned me one day to say that she had passed away. "My mother wanted us to tell you that she was very fond of you."

I sat in my garden that morning and wept, not just for this special earth angel, but the many God had brought into my life at such critical times. She was an unashamed Christian, so was the private detective I had hired to investigate my husband. In the meanwhile I had gathered pretty damning information. I had been told by another reliable source that there was more than one 'other woman' and there was one number in particular that came up with predictable regularity on his telephone records.

A little bird whispered in my ear that this particular 'other woman', Miss Dubai, was a practising sex therapist and that she had had an affair with my husband during the period in which he asked to be reconciled while we were going to therapy with Dr. T.

With this in mind, I recalled an incident during the therapy session we had. My husband had asked Dr. T what a 'narcissist' is. While she explained, I remembered thinking that her description sounded very much like my husband. Then Dr. T wanted to know where he had heard of this personality disorder.

"A friend," he replied in a dismissive way. This was followed by quite a pregnant silence as she looked at him pensively—his 'friend' was obviously a professional psychologist.

I never thought much about the incident at the time, but it would seem that it was the sex therapist, with whom he had had the affair, who'd implied that he was a narcissist—probably during an argument.

Then I also remembered the incident in the conveyancing lawyer's office sometime later, when he fetched a book from his car and gave it to Dr. T. Whether or not he had ever confessed during one of his private sessions with Dr. T about having an affair, I will never know. My informants, however, confirmed that the sex therapist was indeed the published author of the book my husband had brought into the conveyancing lawyer's office and had given to Dr. T. So I decided to pay her a visit.

I took a strong tranquillizer before my appointment with the sex therapist, dressed in my very best 'power suit' and hid a tape recorder in the collar of my jacket. I could tell at first glance that she had no idea who I was.

During the session I played the game for a while, pretending that I was a client in need of her professional services. I asked her how she operated when a couple consulted her for advice. Along this line of questioning I led her into the trap of assuring me that she never became sexually involved with her clients, especially not a married man. Of course, at this point I asked, "So why then are you having sex with my husband?"

It was merciless, I know. But at the time I was so bitter about my life, and in spite of my best efforts at therapy, the healing process had only just begun. I was far from ready to forgive. After the sex therapist had gathered her composure, she started to tell me the story.

"I was set up," she stated. "Your husband's lawyer and I do business together and *he* was the one who encouraged us to meet. I want you to know that I don't see him anymore and I have told all of them I don't want any of them to contact me." A little too late, the damage had been done.

She continued to tell me that my husband had even

proposed to her! (This was also during the time he wanted to be reconciled with me.) He had met her family and had apparently got on well with her father, in particular. Then she assured me again that she had told my husband she wanted nothing more to do with him. She added, "I told him he mustn't try and use his kids to manipulate me either."

I couldn't believe my ears—the children! He involved his children (whom I helped raise) in this illicit affair? Then, as if to establish common ground between us, she said, "This [relationship] has caused me so much trauma I have even been seeing my supervisor for my own therapy!" *Was I supposed to feel sorry for her?*

I waited for her to finish her rather clumsy confession and then I took out the photographs of my beaten and bruised body. She was visibly shocked. She didn't know he could be a physically violent man.

Again and again she confirmed that she wanted nothing more to do with him. In any event, as I also knew, he had already moved on to another woman—the very weekend after they had broken up! But 'the lady doth protest too much', because a few months after our conversation she sent flowers to his daughter for her birthday.

I must confess when I heard this I sent her an SMS saying that I couldn't· believe that in her professional capacity she could send flowers to a girl who must be so confused with four women in her life: her own mother, me, the new girlfriend and her. I did not see this as a kind gesture; I saw it as interfering and unprofessional. The difficulty for me with this gesture was that it commemorated the birthday party which my children and I did not attend as we were not invited and it commemorated the night I had fallen into my husband's trap and allowed him to provoke me so much that I left home. The following evening they celebrated my stepdaughter's eighteenth birthday in a big marquee in the garden of my house.

I was not spared the information that this sex therapist attended the party on my husband's arm, and that she regularly slept over in my bed while we were separated, bringing an overnight bag and her own bed linen. What message was being given to his children? Clearly none of *them seemed to care.*

Sometime later, I also heard that my husband had explained to his children the irrevocable break-up of our marriage was due to the fact that I had an affair! He offered this explanation loud and clear in a public restaurant.

Another hurtful absurdity from his quarter was to raise the ill-fated incident with the Thai prostitute on our honeymoon. The sex therapist told me he had confessed to her that he had frequently visited massage parlours and strip clubs while he was married to me. Yet, during the divorce negotiations he protested in an affidavit that he "had lost respect" for me when I "hired a prostitute on our honeymoon in Thailand."

I was speechless. For a start I didn't hold the purse strings— *he* had invited her to the hotel room, escorted her there on the back of a scooter and paid her—not me. But what was more, only two years prior to this affidavit, on our wedding anniversary and on *that* very honeymoon in Thailand, I had received a love letter from him that expressed everything but a loss of respect for me:

*16th September 2003.*

*OUR MARRIAGE—is not about what you can give me, but what you bring to my life!*
*I know that more than anything you want the best for us. You want to be able to give me everything you think I need, but believe me when I say that all I need is YOU!*
*When I look into your eyes I can see how much you love me. Do you know how deeply that touches my heart? Or how content and fulfilled I am because I've married my best*

*friend and soul mate.*

*The things you desire for our future are important to me, if only because they are important to you!!*

*Don't EVER feel that you have to prove anything to me, because in my heart I know you are capable of fulfilling all your dreams.*

*I chose you as the one person with whom I wanted to spend the rest of my life because I fell in love with the qualities you possess. It's never been about what you can give me, but rather what you bring into my life—happiness ... laughter... friendship ... and a reason to look to tomorrow.*

I LOVE YOU!

To the day, two years later, I was in the Kruger National Park with the Lunch Club ladies. Veronica's newly divorced husband had married his lover and, afraid of pain and loneliness, she invited us along for a 'cake-throwing ceremony'.

She had kept the top layer of her wedding cake as a symbol of the vows she and her husband had made. Now, we all stood on the brow of a cliff as she threw her cake discus-style into the distance. We listened to the dull sound as it exploded on impact somewhere at the bottom.

These magnificent women had taught me a new way of dealing with adversity. I didn't have to despair the way I usually did. From that day on, I realized that there would always be a part of me that was equal to the 'mountain' I faced. However deep I might have to reach inside me to find it—it did not matter—*it was there*. I would overcome.

Suddenly I didn't care if I had to walk out of the divorce court with nothing but my handbag. I finally realized that absolutely *nothing*—not even courtroom victory for my husband—could defeat me *personally*. At the same time I was as ready as ever for a fight and determined that the truth would be known.

When the time came for the trial, my attorneys had to subpoena no less than four women with whom my husband had allegedly had sexual relations during the most recent years of our marriage. I was so looking forward to watching them face each other in court, with each hearing the lies they had been told. *Let them see who the real loony one is. Let them judge for themselves,* I thought. With my habit of keeping a record of letters, documents, photographs, phone messages witnesses, everything and anything to back up my accusations, I was determined that I would not be manipulated, intimidated or silenced in that courtroom. I certainly wasn't afraid of the two sworn affidavits that I had had a lesbian relationship and beat myself up.

However, two days before we were due to appear in court, we settled. You decide! And yes, I did receive substantially more than he had initially offered.

Almost immediately the divorce was official—after all the years of fighting a losing battle, marrying and divorcing the same man *twice*—I received a text message from him on my phone.

"You will always be very special to me. I will never love anyone like I loved you. I thought that we could be friends when this was all over, but you have made sure that will never happen."

"How can any one be a friend with someone who proves to be your enemy?" I replied.

It went through me like a jolt of electricity. Suddenly I opened my mind for the first time ever to consider that he too was messed up and hurting. And then I began to realize that this might be true of all men. Perhaps they simply express their pain differently to women and act out in ways that we don't expect them to.

What had begun as a journey to heal the 'female soul' had brought me full circle to understand that there is not one person—male or female—whose heart has not been broken. Emotional pain is not a female prerogative. It is a *human* condition.

It is said, "We hurt the ones we love the most", and I now fully understand the paradox. As bizarre as it may sound, and in spite of the extraordinary physical and emotional pain this man inflicted on me, I never doubted that he loved me.

This may be difficult for some to fathom. Yet, I will tell you that even my *children,* who witnessed the bruises all over my body, understood that it was possible for me to love him in spite of his violent behaviour − because they did as well.

Five months after our divorce was official, he and I engaged in an sms-conversation. He was attending the Grand Prix in Rio de Janeiro and appeared to be quite chirpy about his life in general. I was hurting so badly at the time, and at some point during the communication I wrote something like, "... I'm finding this so hard and often wonder what the heck I did wrong?"

Strangely enough, I would never have done or said that in the past. Only because I knew it was finally over between us, could I actually express how I felt for the first time.

He replied: "I didn't want to hurt you any more. I knew you wouldn't take me back, would you?"

I didn't respond to his message because the truth was - he was quite mistaken.... Then and there I would have taken him back in a heartbeat! I had to keep that door closed once and for all.

# Abuse Is No Excuse

*One evening an old Cherokee Indian told his grandson about a battle that goes on inside people. He said, "My son, the battle is between two wolves inside us all. One is Evil. It is anger, envy, jealousy, sorrow, greed, arrogance, self-pity, laziness, guilt, resentment, inferiority, lies, false pride, superiority and ego. The other is Good. It is honesty, happiness, peace, love, hope, serenity, humility, kindness, benevolence, empathy, enthusiasm, generosity, truth and compassion."*

*The grandson thought about it for a minute and then asked his grandfather: "Which wolf wins?"*

*The old Cherokee simply replied, "The one you feed."*

Feeding the 'good' wolf is not easy. What makes it so difficult is that I had been conditioned, like most other people, to believe the enemy is *outside* me when indeed it was *within*. It has taken much courage and brutal honesty to admit that my own self-hatred, self-rejection and low self-esteem paved the way for me to attract no less than *two* violent husbands who wiped the floor with me.

The real sad thing, with every betrayal and every beating there was the belief that I deserved exactly what I got! Not that I was bad and deserved this treatment, but that I wasn't emotionally healthy enough to find a man who would treat me with respect.

To this day I believe that as much as my parents and my ex-husbands loved me, they couldn't show it. They demanded love and respect from me, but couldn't reciprocate. I was at their mercy for whatever bits of kindness and approval they would cast my way ... Whether this is actually the truth or not, it doesn't matter—it was my innermost experience. For the best part of my life I have felt unappreciated and worthless, and it used to fill me with such a powerless rage that if I could strike out and hit someone like my ex-husbands did with me, I probably would have.

Yes, they mirrored my own rage. And the *size* of their rage was an exact match to mine.

The main problem, as I see it now, is that I never understood the true meaning of forgiveness. So I would enter into these abusive relationships, expecting my partners to fix my brokenness. And when they failed, which they inevitably did, I felt even more desperate and victimized than before. To stand up and be accountable for myself, as I am doing with this book, is a whole new way of life. I have never been true to myself before. I have lived the life I thought was expected of me and hoped to find acceptance that way.

I chose to be a follower rather than a leader, always walking in my husband's shadow. That way I knew I wouldn't have to take any responsibility and if I should end up in the 'wrong' place, I could blame the situation on my leader.

Now suddenly I am a leader in my own right—with or without followers, it makes no difference—I have taken responsibility for who I am and how I react to adversity. I am learning to validate myself and have taken my first wobbly steps on the path to forgiveness.

It is said that when prisoners who have been chained are set free, they walk for quite some time as if the chains are still around their ankles. The kinds of relationship I entered into with my two violently abusive husbands were de-humanizing. Those who have had similar experiences in these kinds of relationships will identify when I say that the reign of terror in such a relationship is so complete that even long after the relationship is over one feels too guilty to go into another relationship. It feels a disloyal or even an unfaithful act—something that one would certainly be severely punished for.

It takes time to understand and believe that you are suddenly free. In fact, freedom can be a quite scary concept to someone like me who has known the 'safety of chains' for such a long time. Yet, I am willing to learn about this new way of life.

The path of forgiveness has opened the way for many important insights. One of them is that although I need the support of other women which allows me to air my feelings in safety and to get feedback from those who have had similar experiences, there is a danger that I will get too caught up in myself and become disdainful of men and feel superior to them. This not only breaks down gender relations, it defies the value embedded in all relationships ... *No one is your enemy. No one is your friend. Everyone is your teacher.*

This impersonal approach to relationships is difficult to attain, and even more difficult to accept when your face has been punched in by a man twice your size! However, the men who attacked me reflected my own weakness and powerless rage back to me. And when I get onto the bandwagon with other women and start to run down 'all men', I ask myself the question: *Why do I feel so weak as a woman that I must attack men?*

৪৩

The most important lesson I have learnt thus far is that forgiveness, and the joy and freedom it brings, is impossible to achieve while I am intent on seeing myself as a victim. Like so many others, I used to think that to forgive someone means to say, "What you did to me is okay," and I would believe that this gesture made me a good Christian or a better person than the one I forgave.

Today I know forgiveness is the ultimate healing act. It has very little to do with 'the other' and everything to do with my own empowerment.

It would seem that in the end it comes down to a simple choice, as the Truth always does. The price I have been paying for my anger and resentment was too great. I was no longer willing to pay it. I chose freedom for myself—from the chains of abuse, control games and power struggles. I am willing to release my perpetrators from the wrongs they have done to me. What's more, I am willing to let them off the hook *regardless* of what happens to them. Even if life doesn't 'punish' them—I no longer want to bear the burden of resentment, rage and emotional pain. They are free to be whomever they choose to be, and so am I.

With this decision I break the chain with yesterday. And now, when I look at the photographs of my beaten-up face and bruised body, instead of feeling sorry for myself, I want to weep for the person who allowed it to happen—I am beginning to feel compassion for her.

This is not a place I have rushed to. It has taken many days and nights of humbling introspection. My children will one day too get to this place of forgiveness and acceptance. I know this, because the way for them will be prepared by my own self-forgiveness.

To my knowledge, as in my dream many years ago, my ex-husband is still happily travelling down the farm road in his executive car at break-neck speed. I have only just made it back to the top of the hill I rolled down after I jumped out of the car as commanded by that loud inner voice.

It's time to dust myself off and to move on. I have put my beautiful thatched home on the market and in my mind this is the way in which I say my farewells to those I am leaving behind.

I have rekindled my relationship with God and in the

stillness of my heart I enjoy great intimacy with myself and with God. I am beginning to see the 'authentic me'. And who knows? I may even gather the courage and risk-sharing this fearless intimacy with a 'significant other' one day.

One thing is for sure—I am ready and willing to find another way of being in a relationship. And with this I include *all* relationships—my children, my friends, my business associates. I am making room for equal partnerships: relationships in which the other people are as committed and as co-operative as I am.

There is no excuse for abuse in my life anymore. I no longer need to control others in order to feel better about myself, and I will no longer accept being controlled by another either.

Respect, honour, and love—these are the qualities I will build my relationships on, from here on, and let this book be my constant reminder that the good days in an abusive relationship come at a very high price.

I know by now that without honesty and humility, no emotional healing can occur. Therefore it is good for me to admit to you that the temptation to slip back into denial and blame it all on my husbands is ever present. Being the victim still comes easily to me. From time to time I still find myself manipulating others instead of stating my desires with respect for all concerned—including myself.

I also occasionally still get caught up in a power play with someone and fall into the passive-aggressive routine of sulking or stonewalling. But none of these has power over me these days. I view them as bad habits that are in the process of being changed. And I see the other person as my teacher—showing me how far I have come on the road to wholeness and how far I have yet to travel.

I have consciously chosen the way of peace—within and without. At least I now know which comes first, because I have finally got the message my Forever-Friend gave me all those years ago, *"Seek ye first the Kingdom of God and His righteousness and all these things will be added onto you."*

# Dear Reader

After my divorce the road was not easy or without bumps but I was determined to complete the last leg of the journey. It has been long and arduous, but one that was well worth making.

The build up to my divorce was so emotionally devastating that on the day it was finalised, I was devoid of any sense of celebrating my new found freedom – I was curled up in a ball hidden in my home crying. I cannot deny that the pain almost consumed me, the CPTS that followed, plagued me for almost 8 years and took me to the brink of insanity with constant thoughts of suicide. Withdrawal from this abusive and addictive relationship was tough and the only way that I could deal with my emotions was to continue writing in my journal and seek the professional help that I so desperately needed. I earnestly pursued several varied forms of healing modalities - some helped and some hindered the process.

When an abusive relationship ends, surely we are supposed to be happy with a bright future ahead of us, not so? But in reality it was time for me to enter the Death Zone. That space between complete failure and possible death, or the euphoria of reaching the highest point in one's life. Like most people who climb Mount Everest I wanted more than anything to get to the very top and enjoy the spectacular view of my own life and the world around me.

The symptoms of CPTS – (Complex Post Traumatic Stress), that bothered me the most were, reoccurring nightmares, panic attacks, the inability to go out in public, loss of appetite, loss of memory, fear of men and a catatonic state of mind that I couldn't shake. I worked compulsively, to avoid thinking about what I had been through, stayed awake late into the night to avoid the nightmares, which made me exhausted throughout the following day? It was a vicious cycle, but sleeping pills and being tempted to slip back into denial or to avoid the pain was not an option this time.

Many nights in the beginning of recovery, I sat alone drinking wine to drown my sorrows until I realised - just like Bono, *that they could swim.* One night I went onto an internet dating site (which I personally find boring) yet I knew in my heart that meeting someone was not going to heal me – I had to do the work... alone. Little did I know how hard that was going to be. Most people on these dating sites stipulate 'No baggage,' I certainly had my fair share so a new relationship wasn't going to help my healing process.

Robin Norwood, author of *When Women Love Too Much*, had this to say: "In a parallel with the developing disease of alcoholism, dependence on the relationship deepens to the point of addiction. To be without the relationship – that is, to be alone with one's self – can be experienced as worse than being in the greatest pain the relationship produces, because to be alone means to feel the stirrings of the great pain from the past combined with that of the present."

Making a home again was my first task. With very few material possessions from my once – beautiful home hurt me deeply and replacing everything from bed linen and ornaments, to cutlery and crockery was painful. I had some idea of what it must feel like when a person's house burns down, but my daughters encouraged me by saying, "Mom, use this time to create a home that will be 'your' space, and furnish it just the way you want." But they didn't say, "Mom, watch your bank balance."

Throughout my life I was controlled by people who held the purse strings. By the time I was free of all the abuse, and had everything to look forward to including financially security, the one thing I didn't have was the knowledge about investing or the ability to manage my finances.

Suffering with severe CPTS my financial decisions were impulsive and irrational. One of the symptoms of the condition is a shortened sense of life expectancy - I had absolutely no concern for tomorrow. I spent far too much money redecorating, but my home was my personality from the front door to the back and I loved it. It was peaceful and everyone who came to visit complimented me. I enjoyed transforming a section of my garden into a Zen garden complete with a Japanese bridge, water features and a place to meditate called 'Thula Thula.'

In my divorce settlement I asked for one of the 50 or more properties that we owned, but what I couldn't have guessed was that it was the oldest in our property portfolio, the one most in need of repair and upgrading, my ex husband must have laughed victoriously at my foolish choice. By the time I had finished all the repairs, installed a new kitchen and furnished my home, there wasn't much left of my divorce settlement and before I knew it, my beautiful home was up for sale.

For a long time I was reckless with my finances and gave vast sums of money to people less fortunate than myself, I felt compelled to rescue anyone and everyone that I thought was in pain and I couldn't begin to calculate how much money I spent in search of healing and finding the truth.

It's so important not to resist change. It was time to move on with my life and away from everything that was familiar, and anything that could bind me to the past. As I started to piece my life together I knew I had only one way to go and that was forwards. I moved from Johannesburg to Cape Town and rented a beautiful apartment with sea views, it was small but with my daughters all living away from home it was perfect for me. It might sound strange, but for the first time in my life I only had myself to think about which terrified me and I wept buckets. I took long walks on the beach, stopped wearing makeup and having my nails done, dressed down and became real. Please don't get me wrong, it wasn't that I let myself go, I had no reason to perform and be glamorous in a vain attempt to win approval.

After two years and a lot of soul searching it was time for me to move back to Johannesburg and be closer to my daughters and my grandchildren. My emotional state was still fragile and the fear of bumping into my ex and revisiting familiar places from the past still caused me tremendous anxiety, but it was time to face the thing I feared the most, living in close proximity to the man who almost destroyed my life.

The most important of all the healing modalities that I experienced was the treatment I received from Dr. Annemarie Norvello who is a Trauma Psychologist. For the first time in my life someone understood what the problem was with *me,* and the focus was taken off my *abusive relationships* and together with the aid of Five Ducks – yes the little yellow plastic ones - we slowly unpacked all my baggage. You can read more about the Five Ducks on my blog:

**http://abuseisnoexcuse.blogspot.com/**

Four wonderful events on my journey have truly blessed me: The reconnection with Sunshine and her 18-year-old son who was adopted and the birth of two more grand children. Moonie's beautiful daughter who is so much like her mother, her younger brother who is the image of his father and the joyous news that my youngest daughter Star who is pregnant, with another grandson on the way.

The time I spend with my family today, is precious and I value every moment with them. I am fortunate to be an artist and my time is my own, which gives me the opportunity to see my daughters, my grandchildren and my friends as often as I wish, without the tension caused by someone jealous of my affections for them.

My life is so much happier now. I always said, "I want to grow up before I grow old," and I think this is precisely what has happened. The old Cherokee Indian was right after all – the battle is between the two wolves inside us all – Constantly feeding the 'good' wolf (that part in each of us that edifies and encourages) is not easy. But each day I ask for one more step towards that goal.

In your life journey, I hope you find the same PEACE and LIFE PURPOSE that I have found in my own.

Life is truly wonderful.

*Caryl*

Note: Death Zone (noun) – Land at sufficiently high altitudes that there is not enough oxygen to sustain human life.

# How to Contact Caryl

Web site:
**http://www.abuseisnoexcuse.co.za/**

Facebook:
**https://www.facebook.com/groups/343059317922/**

Blog:
**http://abuseisnoexcuse.blogspot.com/**

Video:
**http://www.youtube.com/watch?v=K4sEYGGsetA**

# Pray Don't Find Fault

Pray don't find fault with the woman who limps
or stumbles along the road,
unless you have worn the shoes she wears or struggled beneath
her load.
There may be tacks in her shoes that hurt,
though hidden away from view,
or the burden she bares, placed on your back
might cause you to stumble too.

Don't sneer at the woman who's down today
unless you have felt the blow
that caused her fall or felt the shame
that only the fallen know.
You may be strong, but still the blows
that were hers if dealt to you,
in the self same way, at the self same time,
might cause you to stagger too.

Don't be too harsh with the woman who sins
or pelt her with word or stone,
unless you are sure, yea, double sure,
that you have no sins of your own
for you know perhaps if the tempter's voice
should whisper as softly to you
as it did to her when she went astray,
it might cause you to stumble too.

Author unknown
(Adapted)

# Further Reading

*Behind closed doors: violence in the American family* by Murray A. Straus, Richard J. Gelles & Suzanne K. Steinmetz

*Beyond codependency* by Melody Beattie

*Biblical solutions for the survivors of abuse and rape* by Todd R. Cook

*Breaking free, starting over: parenting in the aftermath of family violence* by Christina M. Dalpiaz

*Children of the self-absorbed* by Nina W. Brown

*Cry salty tears* by Dinah O'Dowd

*Daily meditations for women who love too much* by Robin Norwood

*Empowering survivors of abuse* by Jacquelyn C. Campbell

*Enough about you, let's talk about me* by Les Cartier

*Finding your own North Star* by Martha Beck

*Fresh out of hell* by Alyson Kay

*GRACE the power to change* by Dr. James B. Richards

*Heal and forgive* by Nancy Richards & Marie M. Fortune

*High conflict personalities* by William A. Eddy

*How to stop the pain* by Dr. James B. Richards

*I have life: Alison's journey* by Marianne Thamm

*I'll never do to my kids what my parents did to me!* by Thomas Paris & Eileen Paris

*Malignant self love, narcissism revisited* by Dr. Sam Vaknin

*Men who hate women and the women who love them* by Susan Forward & Joan Torres

*My parents' keeper* by Eva Marian Brown

*Narcissism* by Alexander Lowen

*Running to stand still* by Bearnard O'Riain

*The artist's way* by Julie Cameron

*The dandelion spirit* by Louise Gallagher

*The emotionally abusive relationship: how to stop being abused and how to stop abusing* by Beverly Enger

*The Wizard of Oz and other narcissists* by Eleanor Payson

*Two-part harmony* by Patrick M. Morley

*Toxic parents* by Susan Forward

*What men don't want women to know* by Smith & Doe Staff

*When you love too much* by Steven Arter

*When your perfect partner goes perfectly wrong* by Mary Jo Fay

*Where is God when it hurts?* by Philip Yancey

*Whose life is it anyway?* by Nina Brown

*Why is it always about you?* by Sandy Hotchkiss

*Wild at heart* by John Eldridge

*Women who love too much* by Robin Norwood

*You can't say that to me* by Suzette Haden Elgin